W9-BFL-011

The Aston Webb Front

Buckingham Palace
and its treasures

JOHN HARRIS · GEOFFREY DE

Buckii

INTRODUCTION BY JOHN RUSSELL

PHOTOGRAPHY BY LIONEL BELL
KERRY DUNDAS · SIDNEY NEWBURY

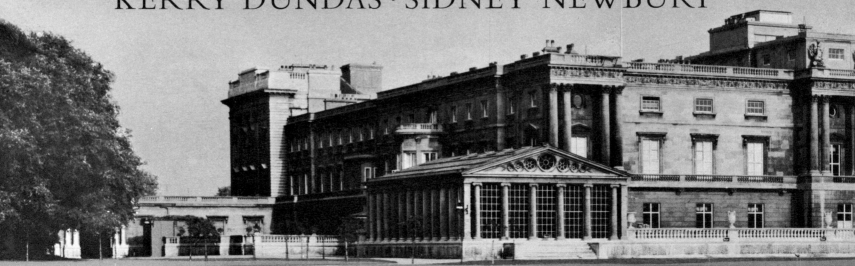

A STUDIO BOOK

BELLAIGUE · OLIVER MILLAR

ngham

Palace

AND ITS TREASURES

THE VIKING PRESS · NEW YORK

Contents

Published in 1968 by
THE VIKING PRESS, INC.,
625 Madison Avenue, New York, N.Y. 10022

Illustrations © Her Majesty The Queen 1968
Text © Thomas Nelson and Sons Ltd 1968
All rights reserved

Library of Congress catalog card number: 62–23206

Printed in Great Britain by W. S. Cowell Ltd

The authors
and publishers
wish to express their
deep sense of gratitude to

Her Majesty The Queen

for her gracious permission to
prepare this account of the
history & contents of
Buckingham Palace
& their appreciation
of the facilities for
research & photo-
graphy that
she has been
pleased to
grant

Introduction

AMONG the inhabited great houses of Europe, none has a personality stronger or more mysterious than Buckingham Palace. That strength, and that mystery, have survived many changes of ownership and a century and more of formal hospitalities. Behind that genial French façade, and behind the ceremonial balcony which serves on great occasions, a complex of imperious inclinations has been preserved intact. Almost everything in Buckingham Palace is there because one known individual liked it, and not because it was thought to be judicious or correct. Buckingham Palace is the residence of the head of the state, with all that that implies. It also includes an office building, a centre of communications, an art gallery open to the public, a set of stables, a post office, and a school; but it is above all a private house in which private life has been going on for a very long time. Its personality is by turns august and reassuring, straight-faced and impulsive, romantic and respectful of protocol, obsessive and practical. It takes very little effort to imagine the costume balls of the 1840's and 50's; but ever since Melbourne called regularly upon Queen Victoria Buckingham Palace has also been the headquarters of the consequential tête-a-tête. At every point the great building refuses categorisation; and the privileged intruder who expects to find himself a superfluous comma in the 'Court Circular' is just as likely to feel, at the end of his visit, that he has stepped out of an unwritten chapter in *Alice Through the Looking-Glass*.

Alice would be quite at home, certainly, in the seemingly unending corridors, none of them less than eighty yards long, which traverse the inner edges of the quadrangle: it needs only a trick of the light on a summer afternoon for us to see her flying in ruched white silk and black patent leather towards the tall panels of looking-glass which make the Principal Corridor a place of continual echoes for the eye. Above all, the scale of Buckingham Palace makes for magic: doors open where we least expect them, and they lead from rooms which can hold two hundred people quite comfortably into the kind of fastidious crevice which might have been designed for one particularly spruce young bachelor. The great house can stun with splendour, where splendour is called for, but its general tone is one of unaffected commodity: the Privy Purse entrance might, for example, be the hallway of a stylish manor house two hundred miles from London. It is enormously *not* the kind of building which a committee could have put together: at the drop of a latch we step from a genuine India, relic of bygone Durbars, to a China fantasticated in the 1820's, and no amount of remodelling has blotted out the fact that strong-minded individuals have had their way with the Palace throughout all its transformations, and that every one of them has left a permanent mark upon it. The Palace has an open-ended history: it is cherished today, as a place to live in, as much as ever it was, and it is not at all the kind of royal residence from which royal persons long to escape. It adapts as easily to family life in the late 1960's as it did to

7

PAGES 8 AND 9
LOUIS HAGHE: THE BALLROOM, BUCKINGHAM PALACE, 17 JUNE 1856

THE EARL AND COUNTESS OF
ARLINGTON AND THEIR FAMILY,
FROM A MINIATURE BY C. NETSCHER
Courtesy of the Earl of Rosebery

JOHN SHEFFIELD, DUKE OF BUCKINGHAM,
AFTER A PAINTING BY
SIR GODFREY KNELLER
Courtesy of the National Portrait Gallery

family life when Queen Victoria's children were growing up: more so, in fact, since the practical side of life has been improved beyond recognition since Queen Victoria complained of its inconveniences. There is nothing of tiresome outward show about Buckingham Palace, in this context; and although I have always doubted that Proust knew quite what he was saying when he made Charles Swann a regular visitor to the private apartments, I wish that he were alive today and could be empowered to bring his gift for particularisation to this aspect of the Palace.

One or two things have been shed along the way. The Duke of Buckingham would no longer hear his nightingales, George III might not find his models of British harbours where he left them, Queen Charlotte would miss her zebra, George IV would find that Nash's dome on the garden front was very soon taken away, and the Prince Consort would miss the frescoes which he commissioned for the Garden Pavilion. But Buckingham Palace is, nonetheless, an undestroyed Pompeii in which changes of taste can be detected, one on top of the other, in perfect repair.

There was never, in all this, a master-plan. The methods employed were pragmatic and accumulatory; and if there was a tradition, it was the one begun by Charles II when he filled St James's Park with rare animals and birds and planted a part of it with blue anemones brought especially from Rome. The site was the grandest in London, and at one time it commanded

Whitehall and the City almost as the Upper Belvedere commands Vienna. Evelyn in his diary for 1673 noted that Lord Arlington, a peer of very recent creation, was living there in royal state. The house was burned down in the following year, but Arlington, not at all deterred, re-built in an even more ambitious style. Arlington House had a grove, a bowling green, a terrace walk, a glass-house full of orange-trees, a stylised wilderness, a chapel with purple velvet in every pew, and stabling for forty horses. When it came up for let in the 1690's, it was the kind of town house which few people could carry off. If not Royalty, then the next best thing: that was what the trustees had in mind, and in John Sheffield, Marquiss of Normanby and soon to be Duke of Buckingham, they found the ideal tenant. A former Lord Chamberlain, he had been the suitor of Princess (later Queen) Anne and had married an illegitimate daughter of James II. He was a man of fixed and ferocious loyalties who had fought with distinction on both sea and land and never hesitated to take the unpopular side in a quarrel. He was also a poet. The National Theatre is unlikely to take his recension of *Julius Caesar* into its repertory, but the poems have something of his own. Imperious, plain-spoken, and adroit, Buckingham was bookish without abdicating from the life of action, and he was worldly without ever sealing off the springs of true feeling. I know of few lines more succinctly dismissive than his

With tame submission to the will of fate
He lugged about the matrimonial weight

and there is a fine cogency about the two lines which Pope was not too proud to quote:

Of all those arts in which the wise excell
Nature's chief masterpiece is writing well.

Buckingham loved the house, and before long he contrived to buy it, and to give it his name. He had town and country in one: for anything as fine, at the time, we should have to wish our-selves across the Alps and outside Turin, where a newly-built road streaked out from the city to the great villa, masterwork of Iuvara, called Stupinigi. Buckingham enjoyed writing to his friends about every detail of the house: the avenue of elms along which carriages came out from the City, and the other avenue, grassed between freshly-planted lime-trees, which served for promenaders; the Latin mottoes, indicative of high satisfaction, which told every passer-by that this was a happy house; and the six-sided *bassin* in the forecourt, with Neptune and his tritons spouting away from morning till night.

The house inside was very grand indeed, and its owner took a special pride in the staircase, with 'eight and forty steps ten feet broad, each step of one entire Portland stone'. Even the ailing had no need to heave themselves up by the iron baluster, so nicely had the rise of the steps been calculated.

The first-floor salon, '35 ft. high. 36 ft. broad, and 45 ft. long', was hung from top to bottom with pictures relating to the arts and sciences. A room of this sort can be genuinely grand, but it can also be pompous and inhuman, like the Faninals' house in Act II of *Der Rosenkavalier*: Buckingham, no *nouveau riche,* was as delighted with the little door which led through to his

PAGES 12 AND 13
LOUIS HAGHE: THE INVESTITURE OF THE ORDER OF THE BATH, 7 JULY 1855

own apartments as he was with the 'niche 15 ft broad for a Bufette' in the parlour below. What he liked most of all was 'a little closet of books at the end of that greenhouse which joins the best apartment', and he regretted not having one curious feature of the earlier house: a long gallery fitted up with a small frame of olive wood with holes and pins for the exact computation of walking a mile. But Buckingham laid such stress on the roses and the jasmine at the back of the house, and on the flower-garden, the 'bathing-place', and the 'kitchen garden full of the best sorts of fruit', that he may have been as great a walker outside as in.

Much of Buckingham Palace as we know it is already present, *en petit*, in Buckingham's account of the house. But the house has, of course, grown enormously: it is twenty, thirty, perhaps forty times as large. This enlargement came about gradually, and almost by accident. When George III bought the house in 1761 he intended, if anything, to democratise it. He decreed that it should be known as 'The Queen's House' and not by any more overbearing name. He simplified the look of it by taking down the iron gates which Buckingham had commissioned from Tijou, doing away with the great baroque fountain, and rigging up two modest little entrances at the side. Doubtless he thought it was grand enough to be King of England without going in for embellishments to keep his subjects at bay. Marriage had changed him, as we may judge from the comments of one experienced visitor: 'I was surprised to find that the levee room had lost so entirely the air of the lion's den. This sovereign don't stand in one spot, with his eyes fixed royally on the ground, and dropping bits of German news; he walks about, and speaks to everybody'.

Queen Charlotte was barely out of her teens when she, too, set a tone which has been kept up at Buckingham Palace ever since. She liked beautiful flowers, and a great many of them. She liked very good pictures, and a superabundance of small objects of art, and the best music, and first-class cabinet-making, and Chelsea vases, and Derbyshire Blue John candelabra, and Wedgwood when it was of the finest possible quality and rather plain. She had spirited children in great numbers and a very large dog. She loved the theatre, and both Kemble and Mrs Siddons were invited to play at The Queen's House. She knew just what was what in the way of new painting, and the portraits of her children which she commissioned from Gainsborough are among the most touching things of their kind. Haydn thought well of her prowess at the keyboard, and her private orchestra included some of the foremost virtuosi of the day. She was very good indeed at needlework, and she adored dancing. Her idea of a ball has not, however, been taken up by her successors: she liked a dance that 'began at half-past six and lasted till one, when the company broke up and retired without any supper'.

All this kept dullness at a distance; and to this day Buckingham Palace is a place that comes instantaneously to life when fun is in question. In one respect only has it lost in character since the days of George III and Queen Charlotte: the removal of the King's Library to the British Museum, and of the royal library in general to Windsor, has severed that harmonious relationship with literature which existed when Doctor Johnson came regularly to read in the octagonal library of The Queen's House and a workshop was set up in the house expressly to bind the King's new purchases.

Life was bound to catch up with The Queen's House. It simply was not practical, at the turn of the century, for the King of England to live in a house smaller than those common among the grandees of the shires, with a railing round it no more than waist-high and a slot-like entrance at the side. George IV had the gift of seeing big, where architecture was concerned, and London was changing in ways that made The Queen's House, as a royal residence, seem antiquated and perverse. Architects had been busy ever since the reign of George II with plans, each more ambitious than the other; and although the King would have settled for a house no more boastful than No. 10 Downing Street (or The White House, for that matter) the whole movement of the times was against this. 'I am too old to build a Palace', said George IV, who had that lasting loyalty to The Queen's House which has affected almost everyone who has lived on the site. (Buckingham's son loved it so much that he asked, unavailingly, to be buried in the garden.)

Had it not been for that loyalty we might well have ended up in Green Park, or elsewhere, with a labyrinthine structure the size of Angkor Vat. As it is, the changes set in motion by George IV were spectacular enough. William IV disliked gilding, and indeed disliked show of any kind, and he made a bold attempt to get rid of Buckingham House altogether and give it to the nation in lieu of the Houses of Parliament, which were burned down in 1834. 'I mean Buckingham House as a permanent gift. Mind that!' he said to the Speaker. 'Pimlico Palace', as it was popularly called, was getting a name for senseless extravagance in the 1830's and Creevey wrote in his diary that 'The costly ornaments of the State Rooms exceed all belief in their bad taste and every species of infirmity. Raspberry-coloured pillars without end that quite turn you sick to look at . . .' Nobody was pleased. Nash was put out because, as he saw it, his commission had been changed from house to palace in mid-career. Parliament was put out because it cost so much. The people were put out because it looked as if the palace would never be made use of. George IV died. Nash died. William IV died. Stagnation set in, and Buckingham Palace was still empty.

Outside of *The Sleeping Beauty* it would be hard to find a greater transformation than that wrought by Queen Victoria, who moved into Buckingham Palace within three weeks of her accession. Within forty-eight hours of moving in she was entertaining a large party to dinner and listening afterwards to 'Thalberg, the greatest pianist in the world . . . *J'étais en extase*!' The Palace to all intents and purposes was hers to inaugurate. One or two survivors of Queen Charlotte's court were still in London: distinguishable by their bizarre way of pronouncing certain words ('goold' for 'gold', for instance, and 'yaller' for 'yellow'), they managed to make Queen Victoria momentarily uneasy about her command of English, but in no other respect did they affect her. She did what she liked: not for the last time, a very young Queen was free to set her own style.

Almost everyone was delighted with that style. Greville found it dull, but then Greville had been struck off the lists because he shouted at table and tried to talk other people down. The Palace quickly became what it is today: affable and efficacious for the transaction of business, great or small, and the best of all accomplices on festive occasions. There are limits, of course, to the freedom of even a young and imperious Queen. Queen Victoria did her duty by *les grands*, and invited them in great numbers; but *les grands* are not always very droll, and there were

evenings over which boredom hung like a catafalque. What Queen Victoria enjoyed most were the confidential talks with her Ministers (above all with the delicious, protective and irreverent Melbourne) and the balls. She had been fond of dancing ever since William IV gave her a 'Juvenile Ball' at St James's Palace on her fourteenth birthday, and during the first years of her reign there was a very great deal of dancing at Buckingham Palace. In particular, the costume balls of 1842, 1845 and 1851 were of historic proportions. Though usually hinged to some aspect of the national interest, they also gave pleasure of a purely frivolous kind. Even on the dance-floor there were moments when things went wrong: Lord Malmesbury in his memoirs describes how, in 1840, the 'Queen danced the first dance with the Duke of Devonshire and valsed after-wards with Prince Albert, but the band played so fast and out of tune that she only took one turn and then sat down, looking annoyed'. But in general all went well, and there were many occasions on which a visitor could verify King Leopold's judgment—that 'There is hardly a country in which such magnificence exists'. The splendour of these entertainments was talked about for decades: readers of Trollope's parliamentary novels will remember that when the Duke of Omnium first got within dreaming distance of being Prime Minister his Duchess quintessentialised her ambitions by saying to herself: 'I'll make Buckingham Palace look second-rate'.

Magnificence does not always make friends for itself, and the curious thing about Buckingham Palace is that gradually it became what it is today: an ark to which a whole people turns instinctively at times of torment or rejoicing. Blore was not a great architect, and he has been generally abused for the east front which he added to Buckingham Palace. Not only did it look like a station hotel, but it was faced with Caen stone, which quickly crumbled and gave the Palace a distressingly mouldy appearance. But one thing he did do: he invented the Balcony. The Balcony is small and narrow and has nothing of grandeur about it: no despot would think of showing himself in so confined a space. But the Balcony works, for our English tastes, in a way that even the Scala dei Giganti in the Doges' Palace would not work for this particular purpose.

It was in 1854 that the Balcony was first put into use. Queen Victoria stood on it to watch the last Guards battalion march out of the courtyard on its way to the Crimea. In July 1856 she was back on the balcony to watch the returning army march past on its way from Vauxhall to Hyde Park; and ever since—but especially in 1914, in 1918, and in 1945—the Balcony has been the very centre of the nation. Few people have any clear idea of what the inside of the Palace is like, or of what goes on there, but almost everyone who was alive at those times of crisis or exuberance will remember for ever what went on in the forecourt. Buckingham Palace has an immediate meaning, for those people, of a kind that neither St James's, nor Hampton Court, or Kensington, nor even Windsor can possibly have.

This is the more remarkable in that England is fundamentally castle-country, and always was. Castles fire our imagination in a way that palaces do not. Castle-people, in a legendary way, are bluff, downright, and self-reliant: you know where you are with them. Palace-people, by contrast, have a name for being intriguing, finicky, fashionable, and false. Palace-life is contrary to nature, we think: 'in palaces, treason' is one of the phrases in *King Lear* which first warns us that

EUGENE LAMI: STATE BALL, BUCKINGHAM PALACE, 5 JULY 1848

dreadful happenings are on the way. Palace-people are corrupt, also: Shelley in *The Cenci* speaks of 'that palace-walking devil, Gold', and although Allan Cunningham was not much of a poet, he spoke for a great part of the nation when he gave a scornful edge to the lines

> *the hollow oak our palace is,*
> *Our heritage the sea.*

There may even be something of foreboding about this prejudice. We may remember, however distantly, what happened to Nonesuch Palace, gone without a trace, and to Whitehall Palace, burned in 1698 all the way from the Banqueting House to the river. We don't even fancy the idea that any one town house should be very much larger than any other town house: and we think distinctly better of Wellington for liking the style 'No. 1, Piccadilly' than we do of Marlborough for browbeating posterity with Blenheim Palace.

So it was not at all a foregone conclusion that Buckingham Palace should be regarded with such steadfast affection. It took character to make it so—the character that kept the Royal Family firmly in London from 1939 to 1945—just as it took character to pick on the things, and to develop the style of life, which are commemorated in this book. As to just how it was done, our records are remarkably few: but we know that it *was* done, and that this book is something more than an unusually scrupulous historical record. Buckingham Palace could be, but is not, the kind of glowering fortress which we find in certain other capitals. It is open to London in a great many mysterious and impalpable ways, just as it is open physically in ways that bespeak an ingenious poetry on the architects' part: looking out, we see London where, and how, we least expect it, and we recognise the truth of what was once said by one of the most perceptive of those who have lived in it: 'I choose to think that Buckingham Palace is not out of the world'.

JOHN RUSSELL
September 1968

The Architecture

JOHN HARRIS

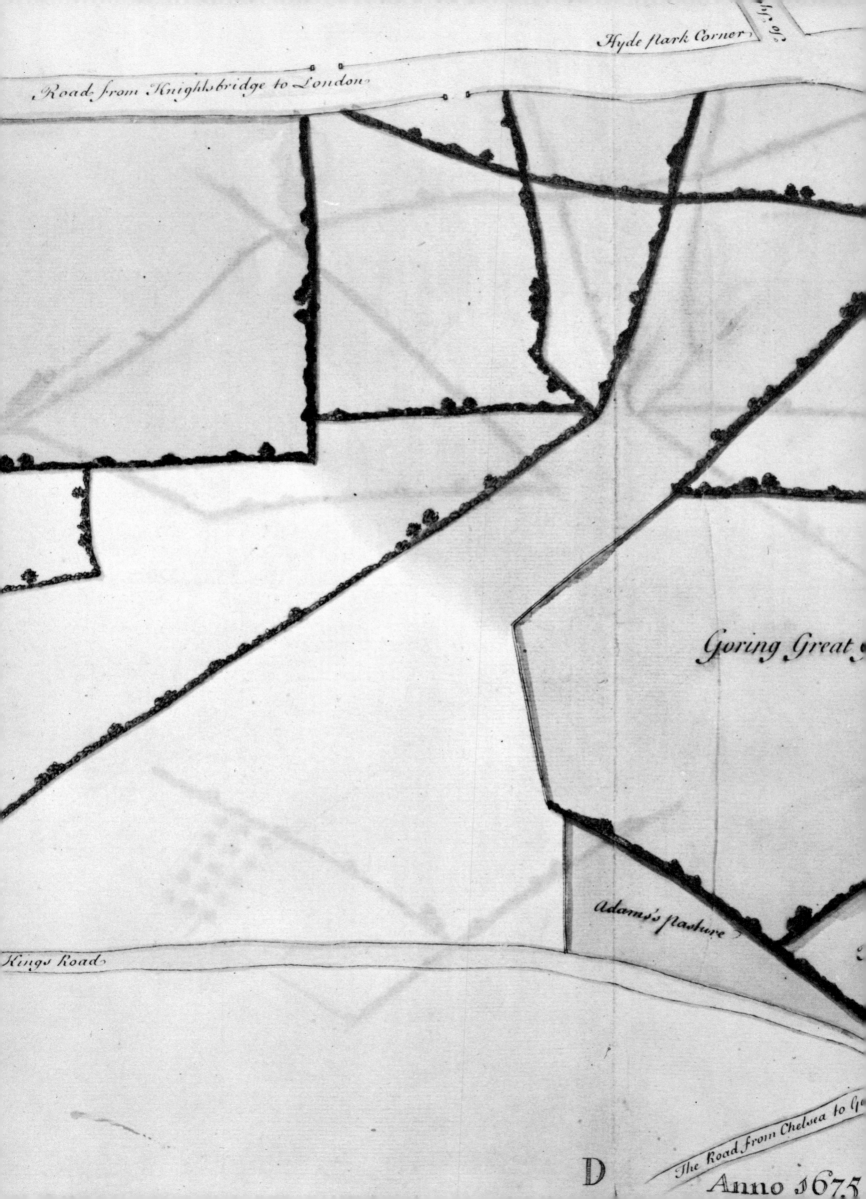

Hyde Park Corner

Road from Knightsbridge to London

Goring Great

Adams's Pasture

Kings Road

The Road from Chelsea to G

D

Anno 1675

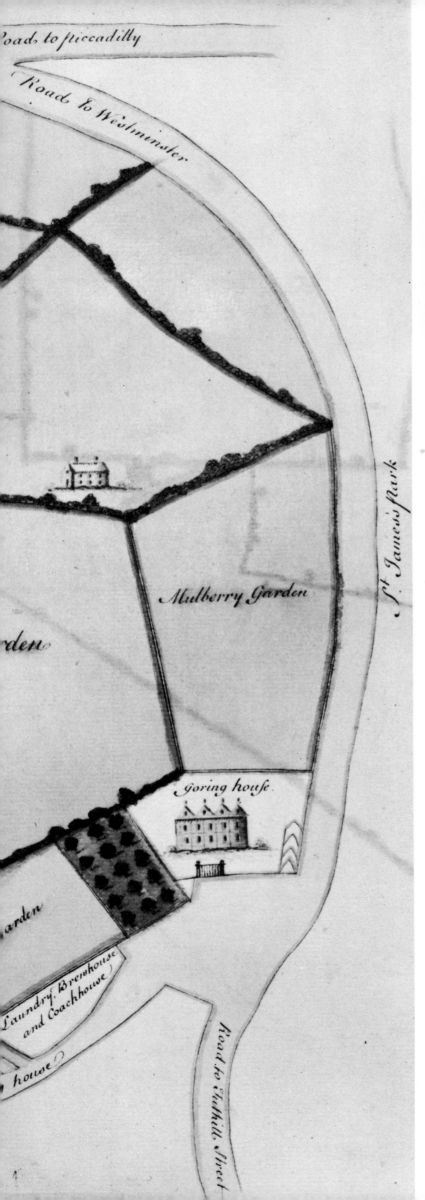

Road to Piccadilly

Road to Westminster

St James's Park

Mulberry Garden

...den

...rden

Goring house

...arden

Laundry Brewhouse
and Coachhouse

...house

Road to Tothill Street

GORING HOUSE, LATER ARLINGTON HOUSE, 1677

THE HISTORICAL BACKGROUND

Lord Goring's purchase[1] of a house and garden from William Blake junior in 1633 initiated the first documented building phase on the site of Buckingham Palace, for he built here 'a fair house and other convenient buildings, and outhouses, and upon other part of it made the ffountaine garden, a Tarris walke, a Court Yard, and laundry yard'.[2] Presumably, he added to the older house, as can be seen in a drawing purporting to show the estate in 1675 – an unremarkable and quite traditional gabled building. The sequence of events, however, is not clear, nor are the plans entirely accurate. In 1677 Goring House was leased to Mr Secretary Bennett, created Earl of Arlington in that year, who had been living there since about 1665. In 1668 Pepys described the house as a 'very fine, noble place',[3] and in 1673 the Countess of Arlington showed John Evelyn 'her new dressing-roome at Goring House, where was a bed, 2 glasses, silver jars & vases, Cabinets & other so rich furniture as I had seldom seene the like'.[4] The following year Evelyn had a very different tale to tell, for on 23 September the house was 'consum'd to the ground, with exceeding losse of hangings, plate, rare pictures and Cabinets; in a word, nothing almost was saved of the best & most princely furniture that any subject had in England'.[5] The 1675 view must show the destroyed house; another view,[6] dated 1677, shows that the house was rebuilt in that year. Despite the discrepancies between the 1677 view and the earlier engraving, the latter is probably the more faithful record. Even so, Arlington's new house[7] was much more sophisticated than its predecessor. It contained a 'long gallery of nine sash windows towards the Park, with a blue marble window slab each, a chimney piece of blue marble and two white slabs, and fifteen pictures at full length with gilt frames'.[8]

SURVEY PLAN OF GORING HOUSE
AND GROUNDS, 1675

BUCKINGHAM HOUSE, 1715

What the artists, J. Kip and L. Knyff, portray here for *Britannia Illustrata*, published in 1715, is Buckingham House completed for Charles Sheffield, Marquis of Normanby, who had been elevated to the Dukedom of Buckingham in a new creation in 1703. We are standing, as Kip and Knyff stood, with our backs to St James's Park and Whitehall and would have approached the house, to quote from the Duke's own words penned to his friend the Duke of Shrewsbury,[9] 'through rows of goodly Elms on the one hand, and gay flourishing limes on the other', to arrive at the 'iron palisade that encompasses a square court, which has in the midst a great basin with the figures of Neptune and the Triton in a water work'. The palisade meant the 'Iron Rails to the Court' and the 'Great Gates', shown in the accounts,[10] cost £230. They must surely be by Jean Tijou, the smith who wrought the Duke's staircase balustrade and was famous for the Great Screen at Hampton Court. A house with quadrant colonnades breaking forward to link with stable wings flanking a courtyard was an innovation for 1702, when this house was begun. Among the few known precedents in England, Inigo Jones's Stoke Bruerne in Northamptonshire was an early example in the 1630's, then came Hugh May's Berkeley House in Piccadilly, built in 1665, and Hackwood Park in Hampshire, designed for the Duke of Bolton about 1685.

Of more immediate interest was the Chateau de Voorst,[11] built about 1698 in Holland for the Duke of Albemarle by an English architect who must either have been connected with the Court or was a member of the Office of Works. Among those chiefly associated with the planning and building of Buckingham House were William Talman (1650–1719) and Captain William Winde (died 1722). In a letter[12] to the Duke of Newcastle, however, written in June 1703, Sir John Vanbrugh warned his potential patron of Talman's irascibility, and that many noblemen had got rid of him with sighs of relief. Talman's contribution would explain the sophistication of Buckingham House, for it was he who had designed many of the great country houses of England. The idea of a principal storey spanned by a giant order supporting a cornice, capped by a pilastered attic, was something of a novelty for a fashionable town house, but by degrees the idea spread throughout England; for example, to Wotton in Buckinghamshire as early as 1704, or to its county neighbour Chicheley in 1720. In the Library at London University there is an account book in the Duke's own hand, *The intire Expence about my House*. It is a fascinating document which gives every detail of the Duke's expenditure. It tells us that among the many craftsmen employed by him, John Fitch was paid £7,000 for brickwork, Edward Tufnell £540 for masonry, Chaplin, joiner, £500, Benson, upholsterer, £740, and Laguerre £400 for painting. It also tells us that the statues of Apollo, Liberty, Equity, Mercury, Truth and Secrecy on the east balustrade, and the Four Seasons facing the garden, were by Cavaliero David. Now, according to the Ashburnham papers,[13] this Burgundian sculptor was an artistic colleague of both Tijou and Laguerre. Yet these same papers say that Buckingham's statues cost £27 each and were carved by John Nost. One can only assume that the Duke misinterpreted the contributions of these two sculptors, and that to David should be ascribed the splendid 'Bason and Statues in ye Great Court', a Baroque fountain costing the then very large sum of £1,497.10.0.

Buckingham House in St James Park belonging to the Most Noble & Potent Prince Gentleman of ye Bed-Chamber to K: Ch: 2d Colonel of the Holland Regiment and Governour of Hull K. James 2d Created Marquess of Normanby by K.Will & Qu: Mary and one of their Mat. most

HENRY WISE THE GARDENER'S PLAN

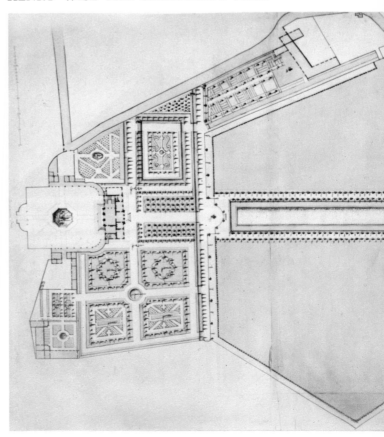

THE GARDEN FRONT

Henry Wise, the royal gardener, has included here, in his plan for the garden, a plan[14] of the house as first proposed by Talman and not by Winde. The sale of Arlington House to Lord Normanby, as he then was, in 1702 would have signalled the moment for laying out gardens, for a garden needs longer to reach fruition than do bricks and mortar. Later, the Duke of Buckingham, as Normanby had then become, tells us[15] that 'Altering Ye whole Garden by Mr Wise & making ye Sweep' cost £1,300, 'Making the Canall in the Medow' £1,000, 'Planting ye New Wilderness' £36.12.6, or such delightful ancillaries as 'Payd the Duchess of Grafton for her Orange Trees' £107.10 and 'Young Lime Trees in ye Medow' £14. The major difference between Wise's plan and the one that was finally carried out is a question of sophistication in the arrangement of the garden rooms and of their front. Wise shows an amply-proportioned front of nine bays with a giant pilastered centre-piece reduced in width but echoing that on the court front. As Campbell's plan, and the early view of the garden front show,[16] an unsatisfactory astylar treatment of eleven bays, divided into bays 4-3-4, has been substituted.

If we were to accompany the Duke on an intimate tour of the house he loved so well, we would enter his Hall, 'paved with square white stones mixed with a dark coloured marble; the walls thereof covered with a sett of pictures done in the school of Raphael', and with him would turn right (north) into the Parlour, where Sebastiano Ricci[17] had painted the cove of the niche at its end. After circuiting through the garden rooms, the Duke would lead us to his 'little closet of books' adjacent to a single-storey greenhouse where he often sat looking on to a 'Wildernesse full of blackbirds and nightingales', known as the 'New Wilderness' and seen in Wise's plan to have been a small parterre garden.

The prominent inscriptions carved round the frieze of the house betray the Duke's character and his feeling for his home: *Sic situ Laetantur Lares* (The Household Gods delight in such a situation); *Rus in Urbe* (Country within the City); *Spectator fastidiosus sibi molestus* (Critics too fastidious harm themselves); and *Lente suscipe, cito perfice* (Be slow to undertake an obligation, be quick to discharge it).

CAMPBELL'S 1715 PLAN

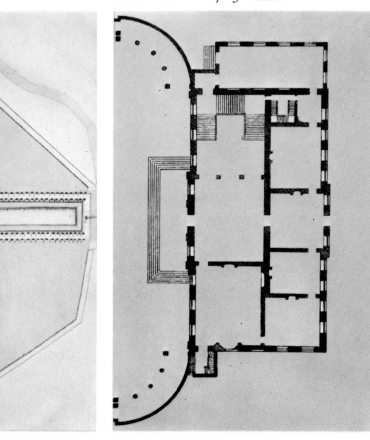

THE QUEEN'S HOUSE

The fate of the house after the Duke's death in 1721 was for it to be cared for but not altered. Because of a falsely drawn-up seventeenth-century lease, the house was found to be built on land partly belonging to the Crown. This is shown by the 1760 survey [18] where the area E, F, G, H, I was the old Mulberry Garden, and K, H, I had been taken out of St James's Park.[19] The Sheffields, finding themselves partly on Crown land, could do nothing but sell out. The major difference between this survey and Wise's plan is the conversion of the north parterre to an asymmetrical walk round a lawn.

The purchase of the house by the Crown in 1761 marked the first stage in its conversion to Buckingham Palace, but in the intervening years it took the name of The Queen's House, a sign that George III's motive was to provide his Queen with a Dower House.

With the aid of a royal purse and a good deal of Treasury tolerance, Buckingham House was transformed[20] between the years 1762 and 1776. What was accomplished can be seen by comparing this 1819 view with Kip and Knyff's view of it in 1715 (pages 22 and 23). The exterior[21] has been given a face-lift or complete re-casing, angle pilasters and statues have gone, new windows have been put in, the forecourt has been raised, and most of the decorative carved embellishments have been scraped away. In essence, Winde's old face has been scrubbed with a neo-classic brush. This applied also to the forecourt buildings, whose open arcades were filled in. But what strikes one most is the withdrawal of formality in the shape of Tijou's iron gates and David's fountain, replaced by a simple iron grille that seemingly invites the public to inspect the Palace in an informal, nonchalant way. In this lies the quintessence of the royal family's aura of domesticity and the key to the anti-Absolutist manner in which they lived.

It matters little perhaps if Chambers's plan[22] is a design or a later survey. It is the only other surviving plan of the house before Nash began to rebuild it in 1825. Here can be seen the first period of aggrandisement, the pattern of which is to remain the same, always preserving much of the old and enclosing it in a new cocoon. Apart from the arrangement of the staircase, the old Duke would still recognise his house. His garden rooms are there, and so is his 'closet of books'. To the north and south, however, the west front has now been extended by symmetrical seven-bay wings. Stepping through his Closet, the Duke would have found the King's Bedroom in place of part of his Greenhouse, and beyond that he would come into the King's Great Library (A)[23] built 1762–66 as the first in a sequence of library compartments needed to quench the King's passion for books. Adjacent was the South Library (B), turned in an east–west direction and having its south wall broken by a segmental bay. On a gallery in this room the King kept his medals and drawings. On to the southern face of the Library was attached the Octagon (C),[24] a most noble galleried apartment lit by seven Diocletian windows. One of the finest rooms in the palace, with a diameter of forty-two feet, in Chambers's *oeuvre* it compares to his Great Room for the Society of Arts (1759) or the Exhibition Room of the Royal Academy (1776). Finally, to absorb the glut of books the East Library (D) was added about 1768 to lie parallel with the Great Library, and was raised another storey in 1774 to accommodate the King's Marine Gallery, where he kept his models of ships and harbours.

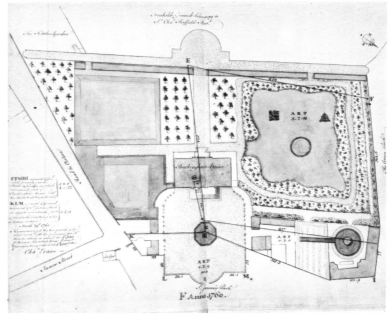

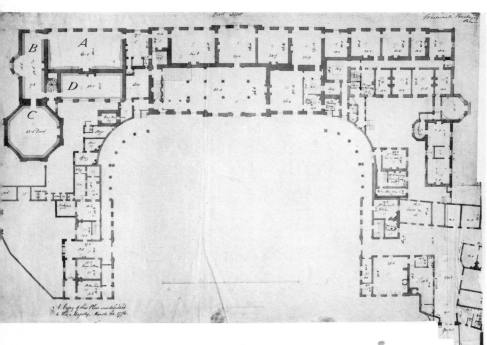

THE OCTAGON LIBRARY
PLAN OF THE GROUND FLOOR, 1838

THE STAIRCASE FROM THE LANDING

QUEEN CHARLOTTE'S SALOON

The relationship between low hall and high staircase can be best seen from the staircase itself. Of the Duke's doing, it is probably based upon suggestions proposed by William Talman. A low, darkish hall adjacent to a colourful painted staircase pleased him. Gone is Tijou's balustrade, replaced in this view by a neo-classical one wrought when James Wyatt re-arranged the stair flights in 1800, supplying at the same time the new and handsome Corinthian screen and airy Palladian motifs supporting the flights. From the first landing we could have enjoyed the splendour of Laguerre's[25] painted story of Dido and Aeneas. On the ceiling Juno asks Venus to cause Dido to fall in love with Aeneas; on the west wall opposite the windows Dido is enthroned in Juno's temple, with Illioneus the Trojan asking for her protection and Aeneas with Achates 'just become visible by the mist's vanishing'; on the south wall was the 'Fatal Feast, at which Dido, hearkening to the sad story of Troy, fell in love with Eneas'; and on the north or Saloon wall (no longer shown in this view by Pyne) was the 'Fatal Cave, where Eneas seems tempting the too willing Queen to take Shelter from the Violent Storm'. Most of the grisaille decoration on this north wall belongs, in fact, to Chambers's phase of alterations, and was painted, according to the accounts, by William Oram. In the old Duke's day the visitor from the staircase was compelled to turn left (west) into an ante-room on the garden front, then right (north) into the Japanned Room lined with 'India Japan Boards'[26], and right (east) into the Saloon.[27]

The Queen's House was divided to provide the King with apartments on the ground floor and the Queen herself with apartments above. In a sense, the splendour of Louis Laguerre's staircase anticipated what lay beyond the illusory recess. Had one already passed through the King's rooms their simplicity and utilitarian character would have heightened the richness of the Queen's Saloon, where she kept her Court. Possibly the Duke would just recognize the proportions of his Saloon, for to quote Walpole in 1783, 'The Ceiling, on which were the Poets and Sheffield, Duke of Buckingham, who built the House, is effaced, & newly painted in the antique taste by Cipriani, as are two more ceilings'.[28] Walpole's comment is not entirely true, for what Cipriani replaced here was Gentileschi's *Apollo and the Muses,* made the centrepiece of a thematic ceiling probably painted by Laguerre and accompanied on the walls by a pantheon of famous persons standing behind a balustrade.[29] Even if the historian would prefer to see the Duke's rather than the Queen's Saloon, hers was not without interest. Its decor was markedly advanced for its date, the 'antique taste' being catered for by a series of grisaille bas-reliefs which were painted by Cipriani, who may have been assisted in their execution by Oram.

The chimney-piece (now in the Queen's Presence Chamber at Windsor) was Robert Adam's sole contribution to this magnificent room. It is shown supporting, as it does today, a marble clock with figures of Vigilance and Patience, made by John Bacon the Elder in 1789.

ADAM AND CHAMBERS

OPPOSITE-
CIPRIANI AND CHAMBERS:
SECOND DRAWING
ROOM CEILING

ADAM: FROM AN ENGRAVING OF THE JAPANNED ROOM CEILING

ADAM: DESIGN FOR A DOORWAY

ADAM: AN ENGRAVING OF A CHIMNEY-PIECE
IN THE SALOON

It will never be possible accurately to evaluate Adam's contribution to Buckingham Palace. Although Joint Architect with Chambers, he was kept in the background. Had he designed anything of more consequence than this chimney-piece[30] and ceiling, he would have included it in the *Works in Architecture*, in which he published pictures of the Japanned Room ceiling and the Saloon chimney-piece in 1778. Although there are no fully itemised accounts for the paintings, Cipriani's responsibility for this Adam ceiling must be assumed from Walpole's comment. The Chambers design, coloured by the painter, is inscribed to the effect that it cost £357.12.0 and that Charles Catton painted the ornamental parts in 'Gold & Colours' and Samuel Norman was paid for 'pasting up the Work'.

Beneath a stone face-lift and an embellishment of the pediment by William Theed the younger, with his noble relief of Hercules taming the Thracian Horses, remains the Georgian Riding House surprisingly unaltered. This drawing[31] is by John Yenn, a pupil of Chambers, who became Clerk of the Works at Buckingham House in 1782. The architect of this building, completed in 1766 at a cost of £5,726, is not known. Although it is probably by Chambers, it is possible that it was designed by Thomas Worsley, for he was not only the King's Surveyor-General and an intimate friend of his, but also a great horseman, who designed his own Riding House at Hovingham in Yorkshire and possessed several designs for riding houses in his collection of architectural drawings.[32]

CHAMBERS:
THE RIDING
HOUSE

NASH AND THE PALACE

In 1798 John Nash[33] exhibited a design for a conservatory for the Prince of Wales, and in this same year married a young woman whom the *ton* regarded as one of the Prince's cast-offs, a former participant in his amorous intrigues at Carlton House. Nevertheless, whatever the rumours, Nash was not immediately favoured. His first royal commission came in 1812, when he built Royal Lodge in Windsor Great Park. Thereafter, the Prince and he were fully in accord with each other's wishes: remodelling Carlton House in 1813; Brighton Pavilion in 1815–21; Regent's Park and Regent Street from 1818, in the sense that they constituted a royal route to Carlton House; a Royal Stand at Ascot Race Course in 1821; and the new Royal Mews at Buckingham House in 1822. There had already been talk of rebuilding Buckingham House in 1819, but 'This object H.R.H. conceives cannot be accomplished for a sum much short of £500,000',[34] and because Parliament would only raise £150,000 the project was abandoned. When the Prince succeeded as George IV in 1820, his ideas were still very vague and any action seems to have been disseminated in talk, minor projects, or simply accepting the *status quo*. Nash may well have resented the opportunity given to Jeffry Wyatt (later Sir Jeffry Wyattville) to remodel Windsor Castle in 1824, but an inglorious end to Nash's career was soon to come, for in June 1825 a bill was introduced into Parliament to enable the revenues of Crown Lands to be applied to the remodelling of Buckingham House. Little did Parliament realise what it had let itself in for.

The circumstances[35] surrounding the genesis of the proposed transformation were summed up in Nash's own words when, on 29 July 1831, he reported to a Select Committee on Windsor Castle and Buckingham Palace in defence of the rise in expenditure over the past five years, from an original estimate of £252,690 to £331,973, then to £432,926, and finally on 15 May 1829 to £496,169.

'Before I enter upon details of the Report it may not be irrelevant to state, that his late Majesty's intentions and commands were to convert Buckingham House into a private residence for himself. A Plan was made upon a small scale, and on my observing that the Plan was being enlarged, I continually urged His Majesty to build in some other situation, and made several Plans for that purpose, using all the arguments in my power to dissuade His Majesty from adding to the Old Palace, but without any effect; for the late King constantly persisted that he would not build a New Palace, but would add to the present house. I then urged His Majesty to pull down the house and rebuild it higher up in the Garden in a line with Pall Mall. To induce His Majesty's acquiescence, I stated the lowness of the present site, and the northern aspect, and recommended that the house should be placed on a level

JOHN NASH, A BUST BY JOHN ROSSI

A DRAWING OF NASH'S FIRST DESIGN
BY AUGUSTUS CHARLES PUGIN

with Hyde Park Corner, and in a line with Pall Mall; a Road or prolongation of which should cross the Green Park as an approach. This proposition I thought had some weight, and for a time I had hopes that my recommendations would be adopted; but one day, either at Buckingham House or Kensington, His Majesty took me to Lord Farnborough, and said good-humouredly, "Long, now remember I tell Nash before you, at his peril ever to advise me to build a Palace. I am too old to build a Palace. If the Public wish to have a Palace, I have no objection to build one, but I must have a pied à terre. I do not like Carlton House standing in a street, and moreover I tell him, that I will have it at Buckingham House; and if he pulls it down he shall rebuild it in the same place; there are early associations which endear me to the spot". Such were nearly the words that passed. From that moment, I never presumed to press His Majesty on the subject of building a Palace, or of removing the site. Plans were accordingly made, and with a rough Estimate, submitted to Lord Liverpool. Before they were decided upon, very considerable additions were commanded, and further Estimates; until at length the Plans nearly as they now are were completed and approved, and I was directed to carry them into execution. The Building being so enlarged, and additions being daily suggested, I began to think the King might be induced to make use of it as the State Palace, and I frequently expressed my fears to His Majesty; but he persisted in saying, he should continue to hold his Courts at St James's, and that he never would hold them at Buckingham House. After the Building was covered in, His Majesty sent for me to Carlton House, and said, "Nash, the State Rooms you have made me are so handsome that I think I shall hold my Courts there".'[36]

Nash's first design, shown below in a drawing by A. C. Pugin, was so hastily prepared that its success was imperilled from the first. This is all that survives from plans that were 'not yet quite finished' early in May 1825. Nash's composition looks paper-thin, and in fact had the insubstantiality of a stage-design. It has a romantic, lively, silhouette, but the parts are unco-ordinated, and however splendid and convincing it might have seemed to George IV, translated into bricks and mortar it was doomed to failure. Spiced as it is with recollections of French neo-classicism, particularly of Gabriel, it is also indebted to Chambers and Soane, two architects whom Nash admired and emulated, and of course, it is no coincidence that it resembles his Cumberland or Chester Terraces in the Regent's Park. Hardly had the walls begun to rise than Nash became aware of how wrong his design was. The wings had to be demolished in 1828, and the ludicrous dome, 'a common slop pail turned upside down', peeping over the portico became a subject for ribaldry. Yet in some of its parts it is still ravishingly beautiful, better than what it had overlaid, or what was to succeed or overlay it.

A ROMANTIC DRAWING OF THE PALACE DRAWN BY JOSEPH NASH IN 1848
BELOW, BLORE'S CLOSING OF THE COURTYARD OF 1847

This attractive romanticised view by the artist Joseph Nash in 1848 perpetuates the Palace as it must have looked before Edward Blore had closed the courtyard view to Whitehall by 1850. Despite Nash's brave and plausible answers to the Select Committee of 1831, he was relieved of any further responsibility for the Palace. He must have cared little, for his King had died in 1830 and an unsympathetic William IV ordered an estimate to be made 'of the expence of completing Buckingham Palace and report generally on the practicability of preparing the Building for His Majesty's reception'.[38] Nash's estimate to the Committee for this had been £11,656; a consortium comprising Wyattville, Soane, Smirke and Seward gave £31,177 as a more realistic figure, and Blore's was £26,177, proof that Nash, as a cartoon cattily said, 'never minds no Estimates'. Blore's figure, however, was for finishing works only. To make the Palace suitable for the Court another £75,000 was required. It meant that the enlargement would cost nearly £720,000.

There had never been any real determination on William IV's part to make Buckingham House into a state palace. After his accession in 1830 it took second place to Windsor Castle in his affections and was even offered to the Houses of Parliament when they were burned down in October 1834. Nevertheless, he wanted it finished and saw that Blore got down to his task. But in June 1837 he died and it was left to his successor Queen Victoria to enter the new Palace in state and to decide that here would be the principal venue for the Court. We have seen that Nash had anticipated this with some consternation, so it was perhaps inevitable that in less than ten years the Queen should have to remind Peel about the 'urgent necessity of doing something to Buckingham Palace', and about the 'total want of accommodation for our little family which is fast growing up'. She hoped that Sir Robert would do something about the exterior, 'so that it should no longer be a disgrace to the country, which it certainly now is'.[39] Blore's plans were considered in May 1846, and in 1847 Parliament voted £150,000 for removing Nash's Marble Arch,[40] then in front of the Palace, building the new wing, replanning the south wing, and adding a new kitchen and Ball Room. The cry went up, 'let Mr Blore take a few lessons in the grandiose and scenic from Greenwich Hospital'; but, alas, he never did, and few would disagree with the writer in *The Builder* on 18 August 1847, who thought the new front built by Cubitt 'little more than an ordinary piece of street architecture'.

THE PALACE TODAY

The inscriptions on Sir Aston Webb's design of 1912 for refacing the palace, conveying George V's comments, are by Viscount Esher, then Secretary to the Office of Works. 'The King approves the parapetting work proceeding on Oct. 1; The King wants to see details of these figures. It is doubtful whether H.M. will like figures in this position; The King is not sure what these are'. Admittedly, Blore's Caen stone had badly decayed during the sixty years of its life, and the King demanded that Webb perform nothing more than a face-lift in conjunction with the Victoria Memorial scheme in front of the Palace; but reflecting now upon Webb's achievement elsewhere, little else could have been expected other than this insipid French *dix-huitieme* façade. In fairness, however, the King's comments show his disapproval of sculptural embellishment, and Webb's preliminary designs were progressively scaled down from a more flamboyant baroque style.[41]

Before the Victoria Memorial scheme, initiated in 1906, this royal palace must have been unique in European capitals as standing not upon an urban square, but within a bosky park and garden. Even now it is closer in identity to many of the European palaces standing in the country, yet on the edge of town. The old Duke was right when he inscribed on his frieze, *'Rus in Urbe'*. In a sense, the formality of the Duke's forecourt, destroyed by George III, was restored by Webb. He placed here a series of ornamental gates with ironwork designed by Walter Gilbert and Louis Weingartner, of the Bromsgrove Guild.

THE GARDEN FRONT

This warm façade in golden-brown Bath stone shows Nash's design at its least disturbed, and also shows him unable to control his long composition. However fine may be the four bays, emphasised by detached coupled columns, or the generous semi-circular bow, the façade lacks any cohering qualities, though less so than the Regent's Park terraces it resembles. Over his unpalatial bow Nash placed his 'slop-pail', the dome that raised so many laughs as it peeped ridiculously over the quadrangle pediment. When Blore removed the dome, he rectified something of the garden front's long-drawn-out character by adding a three-quarter attic surmounted by a square cubic mass in the centre. Yet despite Nash's compositional mistakes, no one could have used Coade stone more successfully. Once again William Croggan is to be congratulated, for his are the capitals and friezes, the trophies, the two long reliefs (1827), designed by Westmacott, of *King Alfred Expelling the Danes and Delivering the Laws,* which flank the bow, and most enchanting of all, the lively Mannerist face-consoles to the first-floor balconies. Two more of Westmacott's reliefs, designed for the Marble Arch but subsequently rejected, were incorporated here: in the attic above the bow is *Patriotism Encouraging Youth in Martial Exercises,* a two-part composition, and two other Nash-period reliefs were used or transported by Sir James Pennethorne when he added the dominating silhouette of the Ball Room to the south. On the exterior of the West Gallery is J. C. Rossi's *Four Seasons* and on the Ball Room a relief by E. H. Bailey. Until recently the front was made even more lively by sculpture that has been dismantled: Rossi's six Virtues[42] on the balustrade of the bow are now laid out,

CROGGAN'S BALCONY CONSOLES

corpse-like, near the Riding House, and another pair of Croggan's fine trophies, once on the central attic, have also gone. As can be seen in Nash's engraved view, there used to be three Ionic Conservatories, but the one placed at the east extent of the north front was removed by Blore to Kew Gardens. Today, the Queen's Gallery and a small private chapel occupy the southerly front. Between them, the raised terrace is decorated with a series of urns, designed in 1827 by Thomas Grimsley and made by Croggan at the Coade works, and later intrusions in J. M. Blashfield's artificial stone.

THE CENTRAL BOW

NASH'S GRAND ENTRANCE AND BLORE'S PORTICO

In passing through the central tripartite entrance from the Forecourt, Nash's Grand Entrance portico on the west side of the Quadrangle would be seen to be framed by the arch, and our view would widen out to embrace the width of this front. Here it is possible to gain some idea of Nash's gay, lively design, a re-interpretation of those picturesque principles expounded so well in Regent's Park. Through necessity Blore converted this quadrangle into a lifeless space by raising Nash's front, filling in the fluted Doric colonnades that provided light and movement on the ground floor, and, in 1847, by enclosing the whole with his new east front. For an example of just how dull Blore could be, we have only to turn from west to east to see an ungainly effort at grandeur, without subtle articulation and relieved not at all by Ternouth's *St George and the Dragon* in the pediment. What a relief to turn back again to Nash's elegant portico, its coupled columns distantly echoing Perrault's portico for the Louvre. Its crowning figures of Neptune, Commerce and Navigation by William Croggan were made in 1827 in Coade stone, an artificial substance resembling terra-cotta. The pediment relief of *Britannia Acclaimed by Neptune* was made by E. H. Baily in 1828, and on the wall behind the portico at first-floor level (outside the Green Drawing Room) are seven roundels depicting the *Progress of Navigation,* signed by J. E. Carew. Of the various sculptors it is Croggan, above all, who gives life to this façade, for his are the splendidly vigorous trophies, the rich, leafy friezes, and the capitals of the orders. When Blore attempted to improve Nash's design by removing the silly dome and raising the attic, he incorporated here Sir Richard Westmacott's two long reliefs carved in 1828 for the Marble Arch. The *Death of Nelson* is to the south, the *Meeting of Blücher and Wellington* to the north.

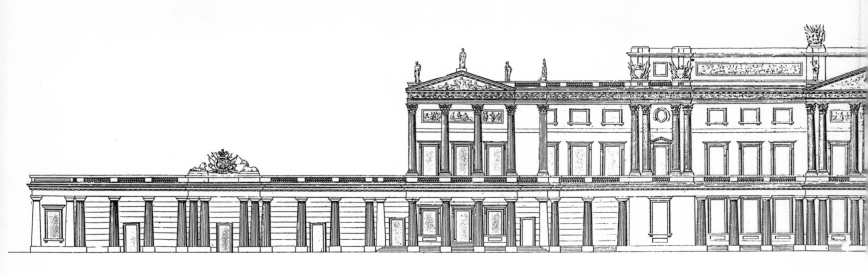

ELEVATION AND PLANS BY LEEDS AND BRITTON

The elevations presented by W. H. Leeds and John Britton[43] are more or less consistent with the Palace as it had been completed in 1837. His plans (to be read in conjunction with the two aerial views on the endpapers), however, are based upon a preliminary design, but cannot be neglected because they are all we have in the way of a plan for a perambulation of the Palace. Fortunately, the practice of cocooning rooms of an earlier epoch means that these plans are still remarkably valid for our purpose. Once we have passed through the Grand Entrance in the Blore–Aston Webb front, and beneath Nash's portico in the Quadrangle, the Grand Hall (a) will be seen to preserve the size and proportions of the Duke's hall. That connoisseur would still recognize the relationship of hall to staircase (b), but the width of his house comprised only the hall and the Marble Hall (c). Today, this Marble Hall, or lower gallery, terminates at its north end (d) with the Ministers' Staircase (not shown on this plan because it was built in 1838–39). On the garden front the Household Breakfast Room is (g), the 1855 Room (f), the Bow Room (e), the 1844 Room (h), the Carnarvon Room (i), the Eighteenth-Century Room (k), and the Orleans' Room (l), the last two forming part of the Belgium Suite. Poor George! His libraries had all been sub-

GROUND FLOOR

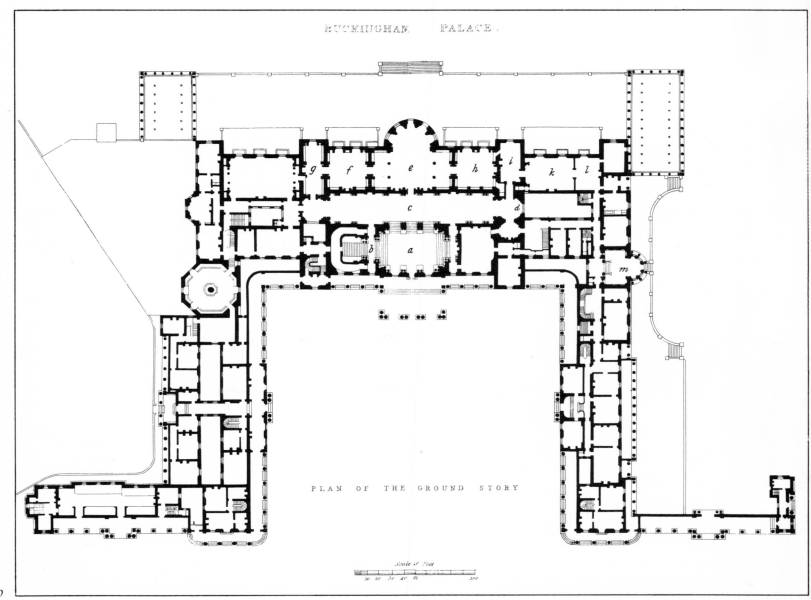

BUCKINGHAM PALACE.

PLAN OF THE GROUND STORY

Scale of Feet

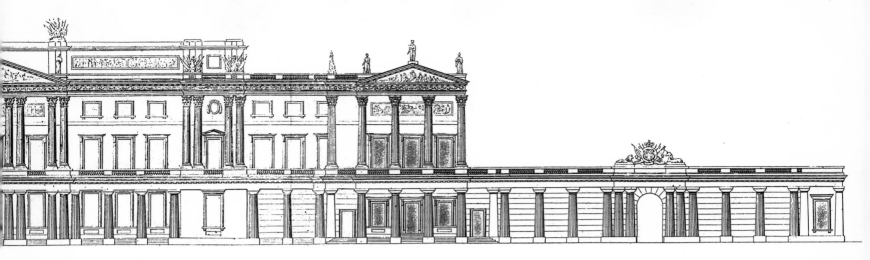

divided or destroyed and the great Octagon received a central iron column for support and was turned into a Chapel intended to receive the Raphael Cartoons. Parts of this Octagon are still embedded in the Palace, as are parts of the Prince of Wales's wing, preserved in the general plan of the Queen's Garden Entrance (*m*). Continuing eastwards the corridor would open to the King's Door, adjacent to which is the King's Waiting Room.

At the top of the Grand Staircase (*a*), the southern arm (*b*) leads to the East Gallery (*c*) and the Ball Room, and the pair of northerly prongs point to the Guard Room (*e*), opening to the Green Drawing Room (*f*) and into the Throne Room (*g*). We can then pass into the Picture Gallery (*h*) or into a room at its north end, today an octagonal vestibule at the head of the Ministers' Staircase. From this vestibule, access is given to the Royal Closet and the principal State Rooms on the garden front: the White Drawing Room (*k*), the Music Room (*i*), the Blue Drawing Room (*l*) and into Blore's State Dining Room (*m*). Beyond its recess Sir James Pennethorne, the queen's favourite architect in 1853, formed the West Gallery to link up with his new Ballroom and the State Supper Room, completing the circuit with the East Gallery.

PRINCIPAL FLOOR

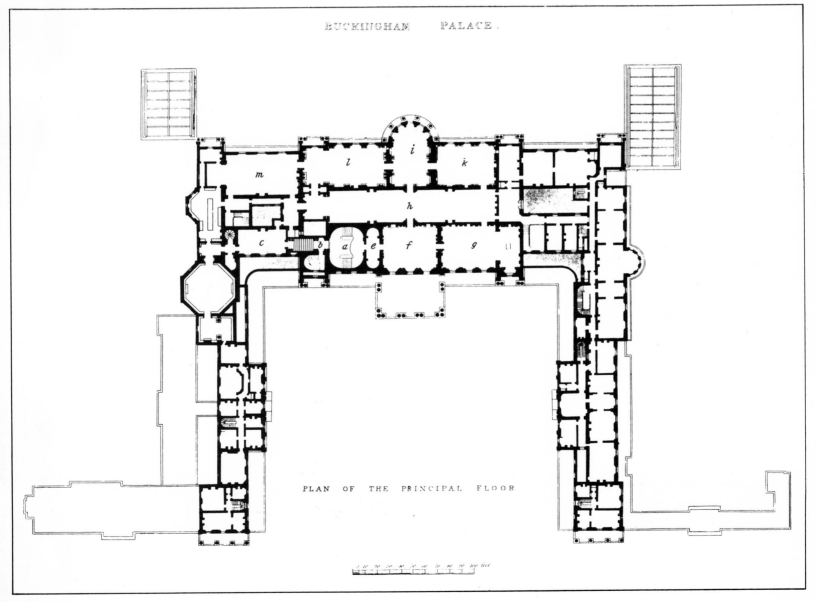

BUCKINGHAM PALACE.

PLAN OF THE PRINCIPAL FLOOR

THE GRAND HALL

One's first emotion upon entering this Hall is of surprise, for here is no spacious apartment, but instead one almost ridiculously low and squashed in its proportions. Nevertheless, the Duke would have recognized it, as would have George III, for here, by virtue of the existing structure, is perpetuated Winde's 1705 hall. But Nash treated it most ingeniously to gain more height and give some impression of spaciousness and light. He scooped out the floor level by the equivalent of eight steps, arranging the outside ground level accordingly, and provided a beautifully ordered system of three tiers of ascent. His is the Corinthian columnar treatment in a beautiful veined milky-grey marble brought from Carrara by Joseph Browne, the sculptor whom Nash was persuaded to send to Italy in 1825 to contract for a suitable stone. The capitals, in chased and gilded bronze, are by Samuel Parker. One can but applaud Nash's use of cross-vistas with side-lighting, and the perspective made by the mirrored sides of the window frames. Today the colour is different. It is the white and gold, reflecting the Frenchified Edwardian taste of C. H. Bessant, who was commissioned to redecorate the Palace almost completely in 1902. Here in the Hall, for example, he obliterated an attractive painted ceiling in the Renaissance style. Prominently placed at its north end stands a lush, encrusted chimney-piece, presumably designed by Nash, and if so, his best, and at £1,000 the most expensive of his in the Palace, supplied in 1829 by Joseph Theakstone, 'the ablest carver of his time'.

THE GRAND HALL, LOOKING TOWARDS THEAKSTONE'S CHIMNEY-PIECE

THE MARBLE HALL, LOOKING TOWARDS THE MINISTERS' STAIRCASE

THE MARBLE HALL

Even here we can be forcibly reminded of the Duke's house, for standing between the two halls, the width from wall to wall is seventy-four feet, the same width as that of Buckingham House. This Marble Hall would mark the site of the garden rooms, the Duke's 'suite of large rooms', his 'bed-chamber' and 'large closet'. To give a sense of movement to the 137 feet of this 'Long Gallery', Nash has used a coupled order against the walls. The chimney-pieces are not his, however; they came from Carlton House and could therefore have been designed by Henry Holland and sculptured by Sir Richard Westmacott. The festoons of fruit and flowers to

each overmantel were in the Centre Room in 1873, and must surely be of an even earlier period than Buckingham House. It would be a nostalgic memento if these were, in fact, part of Lord Arlington's decorations, perhaps from the 'pretty gallery', regrettably demolished by the Duke. At its north end we see the Ministers' Staircase by Blore in 1838–39, when it became obvious that Nash's plan allowed for no handsome means of communication between the two floors of the palace at this north end. It was also important for access to the Belgium Corridor.

THE GRAND STAIRCASE

The Grand Staircase is of greater spatial complexity than the Duke's, and decidedly more than George III's. The first pause occurs on the Grand Hall landing, where a vista is aligned to one of the Marble Hall chimney-pieces. From here one can move forward, looking up to and through the vaulted arm leading to the East Gallery, the State Supper Room and the Ball Room. This third arm, and most happy design of Nash's, may echo something from Borromini's *Perspectiva* in the Palazzo Spada, in Rome, and, of course, in a humble way Bernini's Scala Regia in the Vatican. Turning our backs upon this excursion into Continental baroque, the walls and ceiling surround us in scintillating white and gold with white sculpture high up on the walls. This was not the effect intended by Nash, for his facings were of veined scagliola, or plaster imitating stone, material used in this context in a pioneer way. Its extensive employment by both Joseph Browne and Nash initiated its popularity in the succeeding decades. Yet so quickly did it deteriorate on the staircase that as early as 1834 Blore replaced it or substituted painted marbling. Thomas Stothard designed all the sculptures: long reliefs of the Seasons carved by his son Alfred Joseph, and the whimsical alto-reliefs of playing cupids in the lunettes of the shallow skylight carved by Francis Bernasconi. Above them scintillates the etched glass made by Wainwright, among the most exquisite of the decorative attractions in the Palace. Above all, the sumptuous gilt-bronze, acanthus-scrolled balustrade captures the attention. Made by Parker in 1828–30, and commensurate with its splendour and quality, it cost £3,900 and had few equals in Regency England.

ABOVE, THE GRAND STAIRCASE, LOOKING TOWARDS THE PERSPECTIVA AND THE EAST GALLERY

OPPOSITE, THE FIRST LANDING FROM THE PERSPECTIVA

THE GUARD ROOM

As an ante-room to the Green Drawing Room, the Guard Room provides a pause between the relatively public nature of the Grand Staircase and the place of assembly before the monarchical world of the Throne Room. As a unit in a traditional sequence of planning, Nash had to discover space for it within the wall divisions of the old house, and very roughly his Guard Room is on the site of the Duke's landing. In this small room Nash might be considered at his best and most royal. Here are the first of the fine parquetried floors. The doors were made by George Harrison, enriched with Samuel Parker's metalwork, and set with silver plates, and an ingenious method of lighting by a series of oval apertures filled with convex plates of Wainwright's engraved glass. Through these light plays softly upon William Pitts's relief of *Peace and War* and upon the white pedestalled statuary.

THE GUARD ROOM, WITH THE DOOR TO THE GREEN DRAWING ROOM

THE GREEN
DRAWING ROOM

The Green Drawing Room is really the thinly clothed bones of Queen Charlotte's Saloon, and before her time, of the Duke's. On the east side three windows, central to the Quadrangle, once commanded a bosky view to the Long Canal in St James's Park and to the Georgian silhouette of Whitehall and Westminster. The doorway on the west side now opens to the Picture Gallery, dividing the Palace like a spine running north–south, but in Queen Charlotte's day it opened into the Japanned Room with Adam's ceiling painted by Cipriani. The colours of this Drawing Room, Nash's Saloon, are soft and muted with the off-white and gold of the pilasters and ceiling bringing together the richness of green stamped brocade on the walls and the deep crimson and gold of the Axminster carpet. If the pair of chimney-pieces, by the same sculptor as those in the Music Room, are by Joseph Browne, then they may be of Italian importation, and even by Italian carvers.

THE NORTH-EAST CORNER, WITH THE
DOOR TO THE PICTURE GALLERY

THE GREEN DRAWING
ROOM CEILING

THE THRONE ROOM

The white and gold taste of 1902 once again predominates in a room that should have stone-coloured walls and red silk hangings. Both Nash and Blore call for attention, for this is a 'transition' room, finished after George IV's death in 1830. The ceiling, for example, follows a design laid down by Nash, and this can be said about most of the sculptural decoration. In 1828 E. H. Baily provided the encircling frieze of these events from the Wars of the Roses: north, the *Battle of Tewkesbury*, east the *Marriage of Henry VII and Elizabeth of York*, and west, the *Battle of Bosworth Field*; on the south wall Bellona appears with a group of warriors. To whom to attribute the door from the Green Drawing Room is anyone's guess. Admittedly, its inner surround follows Nash's designs elsewhere, and the flattened pediment is of the same type as the old doors in the Picture Gallery, but the Victories over the door crown William IV.

THE DOORWAY, LOOKING BACK INTO
THE GREEN DRAWING ROOM

ONE OF THE VICTORY CONSOLES

The most beautiful sculptures in this room are Bernasconi's winged Victories supporting consoles under the beam in front of the Throne area, and most happily reaching out to each other by conjoined garlands suspended from the beam. Against the north wall stands the Throne, flanked by carved wood and gilt trophies designed by Henry Holland. These are said to have once decorated the Throne Room in Carlton House.

The Throne Room can be left by a door into the Gallery, or by a secret jib-door near the Throne, leading into the Vestibule at the head of the Ministers' Staircase.

THE ROYAL CLOSET CHIMNEY-PIECE

At the head of the Ministers' Staircase the present Octagonal Vestibule was formed out of an oblong one in 1904. It serves to communicate with the Picture Gallery, secretively with the Throne Room, and westwards with the Royal Closet, a small room facing the first of the State Rooms on this garden side of the Palace. Whatever else may claim interest in this room, all attention is drawn to the chimney-piece, removed from the Throne Room at Carlton House and installed here about 1830, the date of all those parts within the area of its egg-and-dart moulding. But what of the rest? It is fraught with problems, for the bronze and ormolu caryatids, with their pedestals and the applied ormolu frieze and panels, are undoubtedly of Parisian workmanship and are quite un-like anything actually designed by Henry Holland at Carlton House in the 1780's. Whether the chimney-piece was supplied from Paris is, of course, another matter. Many will think it odd to pass from here off axis, into the White Drawing Room. There was no reason for this, but according to Nash's plans it seems always to have been so.

ONE OF THE CARYATIDS

THE WHITE DRAWING ROOM

Here the Royal Family may assemble before passing through to the State Dining Room or Ball Room after they have come from the Royal Closet through a curiously secretive door concealed by a swinging pier-glass and table. Although the most glittering of the State Apartments, its white and gold is not of Edwardian date, as might have been expected, but pre-dates 1873 and supplants a richer and more sombrely-rich scheme in which were pilasters of yellow scagliola by Joseph Browne. Substantially finished in 1831, this room is also a creation by Nash, for Blore only contributed the pier-glasses, with their lusciously baroque terminations, and ordered the flowered Axminster carpet. The ceiling, as in the Guard Room, is decorated with reliefs by Pitts, a series of twelve panels allegorical of the Origin and Progress of Pleasure: *Love awakening the Soul to Pleasure*; *The Soul in the Bower of Fancy*; *The Pleasure of Decoration*; *The Invention of Music*; *The Pleasure of Music*; *The Dance*; *The Masquerade*; *The Drama*; *The Contest for the Palm*; *The Palm Assigned*; *The Struggle for the Laurel*; and *The Laurel Obtained*. The 1831 *Report* to the Select Committee describes these 'as *the sports of boys*, costing £800'.

THE NORTH END: ON THE LEFT IS A CONCEALED
MIRROR DOOR TO THE ROYAL CLOSET

THE MUSIC ROOM

Having reached the centre of the west front, we should remember that we are progressing through the enfilade of apartments added by Nash when he widened the Duke's house on this garden side. In 1831 the parquet floor of this Music Room had nearly been finished and all the pier glasses were in position, so here we have yet another room by Nash untouched by Blore's completing hand. This room is something of a pivot in the Palace. Directly east across the Picture Gallery lies the Green Drawing Room, and southwards will soon be seen the State Dining Room and Ball Room. As an architectural entity it is highly successful, for rather than being just four walls raised beneath a lavish ceiling, the way Nash has used his grand order, encircling the square and semi-circular compartments and giving them a continuity by the arched windows, mirrored pier-glass recesses and arched doors, provides something like a taut cohesion of elements. The colouring is most rich and satisfactory: crimson curtains, ivory walls, the deep lapis-lazuli blue of Joseph Browne's columns, and the bright gilding of capitals, cornices and pelmets. If we look up at the ceiling, it is worth remembering the ceilings at Brighton Pavilion, for in this Nash shows something of his ingenuity at vaulting, perhaps an unconscious debt to Sir John Soane. In the three segmental parts of the square Pitts has given the Progress of Rhetoric, with three reliefs of Harmony (north), Eloquence (east), and Pleasure (south). Only when the Savonnerie carpet is raised can the full beauty of the inlaid floor be appreciated. Here is the high-water mark of the craft in England, a consummate job by George Seddon, the cabinet-maker of the firm Morel and Seddon, who charged £2,400 for the work in 1831.

LOOKING TOWARDS THE BOW
ABOVE, A DETAIL OF THE PARQUETRY FLOOR

THE MUSIC ROOM.
OPPOSITE, THE NORTH–EAST ANGLE

THE BLUE DRAWING ROOM

Before Sir James Pennethorne built the new Ball Room, the Blue Drawing Room, originally known as the South Drawing Room, served in its stead. Although Nash revised his design, Joseph Browne's 1834 chimney-piece may be the only intrusion. The colouring of this room is almost voluptuous: a flock wallpaper of turquoise matrix on shaded umber, a red and gold Axminster carpet, identical to the one in the Red Drawing Room, and thirty columns painted in imitation of onyx over Browne's original pink scagliola. Looking up at the ceiling, we find we are in a two-part compartment of three major bays held by coffered coves, and a slightly lower bay at the south end behind its own tympanum. This second part corresponds to the Royal Closet at the other end of the enfilade. In the tympanums Pitts apotheosises Shakespeare (north), Spencer (south) and Milton (facing north). Stothard had been originally commissioned by Nash, but Blore preferred Pitts's estimates. Not fixed in position until 1835, these memorials to the poets are definitely Victorian, in contrast to the sculptor's more chaste, neo-classical style elsewhere in the Palace.

THE NORTH-WEST ANGLE WITH A GARDEN WINDOW

PAGES 66 AND 67: THE CHIMNEY WALL AND THE MUSIC ROOM DOOR

THE STATE DINING ROOM

This, the last room on the enfilade of the old Palace, and related to Chambers's plan, is above the south wing, or George III's Great Library. At the time of the Select Committee's *Report* in 1831 little had been begun, and Nash's designs were scrapped for Blore's extraordinary restless bracketed ceiling, a powerful design that ought perhaps to canopy white walls instead of the present red damask. Little may have been complete at William IV's death in 1836, for in many medallions Queen Victoria's cipher appears. The style of the chimney-piece here is similar to those in the State Supper Room. It may therefore be by M. C. Wyatt, or by a sculptor in sympathy with his style.

THE DINING ROOM SHOWING ROYAL PORTRAITS

THE WEST GALLERY

In former times, the State Dining Room would have terminated the Palace towards the south, further progression being possible only by turning to the east, above the shell of George III's South Library, and into the Gallery of his Octagon Library, converted by Nash into the Chapel. Until 1853 England's greatest spread of Empire was ruled from a palace with State Rooms no larger than those in a country house, and one of moderate size at that. Blenheim, Castle Howard, Houghton or Kedleston could boast of having more capacious rooms of assembly. It was obvious that something had to be done[44] and in June 1853 Queen Victoria commissioned Sir James Pennethorne[45] to rebuild all those parts of the palace south of the State Dining Room. He built the West Gallery (once called the Approach Gallery) on to the State Dining Room as a link to his huge Ball Room, laid out on the south side of the Palace. We shall see the rest of his work when we pass through the Ball Room and make a circuit towards the north again, passing into his East Gallery, where he rebuilt and extended Nash's galleries leading off the south arm of the Grand Staircase. From the East Gallery opens the State Supper Room. The West Gallery, lighted by simple groups of nine pane fanlights with engraved glass, is a room of almost perfect entity, marred only by the unsympathetic north and south mirror doors. Above these doors are William Theed the Younger's two large reliefs, installed in 1856. To the north is the *Birth of Venus* and to the south *Venus Descending with the Armour of Achilles,* both showing a return to a Renaissance tradition of sculpture as distinct from Pitts's and Stothard's late neo-classicism. Between the West and East Galleries is Pennethorne's quite unremarkable Cross Gallery, a room that does not merit close attention.

WILLIAM THEED'S BIRTH OF VENUS
IN THE COVE OF THE CEILING

THE DOOR FROM THE WEST GALLERY

THE BALL ROOM

It is not Pennethorne's fault that this is now a somewhat stark Georgian baroque room, for its character is almost entirely Edwardian, Bessant having stripped it of all its colourful decorations and articulated its walls with a giant fluted order. Louis Gruner's *cinquecento*-style decorations included wall paintings of the *Twelve Hours* by Nicola Consoni. Following that great architect C. R. Cockerell, Pennethorne initiated here a return to the Italian Renaissance tradition of decorative art. For colour, all one's attention is drawn to the splendid crimson velvet of the Throne Canopy, designed by Sir Edwin Lutyens and created from the Imperial Shamiana used at the Coronation Durbar at Delhi in 1911.

THE BALL ROOM THRONES

THE EAST GALLERY

Nash's plan shows a gallery of half this length, continuing the direction of his *Perspectiva* and leading to the Octagon Library. With sixteen of Consoni's grisaille panels of cupids at play, this is now the sole survivor of Pennethorne's decorations. Nevertheless, it has lost its marbled walls and painted arched compartments containing urns of cascading flowers. Pennethorne was a great pasticheur, as is well shown by the doors so successfully copying the style of the earlier ones. The chimney-piece is not by Pennethorne. It was removed to the East Gallery by Blore from the Picture Gallery and belongs to the set of five supplied by Joseph Browne from Carrara and almost certainly carved by Italian sculptors. In this one, winged female figures symbolical of painting hold laurel garlands which encircle the head of Rembrandt. The most northerly doorway on the west side leads into Pennethorne's Ante-Room, now called the Silk-Tapestry Room.

THE SILK-TAPESTRY ROOM

TWO NEEDLEWORK PANELS AFTER PAINTINGS OF *THE MASSACRE OF THE INNOCENTS* BY TINTORETTO, AND *THE REST ON THE FLIGHT INTO EGYPT* BY BOURDON

This is a by-pass, for it avoids the Grand Staircase and allows access between the Ball and Supper Rooms and the Picture Gallery. It is, in fact, merely Pennethorne's enlargement of a room by Nash performing the same function, and is today named from four Italian needlework panels (now at Hampton Court) of the second half of the seventeenth century, depicting the *Adoration of the Magi,* the *Massacre of the Innocents,* the *Flight into Egypt,* and *Christ in the House of Simon the Leper.* The Picture Gallery is now directly accessible on the north axis.

THE PICTURE GALLERY

However impressive this gallery, 155 feet long, it has nevertheless undergone vicissitudes, first at the hands of Blore in the 1830's and then at Aston Webb's in 1914. The view from the south end is framed by a screen of columns fronting a vestibule for access to the Blue Drawing Room adjacent to the west. Nash's system of lighting, a single series of raised skylights, was replaced by Blore within a few years of its erection by a parallel tripartite system of raised oval and square lights. This again gave way to the present curved roof in 1914. In 1873 the Nash–Blore entrances still remained, although Blore must have done some early rearranging. Each entrance was flanked by pairs of Coade and scagliola busts on pillars made by Croggan and set obliquely to the jambs; these were removed in 1931. Browne's remaining four chimney-pieces honour Titian, Dürer, Van Dyck and da Vinci.

THE NORTH VIEW OF THE GALLERY

BELOW, THE DURER CHIMNEY-PIECE

A DETAIL
OF THE CEILING

THE 1844 ROOM AND THE 1855 ROOM

After descending the Ministers' Staircase a diversion could be made to the semi-state apartments that open to the garden and lie parallel to the Marble Hall. What remains of Nash in these rooms—and we must be wary because much was Georgianised later—is in a mood of restraint. The sequence from south to north is as follows: the Household Breakfast Room, with a late eighteenth-century chimney-piece installed in 1928; the 1855 Room, commemorating the occupation of these rooms by Napoleon III and the Empress Eugènie; the Bow Room, central to the front and redecorated in 1902; the 1844 Room, named because of its occupation in that year by the Emperor Nicholas of Russia; the Carnarvon Room with a chimney-piece said to have come from Carlton House, but more probably French, of about 1820; and the Eighteenth-Century and Orleans Rooms, both with good standard Nash-period chimney-pieces.

THE BELGIUM CORRIDOR

The more northerly garden rooms form part of the so-called Belgium Suite, from which an exit could be made either to the foot of the Ministers' Staircase or directly into the Belgium Corridors. These corridors, vaulted with variations of cross-

vault and saucer domes, are by Nash, indebted, as in the
Music Room, to Soane, and would take one to the Garden
Entrance on the north front, wherein is embedded the ghost
of Chambers's Prince of Wales's Wing.

THE KING'S WAITING ROOM

Beyond the Entrance and occupying the whole of the north wing on the ground floor are the Offices of the Duke of Edinburgh and the Privy Purse. In the centre of the Quadrangle front Nash formed the King's Entrance, adjacent to which is the old King's Waiting Room. Here the chinoiserie chimney-piece, like that in the Royal Closet, forcibly reminds us of the splendour and decorative richness of Holland's Carlton House. This chimney-piece comes from the Chinese Drawing Room, the most exotic of the Prince's apartments, illustrated by Thomas Sheraton in his *Cabinet Maker and Upholster's Drawing Book* published in 1793. This unique engraving is indeed a fortunate survival, for it shows the chimney-piece ensuite with the pair of similarly-styled chinoiserie pier tables now in the Yellow Drawing Room. So close is the style of these tables to that of Adam Weisweiler, that all three may well have been exported from Paris under the orders of the *marchand mercier* Dominique Daguerre, or of William Gaubert, who was something of an *entrepreneur* at Carlton House. When that ravishing neo-classical palace was so unfortunately demolished in 1827, it was an obvious move to install this exquisite chimney-piece in the Brighton Pavilion,[46] where it remained in the Music Room Gallery until it was brought to Buckingham Palace twenty years later.

THE CHIMNEY-PIECE, WITH A PAINTING
BY CORNELIS VAN GIEST.
RIGHT, A CHINESE CARYATID

THE CHINESE LUNCHEON ROOM

At the end of the Privy Wing there is the Privy exit to the main forecourt, and a staircase to the first floor, or Visitors' Apartments facing the Mall across the Blore–Webb east wing. We are now, of course, out of Nash's domain. Ahead, southward, stretches the Principal Corridor, but the first room to see is the Chinese Luncheon Room in the north-east angle of the front.

This gorgeously exotic ensemble is a most delightful surprise, for it is completely made up by Blore and Cubitt from parts of the Brighton Pavilion Music and Banqueting Rooms, combined with rich Chinese-red hangings and bam-boo trellis-like decorative dados. The chimney-piece, reflecting as much of India as of Cathay, was designed by Robert Jones and made by Benjamin Vulliamy and Westmacott. The doors, again of Hindoo derivation, are 'Embellished in imitation of Japan work . . . and above these, in an arched compartment . . . dragons issuing from an expanded flower cup, expressive of the chimera of oriental mythology', were painted by Frederick Crace. There are four paintings in this room, each of them 'inclosed within painted framings of trellis-work, edged by narrow gold mouldings' from Jones's wall decoration of the Banqueting Room.

THE EAST WALL, SHOWING ONE OF ROBERT JONES'S PANELS
ABOVE, FREDERICK CRACE'S DOORS

THE CHINESE LUNCHEON ROOM CHIMNEY-PIECE
WITH FIRE-DOGS MADE BY W. M. FEETHAM IN 1849

THE PRINCIPAL CORRIDOR

The Principal Corridor, extensively redecorated between 1855 and 1873, extends for the whole length of the Quadrangle on its east side. Not only is this a passage of communication, but also a gallery for the display of works of art. We can walk through its mirror-reflecting cross-walls, past two China Pagodas (from the Music Room at Brighton), to reach the Yellow Drawing Room in the south-east angle of the wing, which occupies the same position as the Chinese Luncheon Room at the other end of the corridor.

A PAIR OF YUNG CHENG PORCELAIN PAGODAS ON SPODE PEDESTALS, FROM THE MUSIC ROOM, BRIGHTON PAVILION

THE YELLOW DRAWING ROOM

The chimney-piece ensemble is most striking, a fantastic creation of a European's dream of Cathay, where Mandarins nod in its niches, winged dragons climb round its jamb-columns, and dragon-serpents convolute in its frieze. Made in 1822 for the Brighton Saloon by Robert Jones and Parker, it cost over £922. Blore, it is true, installed the chimney-piece here, but there seems no evidence that he intended a Chinese decor as lush as that of the Luncheon Room. The jasmine-yellow eighteenth-century wallpaper is part of the 'very fine set of India Paper, green ground, colored flowers, birds, etc' supplied in 1817 by Frederick Crace for the Brighton Saloon before it was redecorated by Nash.

THE CENTRE ROOM

Placed in the centre of the main front is the room from which the Royal Family make public appearances on the balcony overlooking the Forecourt and the Victoria Memorial. The chinoiserie concoction is essentially of the late 1920's, but in 1873 the Brighton Banqueting Room chimney-pieces were here, as were the Brighton lacquer doors.

Sir Charles Allom under Queen Mary's direction created a more binding Chinese scheme of decoration by setting the old Imperial Yellow Chinese silk panels here in chinoiserie frames. The overmantels seem suspiciously to have been made up from those in the Brighton Saloon, and from the same room come the doors, decorated with pagodas in rocky scenery.

A YUNG CHENG PAGODA IN THE YELLOW DRAWING ROOM

THE STATE COACH

ONE OF CIPRIANI'S PANELS

Chambers's design[49] for this most magnificent and opulent coach is dated 1760, so showing that it must have taken nearly two years to build, for George II died on 25 October 1760 and George III did not appear in his new state coach for the opening of Parliament until November 1762. To those who know Chambers as the architect of Somerset House, or the author of the great *Treatise on Civil Architecture*, this ravishing rococo design may seem an anachronism in his work. Nevertheless, 1760 was too early a date for neo-classical geometricality to have been applied to a coach whose form favoured the curvaceous lines of the rococo, and in any case if one examines the coach with care many delicious neo-classical motifs will be found to be incorporated. Joseph Wilton carved the coach, G. B. Cipriani painted its seven panels, Henry Pujolas was the varnisher and gilder, and Samuel Butler was the coachmaker. The whole design is richly allegorical: eight palm trees contain the framework, the four angle-trees supporting trophies commemorative of Britain's victories. Under the body are tritons, two in front holding shells with which to herald the approach of the Monarch of the Ocean, two in the rear carrying the imperial fasces with tridents. In the centre of the roof three boys representing the Genii of England, Scotland and Ireland support the Imperial Crown and hold Sceptre, Sword of State, and Ensigns of Knighthood.

ONE OF THE TRITONS CARVED BY WILTON

THE WATERLOO VASE

After a chequered career, this vase came to rest in the garden of Buckingham Palace in this century. Napoleon, passing through Tuscany on his way to the Russian front, had seen a block of marble over fifteen feet high. He asked for it to be preserved and may even have ordered a vase to be roughly blocked out to commemorate his anticipated victories. After Waterloo, however, the Duke of Tuscany presented the block or unfinished vase to George IV, who commissioned Westmacott to carve it for the new Waterloo Gallery at Windsor, but its twenty tons would have sent it crashing to the Windsor dungeons, so in 1836 William IV gave it to the National Gallery, who disposed of their burdensome gift in 1906 by returning it to the King's residence.

THE GARDEN HOUSE

The designer of this gay summer house with its disdainful atlantes is not known, but it may well have been William Kent, or possibly John Vardy. It was originally set up in the Admiralty Gardens around the 1740's and is shown on a plan drawn in 1794.[48] After the Admiralty was extended, a century later, it found a home in the Palace gardens.

THE GARDEN PAVILION

Soon after William Aiton in the mid-1830's had begun the Early Victorian landscaping of the grounds laid out by 'Capability' Brown,[47] a wooden, rustic house was built by the lake, possibly to Wyattville's designs. Louis Gruner, one of the Prince Consort's favourite painters, describes it as 'picturesque and fantastic, without any regular style of architecture'. In 1844 it was chosen as the vehicle by which Prince Albert could encourage experiments in the techniques of fresco painting, then being revived as a suitable medium for the proposed decoration in the new Palace at Westminster. As Mrs Jameson wrote in her preface to Gruner's *Decorations of The Garden-Pavilion In The Grounds of Buckingham Palace* (1846), 'The introduction, or rather the revival, of Frescoe Painting in this country has become, in connection with a great national monument, a topic of general interest, an affair of national importance, and no longer a matter of private or artistic speculation'.

For the central Milton Room, the contributors to a Comus cycle were Dyce, Eastlake, Landseer, Leslie, Maclise, Ross, Stanfield; and Unwins for the lunettes, E. Morley for the painted flowers, and S. Rice for arabesques. W. G. Nicholl moulded the bas-reliefs and stucco decorations; G. B. Stephens carved the chimney-piece; and the Pompeian doors were carved by G. B. Lovati. Flanking this room was the Pompeian Room, with encaustic painting by Agostino Aglio, and the Scott Room, with contributions in the Abbotsford taste by Dallas, Timbrell, Townsend, Stonehouse, Severn, and John and Richard Doyle. Although the *Quarterly Review* of the day had great expectations of this experiment, to our eyes and taste it seems a curiously incoherent scheme, like a cross-section in miniature from one of the contemporary Royal Academy exhibitions. It remained something of an antiquarian toy and like a neglected summer house in a country garden, rotted away until it was demolished in 1928.

THE ARCHITECTURE
CAPTION NOTES

1 My sources are drawn basically from Mr H. Clifford Smith's *Buckingham Palace*, 1931.
I obviously cannot compete in depth with Mr Smith's discussions. This is particularly the case with the earlier history of the site between about 1609 and 1633. I have ignored this completely, because in what is intended to be primarily a pictorial survey, the intricacies of lease and sub-lease, or of what was and what was not the Mulberry Garden, are irrelevent. I hope that my approach in describing the architectural features, first in chronological order, then in order of a suggested perambulation of the Palace, will be no less clear than Mr Smith's admirable but somewhat more complicated form of presentation. The official *History of the King's Works,* due to appear under the editorship of Mr H. M. Colvin, will minutely describe the architectural history of the Palace from 1761 to 1851. The authors of that *History,* in particular Mr Michael Port, whom I have consulted over the Nash–Blore phase of the building, will take into account an array of documents that time has not allowed me to examine. The architectural history of the Palace as we see it today is told with a wealth of detail in two reports: that from the *Select Committee on the Office of Works and Public Buildings,* dated 19 June 1828 (often called the First Report), and the *Second Report from the Select Committee on Windsor Castle and Buckingham Palace,* dated 14 October 1831. In the Royal Library at Windsor Castle there are a number of key documents, among them the *History* of the Palace, known as the Surveyor-General's Report (*see* note 6), and a valuable collection of old photographic albums, the most important being those of 1873.

2 Clifford Smith, *op. cit.,* pp.14 and 11–23 for the history of the site.

3 Pepys, *Diary,* ed. Braybrooke, V, 1877, p.332.

4 Evelyn, *Diary,* ed. de Beer, III, 1955, p.8.

5 Evelyn, *op. cit.,* IV, 1955, p.44.

6 Both plans are from the volume in the Royal Library, Windsor Castle, entitled *Buckingham Palace, History and Plans of the Grounds. From the Sixteenth century. Being extracts from the Surveys, Entries and Records in the Surveyor-General's Office, etc, relative to the freehold and leasehold Estates purchased by His Majesty of Sir Charles Sheffield, Bart., in the year 1762; now called the Queen's Palace.* This volume has been called the Surveyor-General's Report.

7 The architect is not known, nor is that of Arlington's country house at Euston in Suffolk, newly built in the mid-1670's. *See* A. Oswald, 'Euston Hall, Suffolk', *Country Life,* 10 January 1957.

8 Surveyor-General's Report.

9 A letter to the Duke of Shrewsbury, in *The Duke of Buckingham's Works,* II, 1723. For a recent summary of the history of the Duke's house, *see* John Cornforth, 'The Sheffields at Buckingham House', *Country Life,* 12 July 1962.

10 *The intire Expence about my House,* in the Duke's own hand, is MS. 533 in the library of London University at Senate House.

11 For the Chateau de Voorst, *see* Van Der Wijck, 'De Voorst', in *Bull. Van De Kon Ned. Oudh Bond,* 6e ser. Jaa, 16 June 1963.

12 Vanbrugh to Newcastle, Alscot Park Papers quoted in L. Whistler, *The Imagination of Vanbrugh and His Fellow Artists,* 1954, pp.35–36.

13 Ashburnham Papers. *See* transcripts in possession of Mr and Mrs Paul Mellon, ex. R. Gunnis Coll. *See also* R. Gunnis, *Dictionary of British Sculptors 1660–1851,* 1953.

14 Sir John Soane's Museum. Published by David Green in *Gardener to Queen Anne,* 1956, Pl. 29.

15 In *The intire Expence.*

16 In the collection of Mr and Mrs Reginald Sheffield. Reprd. *Country Life, op. cit.,* p.87, Fig. 3. It is also surely relevant that the small cut of the garden front shown in the Duke's *Works* (II, 1723, p.274) is of one conformable to the Wise plan.

17 Entries in *The intire Expence* are ambiguous upon this point. £15 is recorded for 'Painting the Arch for a sideboard by Verget'. The entry concerns the arch, and as it is most unusual in this type of account to mention the maker of a sideboard, a painter must surely be referred to. If so, where does Ricci come into the story?

18 Surveyor-General's Report.

19 *See* P.R.O. Treasury Warrent. Out Letters (gen.), xvii, p.231. Queen Anne to Surveyor-General of Crown Lands, 23 August 1703: 'the Duke of Buckingham, upon rebuilding his house, hath gon further into the Park than he had leave from the Queen to do'.

20 P.R.O. Works Minutes 4/13, 4/14, 5/63. *See also* the *Journals of the House of Commons,* XXXV, p.320.

21 Chambers's first scheme for encasing the house is in his portfolios in the Royal Library, Windsor Castle. Adam's unexecuted project for the same purpose is dated 1761 and is in the Worsley Collection at Hovingham, Yorkshire.

22 Westminster Public Library. Gardner Collection, 39. 16–17. One plan shows the staircase in its 1705 position, the other in the position it was not to acquire until altered by James Wyatt, c. 1800. Wyatt may therefore have been executing suggestions already laid down by Chambers over thirty years earlier.

23 The illustration is from a set of wall plans in the Royal Library, Windsor Castle. They were prepared for surveying the position of easel paintings.

24 B. M. Crace, *Views*, XIII, p.14, dated 1768, shows the Octagon being built and surrounded with scaffolding.

25 According to *The intire Expence*, Laguerre was paid £400. The £230 paid to him by the Duke in his ledger at Childs' Bank (Glyn Mills & Co.) under 12 October 1706 may be part of this larger payment. The painted programme is fully described in *An Account of the Paintings and Pictures at Buckingham House* (B. M. MS. Harl. 6344). *See* E. Croft-Murray, *Decorative Painting in England, 1537–1837*, 1962, p.252.

26 From an inventory taken 20 April 1743, a year after the Duchess's death (Lincolnshire Record Office, Sheffield Papers C/17): 'Lined with India Japan Boards, all the Japan finisht with carving and gilding, all the glass and picture frames the same. Eight carved and gilt flowers fixt in the lower panels'. There were also here 'four sconces in Japan frames and eleven Japan elbow chairs'. In the 'intire Expence Indian Painting all round' cost £15.

27 The first-floor plan is shown in a volume of surveys taken c. 1761: *The Royal Apartments at St James, Kensington, Hampton Court, Windsor Castle, Somerset House, Queens House* (Windsor Castle Royal Library $\frac{4}{16}$–4).

28 Walpole Society, XVI (1928), p.78–Walpole's comment in 1783.

29 *An Account of the Paintings . . .* does not specify Laguerre's responsibility for painting in this Saloon. He may in fact have done no work other than the staircase. Nevertheless, the description of the 'portraiture' frieze around the room is strikingly similar to his scheme executed at Blenheim c. 1720. Vertue, on the other hand (Walpole Soc., XXII, *Vertue Notebooks*, III, pp.6, 97), attributes the ceiling specifically to Antonio Bellucci and says it cost £500, paid by the Duchess. Bellucci came to England in 1716 and left in 1722; the Duke died in 1721, so the ceiling must have been painted about 1720–21. The ceiling was based iconographically upon Gentileschi's 'Apollo lying along upon a Cloud, and the Nine Muses underneath it, each of them playing to him on a several instrument'. This had been originally painted for George Villiers, Duke of Buckingham, and installed at York House. It was removed from there some time after 1670 and may have been one of Lord Arlington's acquisitions after the fire of 1674. Flanking it in Buckingham House, Bellucci–if indeed he was the painter–put up the *Fable of the Peiredes* and *Apollo and Marsyas*. In the coves were the Three Graces, Four Virtues, the Faculties, and Genius and Learning. Between the windows could have been seen Minerva trampling on Malice and Envy and Mercury killing Argus. Another ceiling was painted in the Little Closet. Here *Juno Lulling Jupiter Asleep* cost, according to *The intire Expence*, £20. Already some contradictions have been seen in the Duke's compilation of his *Expence*; did Davie or Nost carve the statues, or did Ricci or Verget paint the Dining Room cove? Therefore the Duke's entry in his *Expence* 'For the Pictures in both the Salon & Closet, £5,060' is indeed mysterious. Does it refer to the wall and ceiling decoration, or was this large sum paid for a collection of easel pictures?

30 The drawing for the engraving is in Sir John Soane's Museum, Adam volumes, XXII, p.57, and varients are XXII, pp.56, 58, all dated 1761.

31 Westminster Public Library, Gardner Collection, 39. 30.

32 The collection of drawings now in the possession of Sir William Worsley, of Hovingham Hall, Yorkshire.

33 *See* Sir John Summerson, *John Nash*, 1935, for a general discussion of the part played by Nash at Buckingham House.

34 B.M., Huskinson Papers, MS. 38, 760, f.206.

35 *See* First and Second Reports.

36 Appendix to Second Report, p.270.

37 The principal collection of Blore's designs for the Palace are in the Victoria and Albert Museum, 8738-1–75; designs for the east front are R.I.B.A. J2/17, 1–2 and for the Grand Hall, J2/17.3; and others in the British Museum and Public Record Office.

38 P.R.O. Letter Books Msc. Buckingham Palace, 1831–34, I. Quoted from Clifford Smith, *op. cit.*

39 Clifford Smith, *op. cit.*, p.54.

40 For the Marble Arch, *see* H. Clifford Smith, 'Vicissitudes of the Marble Arch', *Country Life*, 4 July 1952, illustrating the model in the Victoria and Albert Museum. The Arch, erected by 1834, was taken down c. 1847 and re-erected in its present position by Pennethorne and the landscape designer, William Nesfield, in 1851.

41 Designs R.I.B.A. X10/3.1–22

42 One figure is a later replacement, as is shown by its being signed by Doulton's of Lambeth.

43 Published by W. H. Leeds in his 1838 Supplement to J. Britton and A. Pugin's *Illustrations of the Public Buildings of London*.

44 There had been proposals about this time to appropriate Buckingham Palace for the purposes of a National Gallery, to give over the Trafalgar Square building to the Royal Academy, and to build a new palace in Kensington Gardens. *See The Builder,* 12 January 1867, pp.23–4.

45 Pennethorne's designs are mostly dated 22 December 1852 and are in the Royal Library, Windsor Castle, having been given to King George V in 1934.

46 All my information relative to the Brighton Pavilion comes from two sources: firstly, Henry D. Roberts, *A History of the Royal Pavilion, Brighton,* 1939; second, Clifford Musgrave, *Royal Pavilion,* 1959.

47 Aiton's work is discussed by J. Dennis in *The Landscape Gardener,* 1835, pp.103–6, with illustra-tions. There are two garden plans by Brown in the Royal Library, Windsor Castle, Misc. Portfolios Royal Residences.

48 Thomas Chawner's plan dated 22 March 1794 is B.M. Crace Port. XIII, 7.

49 The design is in the Royal Mews, Buckingham Palace; further designs are Windsor Castle 14000, 17969, 17970; also Sir John Soane's Museum 43/6.[23] The original model of the coach, made by Capitsoldi and Voyers when working in Wilton's studio, is in the London Museum.

50 In the Royal Mews is an engraved design by Samuel Butler, the coachmaker, and John Linnell, the cabinet-maker. They are associated with drawings by Linnell in his album in the Victoria and Albert Museum (92.D.26).

51 The accounts are P.R.O. AOI/1455, roll 71.

The Works of Art

GEOFFREY DE BELLAIGUE

THE OCTAGON LIBRARY, BUCKINGHAM HOUSE
An engraving published by Pyne, 1 February 1818

BUCKINGHAM PALACE became a palace almost against the wishes of its successive owners. Since its purchase by George III in 1762 it has been regarded primarily as a private residence.

In 1723 the Duke of Buckingham wrote with affection about 'a little wilderness full of black birds and nightingales' under the windows of his little closet of books.[1] George III echoing these sentiments improved the garden and enlarged the closet till his library filled five large rooms. He continued to use St James's Palace for ceremonial purposes. When George IV finally decided in 1821 to carry out his plan of taking up residence in Buckingham House he too intended that St James's Palace should remain the setting for his official duties. Accordingly he instructed Nash to 'convert Buckingham House into a private residence for himself',[2] but died before the redecoration was complete. William IV, though he too died before he could take up residence, 'never calculated on the use of Buckingham Palace for any purpose of state as distinct from residence'.[3] Even Queen Victoria, who left Kensington Palace for Buckingham Palace in 1837, continued to make use of St James's Palace for ceremonial functions. It was not till some thirty years after her accession that she finally transferred her 'drawing-rooms' from St James's to Buckingham Palace.

Perhaps because of this approach successive owners have felt little compunction about preserving the interior appearance and furnishings of the rooms left them by their predecessors. A private residence reflects the private taste of the owner. Nor was there at Buckingham Palace the same distinction, which we find in French palaces, between the state rooms, the *chambres d'apparat,* and the private apartments, the *petits appartements.* At Versailles, for example, the former have remained largely unaltered since they were created by Louis XIV in the seventeenth century, whereas the latter were repeatedly transformed in the eighteenth century by Louis XV and Louis XVI.

During the successive refurnishings of Buckingham Palace, furniture was borrowed from other residences. For example, George III brought in pieces from St James's Palace and Kensington Palace. George IV in turn instructed Nash to re-use many of the Carlton House fixtures. The furniture was also to be supplied largely from Carlton House. After his death it fell to William IV and Queen Victoria to set out the Carlton House furniture within its new setting. When Blore built the east wing of the Palace in 1847, Queen Victoria drew on yet another

---

[1]Letter to the Duke of Shrewsbury, in *The Duke of Buckingham's Works,* II, 1723.
[2]*Second Report of the Select Committee on Buckingham Palace* (1831), Appendix, p.270.
[3]Sir Herbert Taylor, quoted by H. Clifford Smith, *Buckingham Palace . . . ,* London (1931), p.52.

treasure house of George IV's. The fittings and furnishings of the new wing were taken largely from the Royal Pavilion at Brighton.

This constant re-deployment of furniture designed for other palaces may suggest that Buckingham Palace, both when it was a 'house' and later a 'palace', was furnished on the cheap. Certainly George III, who was the first to condemn the extravagances of his son, would hardly have spent in the 1760's on one room the equivalent of £45,000, as George IV actually did some sixty years later, on the Music Room at Brighton Pavilion. George III clearly disapproved of lavish interiors filled with highly ornamented furniture. Pyne's description of his apartments at Buckingham House confirms this. He notes that they 'are remarkable for their plainness . . .'[1]

In contrast, George IV cannot be accused of a tendency to cut down on expenses by cheese-paring economies in the furnishing of his palaces. If economies were made, they were forced on him. The public outcry at the high cost of the architectural transformations at Buckingham House carried out in the late 1820's—which was eventually to ruin the reputation of his architect, John Nash—may possibly have inhibited the King from placing a large number of fresh commissions with English furniture makers.

After George IV, both William IV and Queen Victoria were anxious to restore the public image of the monarchy, which had suffered seriously during the Commons' debates on George IV's finances. They were certainly in no mood to spend vast sums on furniture—which would have been condemned as an irresponsible waste of public money lavished on frivolities.

Despite this overall picture of economies in the successive furnishings of the Palace, whether by choice or by necessity, the records and the engravings reveal, notably in the eighteenth century, a high regard for interior design. For example, George III's Octagon Library (page 102), though sparsely furnished, is furnished with taste. In the centre is an eight-sided writing desk which is both practical and aesthetically appealing, its eight sides echoing the plan of the room. This desk supports in the centre a four-sided clock by Eardley Norton (page 158), where it can be seen to full advantage. Its square plan varies the octagonal theme but preserves the overall angular pattern of this interior.

One of the most costly schemes of decoration undertaken for George III was the creation of the New Japan Room (page 105), for which William Vile was paid £572.12.0. Significantly, Vile re-used the lacquer panels which had decorated the Duke of Buckingham's 'Old' Japan Room. He refixed on the walls the old panels which he had touched up, added fresh ones where necessary, and fitted 'Carved & Gilt Mouldings round the panels'.[2] In the engraving we can see between the windows two gilt tables—possibly by James Moore, c. 1720—which stand under two mirrors in lacquer and gold. These mirrors (page 118), though they also antedate by some twenty years the redecoration of the room, were made to tone in with the general scheme, Vile being paid £2 'for Cleaning & new Gilding 2 Japan Glass Frames & new drawing the Ground in Japan'.[3]

The records bring to light other arrangements of rooms where the furniture was made to

[1]W. H. Pyne, *The History of the Royal Residences . . .* , Vol. II: *The History of Buckingham-House* (1819), p.8.
[2]Public Record Office, L.C.9/308, 22, Quarter to Lady Day 1763.
[3]Public Record Office, L.C.9/309, 35, Quarter to Midsummer 1763.

harmonise with the wall decoration. For example, in 1767 John Bradburn supplied a press for books for Queen Charlotte's Keeper of the Robes, Mrs Schwellingburgh, at a cost of £25.16.0. The mouldings to the two drawers of the lower stage were designed 'to match the Room' and the cornice at the top was intended 'to suit that of the Room . . .'[1]

Where, however, the particular interests of the King or Queen were involved, aesthetic considerations were liable to be sacrificed. For example, Queen Charlotte, who was deeply musical and a passionate admirer of Handel, whose works she herself used to play on the organ, had installed in the New Japan Room the organ crowned by Roubiliac's bust of Handel, which are visible in the engraving. Unlike the mirror, the organ has not been toned in with the japanning on the walls. Furthermore, it is out of scale with the rest of the furnishings and fixtures in the room. Sandwiched between the wall and the fireplace, it serves as a pendant to the door-case to the right of the fireplace. It is unsuited to this role, as it is bulkier, broader and taller than the door-case. Clearly, in a conflict of interests between the symmetry of a wall elevation and the Queen's convenience as a musician, it was the former which was compromised.

In the case of George IV, though no direct evidence has yet come to light, we can safely infer that careful thought was given to the overall effect of a room's furnishings in relation to its panelling and hangings. For his first apartment in Buckingham House, granted him at the age of eighteen in 1780, William Gates made most of the furniture (page 211, for example). On one bill for a pair of 'superb tripods or therms', Gates indicates that they had been designed by George IV himself.[2] If Sheraton's engravings of the Chinese Drawing Room at Carlton House (pages 120 and 121) are taken as a yardstick of George IV's taste before 1800, then his first apart-

[1] Public Record Office, L.C.9/314, 61, Quarter to Midsummer 1767.
[2] Ralph Edwards and Margaret Jourdain, *Georgian Cabinet-Makers* (1955), p.83.

THE NEW JAPAN ROOM, BUCKINGHAM HOUSE (ALSO KNOWN AS THE QUEEN'S BREAKFAST ROOM)

ment at Buckingham House must have been of equal sophistication, each piece (including the tripods) being considered in relation to the whole, both as to scale and decoration.

As regards the final plans for Buckingham House, we do not know, alas, how he intended to display his English and French furniture in Nash's setting, though it is safe to assume that the presentation would have been more exciting and more dramatic than that realized by his immediate successors.

The reference to French furniture introduces another factor which would have affected the arrangement of the rooms. Buckingham House was intended by George IV to contain his collections, largely of French works of art. On the evidence of Pyne's engravings of Carlton House, he would not have re-created 'period' rooms. In contrast, therefore, to those rooms for which the furniture was specially designed, such as the Chinese Drawing Room at Carlton House and later the Banqueting and Music Rooms at Brighton Pavilion, George IV would have arranged his furniture at Buckingham House much more loosely, mingling styles and mixing works of art made in different countries, in the same way as they are shown today. There is a precedent for this in George III's Buckingham House.

In Zoffany's painting of Queen Charlotte at her dressing-table, c. 1765 (illustrated on page 226), she can be seen seated in an arm-chair in the Kent style of c. 1740. The console table in the corridor is also English. The carpet, though probably made in England, is of Persian inspiration.[1] Against the wall is a French regulator clock in the full Louis XV style and under the mirror are two Chinese porcelain mandarin figures.

On a visit to Buckingham House about 1783, Horace Walpole commented on Queen Charlotte's collection of 'modern jars of Chinese porcelaine, many of Chelsea porcelaine & a few of Seve'.[2] If we exclude the reference to Chelsea pieces, this comment could have applied equally well to Carlton House. But whereas George IV displayed his porcelain on chests of drawers and chimney-pieces, as was the practice in France in the eighteenth century, Queen Charlotte seems mainly to have followed the seventeenth-century habit of aligning them above door-cases (page 105) and of placing them on brackets on mirrors. In 1767, for example, we find Bradburn supplying a chimney glass for the Queen's closet fitted with '46 Brackets for China'.[3]

The biggest expenses which George III sanctioned were related to his collections of books, maps, coins, clocks and scientific instruments. While his cabinet-makers continued to supply canopies of State, crowned pier-glasses and State beds for St James's Palace, they were employed at Buckingham House in producing and altering bookcases, map presses, medal cabinets and writing-desks, all 'By His Majesty's Direction'.

Of these early collections little, apart from the clocks, survives in Buckingham Palace. From Queen Charlotte's collection, sold at Christie's in 1819, for the record sum of £59,601,[4] only

---

[1] I am indebted to Miss Wendy Hefford for this information.
[2] Horace Walpole, 'Journal of Visits to Country Seats &c', ed. Paget Toynbee, *Walpole Society,* Vol. XVI (1927–28), p.78.
[3] Public Record Office, L.C.9/314, 89, Quarter to Xmas 1767.
[4] Annotated copy of the sale catalogues of Queen Charlotte's property, 1819, preserved in the Royal Library, Windsor Castle.

a few pieces bought by George IV are still in the Palace. George III's superb collections of books and medals now belong to the British Museum. His scientific instruments are in the Science Museum. These depletions are, however, offset in part by collections formed subsequently. The most recent addition is Queen Mary's collection, which in content reminds one of the 'innumerable Knick-Knacks' brought together by Queen Charlotte, to which Mrs Philip Lybbe Powys admiringly refers in her diary in 1767.[1]

Pyne, in a particularly unattractive phrase, writes, 'the genius of connubial felicity laid the first stone of Buckingham-House'.[2] If we examine the bills submitted by the court cabinet-makers in the 1760's, the point he is making emerges with greater clarity and in plainer language. Furniture was supplied to scale. In 1766 Katharine Naish supplied an 'Elbow chair' for Prince Frederick (then aged three) which was 'Made very high in the Seat for His Highness to Sit at Table, . . .'[3]

Accessories were provided for pets and hobbies. In 1762 and 1763 William Vile, one of the greatest of English cabinet-makers, was busy with orders for bird-cages, monkey-houses (originally intended for St James's Palace), a silk-worm stage and a fish-net handle. For the Prince of Wales, aged one, he made a mahogany plough with brass wheels—which he had to reduce in height by two inches on the King's instructions.[4] For his master's dogs, Vile and his partner, John Cobb, were providing cushions at £1 each. In 1763 Vile made '2 Hand Umbrella's for their Majesties Use',[5] and in the same year a 'Mohogany Tea Kettle Stand' for the Queen.[6]

The note struck is one of domesticity. It is one which is repeatedly heard both in the nineteenth and twentieth centuries. When, for example, Queen Victoria wrote to Peel in 1845 about the need for enlarging the Palace, she did not allege lack of space for receptions but 'The total want of accomodation for our little family, which is fast growing up'.[7]

Today, in the arrangement of the rooms, the debt to the past is evident. The same factors, aesthetic appeal, practical considerations, convenience, still operate as they did in George III's day. At the same time, in the actual location of individual works of art there is little sense of continuity. It is surprising to find how often even the most massive works of art have been moved. For example, Canova's colossal marble group of 'Mars and Venus' (page 182), ideally situated in its present position at the foot of the Ministers' Staircase, is shown in a 1933 photograph at the other end of the Marble Hall, and before that in 1914 on the first floor next to the Picture Gallery. Buckingham Palace continues to reflect, in this sense, the individual taste of its owners. It still remains essentially a private residence.

NOTE. George IV (1762–1830), Prince of Wales from 1762–1811, then Prince Regent up to his accession in 1820, is referred to throughout as George IV.

[1] *Passages from the Diaries of Mrs Philip Lybbe Powys*, ed. E. J. Climenson (1899), p.116.
[2] Pyne, *op. cit.*, p.2.
[3] Public Record Office, L.C.9/314, 6, Quarter to Xmas 1766.
[4] Public Record Office, L.C.9/309, 54, Quarter to Michaelmas 1763.
[5] Public Record Office, L.C.9/309, 54, Quarter to Michaelmas 1763.
[6] Public Record Office, L.C.9/309, 10, Quarter to Midsummer 1763.
[7] Letter from Queen Victoria to Sir Robert Peel, dated 10 February 1845. Quoted by Clifford Smith, *op. cit.*, p.54.

WHEEL BAROMETER
BY TOMPION

A wheel barometer of oak and walnut, veneered in burr walnut and enriched with gilt bronze mounts, which include two bearded figures, each holding a rayed face of the sun. Made about 1695, reputedly for William III, whose cipher used to be contained within the escutcheon at the top.[1] The silvered dial is signed, *Londini/Tho Tompion fecit* (Thomas Tompion, 1639–1713). The dial at the base is a twelve-month perpetual calendar.

Though it was converted into an aneroid barometer in the nineteenth century, originally it was of the siphon type (where two glass weights are attached to a cord over a pulley, one hanging free and the other resting on the surface of the mercury in a siphon tube; the hand attached to the arbor of the pulley turns as the pulley revolves). This type of improved barometer – which made it easier to read the rise and fall of the mercury – was invented by Robert Hooke and was perfected in 1678 at Tompion's workshop. Zacharias von Uffenbach was probably referring to the barometer here illustrated when he wrote, after a visit to Kensington Palace in 1710: 'We saw here a barometer of Tompion with a round disc as a clock'.[2]

Height, 40 in; *width*, 16½ in; *depth*, 3¾ in.

GESSO TABLE BY MOORE

A table of pine decorated with carved and gilt gesso and supported on tapering baluster legs. The decoration of both the apron on the front and the table top incorporates the crowned cipher of George I and the rose and the thistle.

Made for George I by James Moore (fl. c. 1708–26), whose name is incised in the gesso above the crown on the top, this piece of furniture probably dates from about 1714.

Moore specialised in furniture decorated in this technique. Gesso is a composition of whiting, linseed oil and glue; when applied thickly on woodwork and left to dry it offers a smooth hard surface suitable for carving.

The rose and the thistle were obvious choices for the decoration of works of art destined for the royal Houses of England and Scotland. William Pickering used these same devices in conjunction with the fleur-de-lis on a suit of armour made for Henry Prince of Wales, c. 1610 (now at Windsor Castle). Over two hundred years later, John Gibson embellished the hem of Queen Victoria's cloak with a posy composed of the rose, the thistle and the shamrock (see page 187).

Height, 33 in; *width,* 56¾ in; *depth,* 26¾ in.

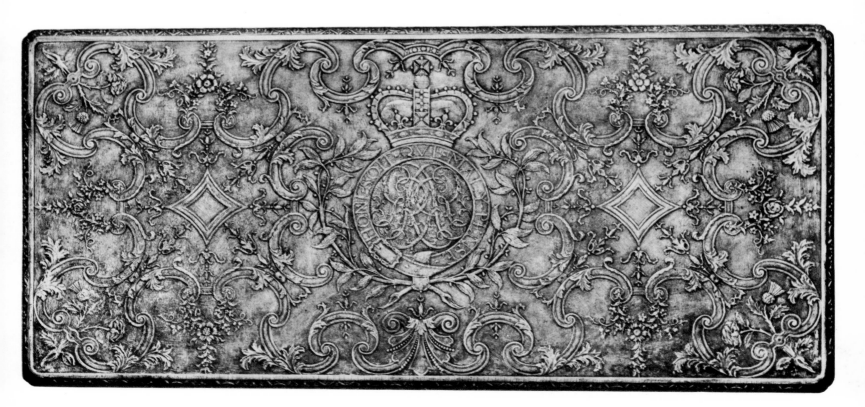

QUEEN ANNE SIDE-TABLE

An early eighteenth-century side-table, made in England, of pine and walnut supporting a slab of *verde antico* marble. The cabriole legs, which are carved with stylised palmettes at the knees, terminate in horses' hooves complete with fetlocks.
It has been suggested that this table was made for Queen Anne at Kensington Palace.[3] Together with three other tables identical in design, this one can be seen in the engraving of the Queen's Gallery at Kensington, published by W. H. Pyne over a century later, on 1 September 1819.[4]

Height, $31\frac{1}{2}$ in; *width,* $77\frac{1}{4}$ in; *depth,* 31 in.

Flanking the table are two mahogany hall chairs (below) from a set which Clifford Smith has identified in the accounts as having been supplied by Katherine Naish in 1766 at a cost of 45/– each for Buckingham House.[5]

Height, $38\frac{1}{4}$ in; *width,* $20\frac{3}{4}$ in; *depth,* $20\frac{3}{4}$ in.

STOOL, POSSIBLY BY WILLIAMS

One of a set of fourteen stools supported on scrolled legs. On the frame of one of them the date 173[1 ?] is marked in ink next to the initials E.S. (possibly the initials of the craftsman who made the stool).

Clifford Smith suggests that these stools, which came from Kensington Palace, may have been made in the workshop of Henry Williams (flourished 1728–58) who supplied furniture for Hampton Court and who frequently decorated the legs of his furniture with a scale pattern similar to that on these stools.[6]

Height, 19 in; *width,* 27½ in; *depth,* 20½ in.

BUREAU-CABINET BY VILE

A bureau-cabinet, of oak veneered in mahogany, which is fitted in the lower stage with four drawers below a drop-front writing flap disguised by two false drawers. Clifford Smith has identified this bureau-cabinet as the one supplied by the cabinet-maker William Vile in 1762 for Queen Charlotte's apartments in St James's Palace at a cost of £71.0.0.[7]

The cabinet is exceptionally well constructed. The dovetails are in themselves works of art, so minute and fine are the joints. The fretwork panels are also examples of virtuoso skill. They are not pieced together; in each case they are cut with geometric precision out of a panel, and the panel, though only 3/32 to $\frac{1}{8}$ of an inch thick, is itself made of three-ply mahogany so as to guard against warping.

Though the construction and carving of this piece are faultless, the general design is open to criticism. The bowed sides of the lower stage, for example, seem out of character with the flat panels of the upper stage. It is possible that the upper stage is a later replacement. In 1767 John Bradburn submitted for the Queen's approval a drawing of a glass case to stand on top of her secretaire in Richmond Lodge.[8] In the same quarter he supplied the case itself at a cost of £24,10.0. The description of this case corresponds exactly to that of the upper stage of the secretaire as it appears today, but without the canopy.[9] The canopy, which is built separately, may, however, belong to the original Vile cabinet.

Height, 84 in; *width,* 37 in; *depth,* 18 in.

WORK-TABLE BY VILE

A work-table, of oak veneered in mahogany; the legs, which are of solid mahogany, are carved with scrolls and foliage. Fitted with three drawers, the top lifts up to give access to the well above these drawers. A book-rest can be fitted into slots on the outside of the table top, for use when the top is raised.

Made by William Vile for Queen Charlotte's apartments at Buckingham House at a cost of £9.15.0, it is described in the Lord Chamberlain's accounts for the last quarter of 1763 as 'a neat mohogony Work Table with Shape Legs neatly Carved & a Scrole on the foot & a Leaf on the knee a Carved finishing to the rail, one half of the top divided into 12 Compartments the other half open & the top made to fold over behind, . . .'[10]

Height, 31½ in; *width,* 38¼ in; *depth,* 27¾ in.

BOOKCASE BY VILE

A break-fronted mahogany bookcase of architectural proportions. Ingenious use has been made of the space available for cupboards and shelves. In the lower stage, in order to ensure the maximum amount of space for the flanking cupboards, their doors are hinged to the sides of the bookcase, and the pilasters, which are attached to the front of these doors, are themselves fitted as shallow cupboards. The panels are decorated with finely carved applied ornaments, which include garlands, scroll motifs, floral swags suspended from lion masks, and wreaths. Of particular beauty is the carving along the entablature.

The bookcase was made by William Vile in 1762 for the furnishing of Buckingham House.[11]

It has recently been suggested that the very fine delicate carving on Vile's furniture was carried out not by Vile himself but by John Bradburn, who was employed by Vile up to the end of 1763 before he succeeded Vile as cabinet-maker to the Great Wardrobe.[12] In the clock-case which Bradburn probably supplied in 1765 for the Eardley Norton clock (page 158), the carving is of the same character and of the same quality as on this bookcase.

A plaque fixed to one of the doors records that George IV presented this bookcase to his sister-in-law, Augusta, Duchess of Cambridge. In 1904 it was given to H.M. Queen Mary, then Princess of Wales.

Height, 105 in; *width*, 103 in; *depth*, 26¼ in.

GLOBE SEWING TABLE BY MORGAN & SANDERS

A globe-shaped sewing table, *c.* 1810, which is of pinewood veneered on the outside in mahogany. It rests on slender tripod supports which are fitted with satyrs' heads and hooves carved in pearwood partly gilt. The upper segment of the globe, which is painted with the signs of the zodiac disposed in three bands, rotates backwards 90° and reveals satinwood trays, drawers and compartments for sewing materials in the floor of the table. Inset into the upper segment is a mirrored recess flanked by brickwork in maple veneer. The mirror, which pulls out, conceals a further nest of drawers.

This table was made for Queen Charlotte by the London firm of Morgan & Sanders, who had bought the right to manufacture globe tables of this design from the inventor George Remington in 1808. In a eulogistic article on the firm of Morgan & Sanders, which appeared in the February 1810 issue of R. Ackermann's *Repository of Arts, . . .* , the writer records that 'It [the Remington table] has already obtained the patronage of her Majesty and the Royal Family, who are ever the foremost to encourage real merit'.[13]

Height, 37 in; *diameter of globe,* 16¾ in.

SERVICE OF CHELSEA PORCELAIN

Part of a service of Chelsea porcelain completed in 1763. Decorated in underglaze 'mazarin' blue, richly gilt and painted with flowers and birds on a white ground, the pieces are marked on the underside with an anchor in gold.

This service of soft-paste porcelain ranks among the finest productions of the Chelsea manufactory. The decoration, which includes butterflies in gold gaily scattered on the blue ground next to the principal scenes of birds and flowers painted in bold colours in a landscape setting, is perfectly in character with the ebullient rococo shapes of the individual pieces. The *chef d'oeuvre* is probably the epergne, the centre-piece, built round a wooden core.

Horace Walpole, while admiring the opulence of this service, condemned it for being in bad taste. In a letter to Sir Horace Mann, dated 4 March 1763, he wrote, 'I saw yesterday a mag-

nificent service of Chelsea china, which the King and Queen are sending to the Duke of Mecklenburg. There are dishes and plates without number, an epergne, candlesticks, salt-sellars, sauce-boats, tea and coffee equipages; in short, it is complete; and cost twelve hundred pounds! I cannot boast of our taste; the forms are neither new, beautiful, nor various. Yet Sprimont, the manufacturer, is a Frenchman [Nicholas Sprimont, 1713–71]. It seems their taste will not bear transplanting.'[14]

The Duke of Mecklenburg to whom the service was presented was Queen Charlotte's brother, Duke Adolphus Frederick IV of Mecklenburg-Strelitz. It remained in the ownership of the ducal family up to 1919. In 1948 it was presented to H.M. Queen Elizabeth the Queen Mother.

Height of epergne, $25\frac{3}{4}$ in; width, $27\frac{3}{4}$ in; depth, $23\frac{1}{2}$ in.

LACQUER MIRROR RESTORED BY VILE

The mirror-frame, which is of pine, is mounted with panels of English lacquer in the Chinese taste within mouldings of carved and gilt wood. This mirror can be identified as one of a pair in the engraving published by W. H. Pyne of Queen Charlotte's Japan Room at Buckingham House (see page 105). Made about 1740, they were restored in 1763 by William Vile, who was paid £2 'For Cleaning & new Gilding 2 Japan Glass Frames & new drawing the Ground in Japan'.[15] The New Japan Room, as it was called in the accounts of 1763, was completely refurbished by Vile, who received in the first quarter of 1763 the large sum of £572.12.0 for restoring, adapting and replacing the lacquer panels fitted to the walls.

Height, 58 in; *width,* 43½ in; *depth,* 2½ in.

TABLE ATTRIBUTED TO LEVERTON

An English side-table, *c.* 1775, of walnut and pine, carved and gilt, incorporating decorative elements cast in composition, also gilt. The dove-grey marble top is inlaid with a chequer-board pattern of 160 squares of specimen marbles. It has been suggested that this table, which came from Woodhall Park, Hertfordshire, was designed by the architect, Thomas Leverton, who built the house between 1777 and 1782.[16] There is, however, no documentary evidence to support this.[17] A table similar in style and construction is in the Metropolitan Museum, New York. Its frame was probably made in 1794 by Ince and Mayhew, and the marble top by John Wildsmith (bill dated 28 July 1759).[18]

Height, 32¾ in; *width,* 57¾ in; *depth,* 27 in.

INDIAN CHAIR OF SANDALWOOD AND IVORY

Part of a set of fourteen chairs, two settees, two small cabinets and two desk arm-chairs made in India, *c.* 1770, of Indian sandalwood mounted all over with panels of engraved ivory. The chairs resemble in shape some of Chippendale's designs. An unusual feature, however, is the carving of stylised palmettes or shells flanking the rearmost claw on each foot. The ivory, which is secured to the frame by ivory pins, is engraved with a mixture of western and oriental motifs. The acanthus leaves on the knees repeat the traditional low-relief carving on English furniture of the mid-eighteenth century; the monstrous heads, on the other hand, which are treated in low relief, have no equivalent in the English furniture maker's repertoire. With their curled trunks, globular eyes and fanged mouths—the teeth are high-lighted by red lacquer separating the fangs—they are clearly of Eastern inspiration.

The early history of this set of furniture has been fully described by Clifford Smith.[19] Made in Madras, *c.* 1770, for Alexander Wynch, then Governor of Fort St George, they were bought by George III for Queen Charlotte in 1781. On the death of the Queen in 1819 they were put up for auction at Christie's and bought for Brighton Pavilion by George IV.

Chair: *height,* 39⅛ in; *width,* 24½ in; *depth,* 22⅛ in.

THE CHINESE DRAWING ROOM, CARLTON HOUSE

THE CHINESE DRAWING ROOM, CARLTON HOUSE
Detail of engraving published by Sheraton, 6 October 1793

Even before George IV began transforming Brighton Pavilion in 1802 into a fantasy of the East, he had already experimented with the Chinese style at Carlton House. The two engravings shown here, published in Thomas Sheraton's *Cabinet-maker and Upholsterer's Drawing Book* (1793),[20] record the appearance of George IV's first venture into *chinoiserie*, his Chinese Drawing Room designed by Henry Holland, which was situated on the ground floor of his London residence. Though this decorative scheme lasted only a few years, the furnishings have survived. We can follow their moves first to the Rose Satin Drawing Room on the first floor at Carlton House, where they can be seen in Pyne's engraving, dated 7 December 1817; then to Brighton Pavilion, to the Music Room Gallery (engraving published by John Nash, 1 July 1824); finally to Buckingham Palace in 1847 and 1848, where they have remained to this day (*see pages 122–27*).[21]

ABOVE: THE ROSE SATIN
DRAWING ROOM, CARLTON
HOUSE

Engraving published by Pyne,
7 December 1817

THE CHINESE DRAWING ROOM,
CARLTON HOUSE

Engraving published by Sheraton,
1 November 1793

PIER-TABLE FROM THE CHINESE DRAWING ROOM, CARLTON HOUSE

Pier-table of oak veneered in ebony and pewter and richly decorated with gilt bronze mounts. It was designed to stand opposite the fireplace in George IV's Chinese Drawing Room at Carlton House. Sheraton, writing in 1793, noted that the Chinese caryatids, which stand in niches, with arms crossed, on either side of the fireplace, were 'answerable to those which support a table on the opposite side, ...' Other features in common are the griotte marble and a number of gilt bronze motifs, including the roundels on the sides containing peacocks in silhouette.

For further details, *see* page 126.

Height, $36\frac{7}{8}$ in; *width,* 66 in; *depth,* $20\frac{1}{2}$ in.

THE 'DRUMMER BOY CLOCK'

Known as the 'Chinese Drummer Boy Clock', this clock is of gilt and enamelled bronze. It was made, *c.* 1792, for the Chinese Drawing Room at Carlton House, and can be identified on the chimney-piece in the second of Sheraton's designs. The decoration of the canopy, painted in the form of scales, was clearly intended to match that of the canopies crowning the niches on either side of the chimney-piece on which it stood (pages 120–21). The cushion and clustered columns in imitation of bamboo which now support it on its rocky base are a later modification. They were added by Vulliamy in 1811.[22] It is just possible to discern these additions in Pyne's illustration of the Rose Satin Drawing Room at Carlton House (pages 120–21). The clock was despatched to Brighton on 6 November 1819, where it remained until its final move to Buckingham Palace. Its dial and movement by Charles Frodsham (latter numbered 890) were probably inserted about 1870. Hitherto this clock has been considered English; fresh evidence suggests that in fact it must have been made in France. In his bill of 1811, Benjamin Vulliamy, the court clockmaker, described it as 'a French Clock in a Chinese Case'. Two years later in a bill for its cleaning his son added the clockmaker's name, 'Maniere' (probably C-G. Manière, master 1778–1810).[23]

Height, 29 in; *width,* 13½ in; *depth,* 6¾ in.

CANDELABRUM IN THE CHINESE TASTE

One of a set of six candelabra, of gilt and enamelled bronze, which are fitted with four lights each. Though Holland's estimates of November 1789 mention eight candelabra, only six were in fact made for the Chinese Drawing Room.[24] The distinctive dragon, which forms the terminal to the central rod of the candelabrum, recalls those which support the drapery on the pier-table between the windows in the Carlton House Drawing Room (page 120).
The bronze manufacturer who supplied these pieces is not known. If the clock was made in France, it is conceivable that the candelabra, which resemble it, are also French.

Height, 30⅛ in; *width,* 13¾ in; *depth,* 8¼ in.

BLACK SEVRES VASE

One of a pair of vases of hard-paste Sèvres porcelain decorated with *chinoiserie* scenes in platinum and gold on a black ground (*fond écaille*). The sources of some of these designs can be traced to engravings after Jean Pillement (1728–1808).

These vases, which are undated, were probably made about 1792. In addition to crossed Ls under a crown, they are marked in gold on the underside with the letters GI and I respectively –the marks of an unidentified painter in the Sèvres manufactory.[25]

The gilt bronze mounts, in particular the dragons, are strikingly similar to those on the pier-table made for the Chinese Drawing Room at Carlton House (page 126). Appropriately, when George IV bought the vases from the dealer R. Fogg in October 1812, he had one of them placed on each of the two pier-tables (pages 122 and 126), which by then had been moved to the Rose Satin Drawing Room (pages 120–21).

Height, $16\frac{5}{16}$ in; *width,* $13\frac{7}{8}$ in.

PIER-TABLE FROM THE CHINESE DRAWING ROOM, CARLTON HOUSE

The pier-table, which now supports an ivory cabinet originally bought by George III in 1781 (*see* page 119) and two Chinese porcelain vases, was made *c.* 1790 to fit between the windows in the Chinese Drawing Room at Carlton House. Of oak veneered in ebony, it was described by Sheraton in 1793 as 'richly ornamented in gold. The top is marble, and also the shelf at each end; the back of it is composed of three panels of glass. . . .'

Jutsham records that, when the Chinese furniture at Carlton House was sent to Brighton in 1819, this table, together with the other made for the Chinese Drawing Room (page 122), was delivered to Mr Bailey on 23 September, 'as patterns to make Two others by & to be sent to Brighton'. Three of the four tables can be seen in the engraving of the Music Room

Gallery at Brighton Pavilion published on 1 July 1824. Two are now in the Principal Corridor and two in the Yellow Drawing Room at Buckingham Palace.

They have been attributed to Robert Campbell,[26] but more recently, on stylistic grounds, to A. Weisweiler.[27] Still more recently it has been suggested that they were made wholly in England, but that their design was modelled on French furniture then in England.[28]

While it is now possible to establish, by means of Jutsham's day-books, that two are copies made by Bailey & Saunders, *c.* 1819, the maker of the original two must still remain in doubt. On the evidence of the construction of the two originals, it seems most likely that they were made in Paris.[29] *Height,* 36$\frac{1}{16}$ in; *width,* 68$\frac{7}{8}$ in; *depth,* 20$\frac{3}{4}$ in.

BERGERE BY HERVE

Bergère, of beechwood, carved and painted in green and white, originally gilt.

It forms part of a set of six chairs, four arm-chairs and four *bergères* made in 1790 for the Chinese Drawing Room at Carlton House by Francis Hervé, a joiner of French extraction living in London.[30] The Chinese figure seated on a cushion which is perched on the top rail was added by Hervé in 1792, presumably to echo the figure of a Chinese drummer boy, also seated on a cushion, which forms part of the clock-case (page 124).

In view of the origins of Hervé, it is perhaps understandable that the chairs should betray a strong French influence. The straight, reeded and tapering legs, the cut-off corners of the top rail of the back, the rosettes carved within square frames above the legs and even the bird's-head terminals of the arm-rests can be paralleled on stamped pieces of furniture of the Louis XVI style made in Paris (cf. pages 215 and 216, for example).

However, what is quite exceptional, and for which there is no counterpart in France, is the piercing of the rails in order to lighten each piece materially and to enliven the surface visually by allowing light to filter through these struts.[31]

Height, $40\frac{3}{4}$ in; *width,* $35\frac{1}{2}$ in; *depth,* 26 in.

THE ROYAL PAVILION, BRIGHTON

In the place of two modest-sized rooms at the north and south end of the east front of Brighton Pavilion, John Nash erected in 1817 two immense halls to serve as a Banqueting Room and a Music Room. The decoration, which was in the hands of Frederick Crace, and the furnishings, which were supplied largely to the designs of Robert Jones, were not completed before about 1821. Their cost amounted to the astronomical figures of £41,886.4.0 and £45,125.15.10 for each of the two rooms.[32] Visitors were overwhelmed by the magnificence and the luxury of it all. Brayley writing about the Music Room in 1838 confessed himself unable to 'convey to the mind or imagination of the reader an appropriate idea of the magnificence of this apartment; . . .'[33] This is perhaps understandable if, as has recently been suggested, this room was designed with the Palace of the Great Khan at Shandu in mind, which Marco Polo visited in the fourteenth century.[34]

Some of the furnishings of these two rooms are illustrated here and on the next two pages.

ARM-CHAIR
BY BAILEY & SAUNDERS

An arm-chair, of beechwood and pear-wood, elaborately carved and partly gilt. The decorative elements include bat's-wing motifs under the side rails and scaling on the front rail. The arm-rests are supported on the heads of two monsters which seem to be a cross between an alligator and a bird of prey. This arm-chair forms part of a set of four arm-chairs, twelve chairs and eighteen 'Runners' supplied by the firm of Bailey & Saunders in 1817 for the Music Room at Brighton, at a cost of £1,517.[35]

Height, 37¼ in; width, 25¼ in; depth, 28 in.

CHANDELIER
BY PERRY

The chandelier, which is in the form of a water-lily, is of painted and cut-glass suspended on a green-lacquered bronze stem. It was one of nine (eight of this size and one larger) supplied about 1818 by William Perry, lamp and lustre manufacturer, for the Music Room in the Royal Pavilion at Brighton. They cost £4,290.12.0.

Diameter, 52 in.

THE 'ROCK CLOCK'

A French eighteenth-century clock of gilt bronze richly chased with stylised foliage and pelt motifs and mounted with human figures treated in the round. Built in two sections, the upper one, which contains the clock-case, tapers at the top and bottom and is in the form of a conventional Louis XV cartel clock.

Known as the 'Rock Clock', it stood on the chimney-piece in the Music Room at Brighton Pavilion. Writing in 1838, E. W. Brayley described it as 'a superb time piece, of curious and elaborate design: the base exhibits a rock and palm tree; around the latter a dragon is entwined and appears to be darting its sting at a figure behind, who wields an uplifted spear. At the top are Venus and Cupid, with the Peacock of Love; and below them is the god Mars, who is climbing upward as though to view the beauties of the Paphian Queen'.[36]

Purchased in Paris, this clock was despatched to Brighton on 13 October 1819, six days after its arrival in London. At that time its movement, so Jutsham informs us, was by 'Ragot a Paris'.[37] The present dial and movement are by B. L. Vulliamy (the latter numbered 739) and were inserted in 1820.[38]

Height, 48½ in; *width,* 24 in; *depth,* 13 in.

SIDEBOARD BY BAILEY & SAUNDERS

One of eight sideboards of pine and beechwood, veneered in rosewood and satinwood. Fret-work panels in brass decorate the apron and the superstructure at the back. Flanking the legs are dragons of monstrous appearance in carved and gilt wood. Tufts of hair sprout from their chests and wings and folds of flesh overhang their globular eyes. The design of the tables is attributed to Robert Jones. Documents reveal that they were made by Bailey & Saunders in 1817 for the Banqueting Room at Brighton Pavilion at a cost of £4,129.3.0.[39]

In the engraving of the Banqueting Room published by John Nash on 1 December 1824, these sideboards can be seen in their original setting. It is not clear exactly how they stood against the walls. It is important to know this, as three of the sideboards in their present condition have no back legs—they are secured by screws driven into the wall. It is probable that they were all like this and that the back legs now on the other tables were later additions. If this is so, the craftsman responsible for these alterations may have been a certain T. Haig, who stamped his name on the back of the capitals to the rear legs on two of the tables.

Height, 38 in; *width*, 88 in; *depth*, 24 3/16 in.

GRAND PIANO BY MOTT

The grand piano is of walnut inlaid with brass and is supported on a monopodium springing from a triangular-shaped base which rests on three feet in patinated bronze chased with scroll and shell motifs.

On 1 February 1817 Isaac Mott took out a patent for a grand piano incorporating various structural improvements of his invention. The Buckingham Palace piano bears two inscriptions, which indicate that it was made by I.H.R. Mott and that it is his 'Patent Sostenente Grand'.[40] In addition, his name is stamped twice within the rim of the piano, together with the date *AD 1817*. This piano must be, therefore, one of the first which Mott produced by virtue of his patent.

Acquired by George IV, the piano was placed in the Music Room Gallery at Brighton Pavilion. It can be identified in the engraving of this room published by John Nash on 1 July 1824. The music stool also came from Brighton Pavilion, and is probably the one which stands in front of Mott's piano in Nash's engraving of the Music Room Gallery. It is of oak painted with alternating anthemion and lyre motifs in gold on a green ground. Its seat, mounted on a central threaded spindle in steel, can be raised about six inches in height.

Piano: *height,* 36 in; *length,* 97 in; *width,* 46½ in.
Stool: *height,* 20$\frac{13}{16}$ in; *width,* 19 in.

THE 'KYLIN CLOCK'

The clock, of gilt bronze and Chinese porcelain, is of unusual design. The movement is fitted into the shoulders of a *famille verte* vase of the late eighteenth century above two seated kylins of Ch'ien Lung porcelain (1736–95). Framing the clock-cylinder and entwined like ivy round the kylins are tendrils of lotus and sunflower plants in gilt bronze. The cylinder is crowned by a group of Japanese porcelain figures. The base, in gilt bronze, is inset with open-work Chinese porcelain panels similar to those forming the balustrades of pagodas. The scrolled support in gilt bronze on which the clock now rests is not part of the original design.

The clock used to stand on the chimney-piece in the Saloon at Brighton Pavilion. The dial and movement (the latter numbered 742), which are by B. L. Vulliamy, date from 1820. Another clock similar in design–but without the lotus and sunflower embellishments in gilt bronze–is in the Residenzmuseum, Munich.[41]

The mounts to both clocks are probably French, though in the case of the Buckingham Palace version, the additional ornaments are most probably English, and may have been supplied by Vulliamy in 1820.

Overall height, 39¼ in; *width,* 32 in; *depth,* 14½ in.

REGENCY KNEE-HOLE WRITING-TABLE

This knee-hole writing-table, fitted with five drawers on each side, is of oak veneered in purplewood; the drawers are of solid mahogany. It formerly stood in the Library at Brighton Pavilion, and still bears the Pavilion brand mark. It can be identified among the furnishings of the library in an engraving published by John Nash in January 1824.

The beauty of this Regency table lies in its simplicity of design, discreetly underlined by a boxwood fillet which frames the face of each drawer as well as the side panels, and runs along the apron on all four sides. The gilt bronze mounts are few and unobtrusive. The table top is covered in red morocco leather stamped with a tooled border.

Height, 31 in; *width,* 73½ in; *depth,* 34¼ in.

INKSTAND WITH A LION, AFTER CANOVA

The inkstand is of mahogany, veneered in kingwood, and enriched with gilt bronze mounts in the neo-classical taste. The paperweight is a reduction in patinated bronze of one of the pair of lions by Canova which forms part of his tomb of Pope Clement XIII in St Peter's, Rome (1787–92). The lions are described in a work on Canova as being in an attitude of 'supremo cordoglio' (deepest sorrow).[42] It is appropriate that George IV, who acquired the inkstand, should surround himself with reminders of this sculptor, whom he greatly admired and who in turn, we are informed, considered himself indebted to the English king 'for the halo of glory which shed fresh lustre' over his last days.[43]

Height, 8¼ in; *width,* 19¾ in; *depth,* 12¼ in.

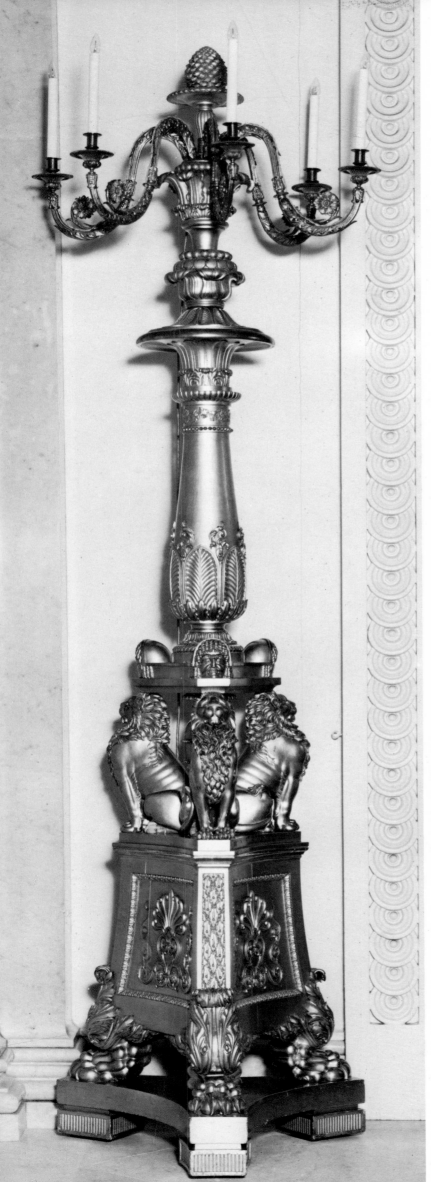

BEECHWOOD AND GILT BRONZE CANDELABRUM

One of four five-light candelabra of beechwood, carved and gilt. The candle-arms are in gilt bronze.

Their history is confused. Clifford Smith, quoting from the Carlton House accounts for March 1811, identifies them as the '4 very large Elegant Candelabras for Saloon, superbly carved and double gilt to design', which were made by Tatham, Bailey & Saunders at a cost of £170 each.[44] It seems more likely, however, that they are the four candelabra which Jutsham describes in his Receipts Ledger in May 1829; two of these, according to Jutsham, had been 'recently made by Mr Morel, to match the [other] Pair . . .'[45] The one difference is that in the inventory they are described as having scroll branches for nine lights, whereas the one illustrated is fitted with five branches. It is probable that their tops were altered at a later date. A comparison with the drawing of one of these candelabra in George IV's Pictorial Inventory reveals that at that time, *c.* 1827, the candle-arms were of a different design and attached lower down the shaft. The drawing does not, however, show clearly the number of arms.

Height, 111½ in.

DINING-ROOM CHAIR, POSSIBLY BY TATHAM

One of a set of beechwood chairs, carved and gilt.[46]

These chairs can be recognised in Pyne's engraving of the Dining Room at Carlton House published on 1 August 1817. Some were later moved to the Music Room Gallery in the Royal Pavilion at Brighton.

Clifford Smith has identified this set in the accounts as '60 Antique Chairs . . .' presumably because of their legs, which are shaped like those depicted on classical vases. They were supplied by Tatham & Co. on 5 January 1813 for Carlton House at a cost of £502.8.0.[47] On the documentary evidence available, however, it seems hazardous to make an unqualified attribution to Tatham.

Height, 32¼ in; *width,* 18 in; *depth,* 21¼ in.

GEORGE IV AND THE ARTS OF FRANCE

While the works of art so far described have been shown in their setting in the State rooms of Buckingham Palace, those illustrated on pages 138 to 147 are taken out of their normal context; they have been photographed as they were displayed in the exhibition, 'George IV and the Arts of France', at The Queen's Gallery in 1966. All the pieces described come from Buckingham Palace.

CHEST OF DRAWERS BY BERNARD II VAN RISAMBURGH

The chest of drawers[48] dates from the mid-eighteenth century and was made by one of the most talented *ébénistes* (cabinet-makers) working in Paris at the time, Bernard II Van Risamburgh (master before 1730–1765/6). It is of oak veneered in ebonised wood and decorated with panels of Japanese lacquer, overlaid in places with European lacquer. The serpentine handles to the two drawers are composed of raised gilt bronze mouldings and loops of stylised tendrils. The slab is of red griotte marble.

The addition of European lacquer to the oriental panels suggests that at the time of mounting they may have been in need of repair, or that their design required adapting so as to harmonise with the bronzes. That panels were touched up in this way in the eighteenth century is shown by an entry in the day-book of the dealer Lazare Duvaux. The entry, dated 9 September 1752, refers to the repair of two chests of drawers for Madame de Pompadour: 'rétabli les corps & tiroirs, regratté l'ancien vernis en aventurine & refait en noir à neuf par Martin, rétabli le lacq, & ajouté des reliefs pour cacher les défauts, . . .'[49]

The Chinese jars,[50] which are of late seventeenth-, early eighteenth-century grey *craquelé* celadon porcelain, are fitted with elaborately scrolled gilt bronze mounts made in France. The mounts can probably be dated to within five years. They are struck with a small crowned C mark, the stamp which was punched to indicate the payment of a tax levied in France on all bronzes between 1745 and 1749.

For a description of the clock, *see* page 200.

Chest of drawers: *height*, $35\frac{3}{8}$ in; *width*, 63 in; *depth*, $25\frac{5}{8}$ in.
Chinese jars: *height*, $14\frac{9}{16}$ in; *width*, $16\frac{3}{16}$ in.

CORNER–CUPBOARD BY BERNARD II VAN RISAMBURGH

The corner-cupboard,[51] which is one of a pair, was also made by Bernard II Van Risamburgh (master before 1730–1765/6), whose stamp *BVRB* is struck three times on the carcase next to the monogram of the furniture makers' guild, *JME (Jurande des Menuisiers Ebénistes)*.

Constructed of oak, the corner-cupboard is decorated with a panel of Japanese lacquer overlaid with rococo gilt bronze mounts. The foot in the centre of the apron was added later to prevent the cupboard from tilting forward when the door is opened. The slab is of alabaster.

Displayed on the corner-cupboard is an early eighteenth-century Chinese vase of blue porcelain fitted with scrolled and foliate gilt bronze mounts made in France in the mid-eighteenth century. It is one of a set of three vases, similarly mounted, which was purchased by George IV in July 1818.[52]

Corner-cupboard: *height*, $37\frac{5}{8}$ in; *width*, $33\frac{11}{16}$ in; *depth*, $25\frac{1}{8}$ in.
Vase: *height*, 26 in; *width*, $13\frac{3}{4}$ in; *depth*, 10 in.

SIDE–TABLE BY WEISWEILER

A French side-table of the last quarter of the eighteenth century[53] supports three soft-paste Sèvres vases, green ground, which are slightly earlier in date.[54]

The table, which is stamped by A. Weisweiler (master 1778), is of oak veneered in ebony. It is inset on the front and sides with four panels of *pietra dura* and plaques of reddish jasper, and is enriched with gilt bronze mounts elaborately chased. The legs are of cast iron and the slab is of red granite. The bronze plaque of the front, inscribed *DOCTRINA,* was evidently a popular decorative motif. It is incorporated into the design of the chimney-piece in the Royal Closet (page 56) and was also used by David Roentgen on a desk sold to Catherine the Great in 1783.[55]

DETAILS OF THE WEISWEILER TABLE AND GARNITURE

Two of the four mosaic panels, which may have been made in the seventeenth century, can be identified in a drawing of a projected sideboard (here illustrated) dated 7 September 1784.[56] The detail shown above corresponds to the third panel from the top in the drawing. The sideboard does not appear ever to have been manufactured. On this evidence the table must post-date 1784. It was acquired by George IV in 1816 from the Parisian dealer, Rocheux.[57]

Height, $38\frac{5}{16}$ in; *width,* $57\frac{1}{2}$ in; *depth,* $23\frac{1}{4}$ in.

The centre vase, known in the eighteenth century as *Vase Tourterelles* from the doves mounted on each side, is painted on the front with a mythological scene in the manner of Dodin which represents Cupid pointing his arrow at Venus, and on the back with a spray of flowers. Its original crown-shaped cover has been lost (cf. vase on page 146) and another substituted in its place. This vase, which is unmarked, dates from *c.* 1770.[58]

Height, $19\frac{1}{2}$ in; *width,* 11 in.

The two other vases, *c.* 1768, which are also unmarked,[59] are painted on the front with scenes of children at play which derive from paintings by J-H. Fragonard entitled *La Bascule (The See-Saw)* and *Le Colin Maillard (Blind-Man's-Buff)*. The colours in the reproductions on the vases bear no relation to those of the actual paintings. The immediate sources copied at the Sèvres manufactory were probably J-F. Beauvarlet's engravings of these paintings published in 1760. The vases were acquired by George IV in May 1829.[60]

Height, $16\frac{15}{16}$ in; *width,* 8 in.

'TABLE OF THE GRAND COMMANDERS'

Of hard-paste porcelain with gilt bronze mounts, this table, known as the 'Table des Grands Capitaines', was commissioned by Napoleon in 1806, together with three other tables similar in character, from the Sèvres manufactory. Completed in 1812, it remained in store up to 1817, when George IV applied through diplomatic channels for permission to buy it. Instead of acceding to this request, Louis XVIII seized the opportunity of offering the table as a gift.[61] So delighted was George IV with this present that in all subsequent official portraits wearing the Garter and Coronation robes, he chose to be painted by Sir Thomas Lawrence with his right hand resting on the edge of this table.

The stem, in porcelain and gilt bronze, is in the form of a bundle of pikes. The porcelain top is painted in the centre with the head of Alexander the Great encircled by scenes of his triumphs depicted in imitation low relief. In an outer circle are the heads of twelve commanders from antiquity, each shown above a scene recalling a notable event in his career. Hannibal, for example, is represented crossing the

Alps, Pericles building the Parthenon, and Caesar turning away in distress from the severed head of Pompey.

For the thirteen heads and the twelve scenes of the outer circle, L-B. Parant (who signed and dated the table top, 1812) received the highest sum, namely 8,000 francs out of a total of 29,025 francs.[62] The specification for this table reveals that the heads were to be copied from antique medals supplied by E-Q. Visconti, curator of antiquities at the Louvre. Though a number of medals can be related to the heads reproduced on the table, engraved stones and antique cameos were also used as models. The head of Themistocles, for example (*see* detail on page 145), corresponds exactly to an engraving of a gem (also illustrated) which Visconti published in 1808 in the first volume of his *Iconographie Grecque. . . .* In his commentary on the engraving Visconti notes that the dolphin, which is shown under the head, symbolises Themistocles' crushing victory over the Persian fleet at Salamis in 480 B.C.

Height of table, $36\frac{3}{8}$ in; *diameter,* $40\frac{15}{16}$ in.

145

CABINET BY CARLIN

A late eighteenth-century French cabinet, which is of oak veneered in ebony and inset with nineteen plaques of *pietra dura*. It is enriched with chased gilt bronze mounts and fitted with three cupboard doors, the flanking ones disguised as drawers by the three *pietre dure* panels inset into each one.

Two of the marble plaques are signed on the back by a Florentine, G. A. Giachetti, who was employed in the Gobelins manufactory in the latter part of the seventeenth century to make mosaic panels. His panels, originally intended for mounting on contemporary pieces of furniture designed for Louis XIV, were re-used a century later on modern furniture, such as on this piece stamped by the Parisian *ébéniste*, M. Carlin (master 1766–85).[63]

The cabinet was probably supplied by the dealer, D. Daguerre, some time before 1778 to the singer Marie-Joséphine Laguerre, famous for her extravagant living and her fine voice, 'son organe sonore'. She died in 1782, aged twenty-eight, after a short but tempestuous life. The cabinet was acquired by F. Benois for George IV some time before 1829.

Height, $41\frac{7}{16}$ *in; width,* $60\frac{1}{16}$ *in; depth,* 23 *in.*

This cabinet supports a *garniture* of soft-paste Sèvres vases similar to that on the Weisweiler table (pages 140–41), only in this case the ground colour is blue, not green.

The centre vase, *c.* 1770, which is unmarked,[64] is painted on the front with a pastoral scene and on the back with a trophy of gardening implements. It was acquired by George IV in May 1829.[65]

Height, $20\frac{1}{4}$ *in; width,* 11 *in.*

The flanking vases, *c.* 1768, which are also unmarked,[66] are painted on the front panels with figures representing on the one a troubadour and on the other a woman with two children, which are copied from engravings by J. Daullé (1703–63) after two paintings by J. Dumont le Romain.[67] On the side and back panels are painted trophies and flowers. The bronze bands separating the cover from the lip of the vase are later additions.

Height, $15\frac{3}{4}$ *in; width,* $6\frac{1}{2}$ *in.*

CANDELABRUM FROM THE THOMIRE WORKSHOP

One of a pair of eight-light candelabra in malachite and gilt bronze in the form of a column resting on a square base. Though stamped *THOMIRE A PARIS*, they are probably by P-P. Thomire's successors, his two sons-in-law, A-A. Beauvisage and L-A-C. Carbonelle, to whom he handed over the family business on his retirement in 1823. They were purchased in Paris by François Benois for George IV in May 1828.

Height, $69\frac{5}{16}$ in; *width,* $23\frac{1}{2}$ in.

PEDESTAL BY THOMIRE

The pedestal supporting the candelabrum, of which there is also a pair, comes, too, from the Thomire workshop. Delivered to Carlton House in July 1813, they can be ascribed to P-P. Thomire (1751–1843), and were supplied as stands to the Thomire candelabra (page 163. *See also* Pyne's engraving on pages 120–21).

The pedestals are of oak veneered on three sides with amboyna and on the back with mahogany.

The design for the central motif in gilt bronze on the front panel is copied from the frontispiece to the fifth book of C. Percier and P-F-L. Fontaine, *Palais, Maisons et Autres Edifices Modernes, Dessinés à Rome, . . .* (Paris, 1798) (*see* detail). Another example of a Percier engraving being reproduced on a piece of furniture is provided by the bronze plaque on the desk illustrated on page 209.

Height, $43\frac{11}{16}$ in; *width,* $15\frac{13}{16}$ in; *depth,* $15\frac{13}{16}$ in.

LONG-CASE AND
PEDESTAL CLOCKS

LONG-CASE CLOCK BY TOMPION

A long-case equation clock, fitted with a perpetual calendar, which was made for Prince George of Denmark, *c.* 1703; of oak veneered in burr walnut and ornamented with water-gilt brass mounts.[68] The clock face, which is pierced to reveal dials showing the day of the week, the day of the month, and the month of the year, is signed: *Thos Tompion/Edw Banger/ London.* Thomas Tompion (1639–1713) was in partnership with his nephew, Edward Banger, from 1702 to 1707.

One of Tompion's inventions was the construction of a mechanism which needed winding only once a year. The mechanism of this clock, which is built on this principle, can run for 390 days.[69] George III, who was himself a keen horologist, selected this clock from among those at Kensington Palace for the furnishing of his new residence, Buckingham House.[70]

Height, 110¼ in; *width,* 23½ in; *depth,* 13 in.

BAROMETER AND CLOCK BY CUMMING

A monumental barometer and clock by Alexander Cumming, which was commissioned by George III.[71] It was sold to the King on 14 February 1765 for the large sum of £1,178.[72] A detailed description of its mechanism is given by Clifford Smith.[73] Its case is of the finest quality. Made of kingwood and mahogany, with an interior fitting of carved ivory, the exterior is mounted with chased gilt bronze ornaments. The chasing of the two military trophies flanking the laurel garland (*see* detail) rivals that of the best silversmiths. Also of particularly fine quality are the floral swags suspended from lion masks. It is interesting to compare this motif in bronze with a similar one in wood on the Vile bookcase made in 1762 (page 114).

Height, 95¾ in; *width,* 22¾ in; *depth,* 18 in.

MONUMENTAL PEDESTAL CLOCK

A French pedestal clock of monumental proportions, made of oak veneered with tulipwood, purplewood, and mahogany. The case and pedestal are enriched with lavishly chased gilt bronze mounts; the seated female figure and three *putti* are in patinated bronze.

The case, though stamped by the Parisian *ébéniste* (cabinet-maker), F. Duhamel (master 1750–1801), corresponds in style to the period of 1735 to 1740. As *ébénistes* were not permitted to stamp pieces of furniture till they had become masters of their guild, it is probably unwise to regard Duhamel's signature in this instance as evidence that he made the clock-case. He could have stamped the clock at a later date if he had repaired it or if he had acted as dealer and it had passed through his hands in this capacity.

When the clock was bought by Lord Yarmouth for George IV in June 1816, it was described at the time of its purchase as having formerly belonged to the Palace of Versailles.[74] In the absence of any French royal inventory marks, this tradition is hard to confirm, though it may well be correct. At all events, it was much admired by George IV, who had it placed in a commanding position at Carlton House, where it can be seen at the foot of the Grand Staircase in the engraving published by W. H. Pyne, *c.* 1818 (here illustrated). Like so many other clocks in the royal collection, its French movement and dial–by J-B. Farine (died 1777)–were replaced by B. L. Vulliamy, who designed the present dial, showing the

GRAND STAIRCASE, CARLTON HOUSE
Engraving published by Pyne about 1818

150

days of the month, the moon's age, etc., and inserted the movement bearing his name and the number 903. The detailed account of these alterations, effected in 1821, is contained in the Vulliamy papers preserved in the library of the British Horological Institute.[75]

Overall height, 108⅝ in; width, 33 in; depth, 17 in.

LONG-CASE CLOCK BY BREGUET

A French long-case astronomical clock by A-L. Breguet (1747–1823) in a mahogany and glass case enriched with gilt bronze mouldings. It is fitted with a heating device; in the base is a tray for burning charcoal which is linked to a chimney which runs up the back of the case.[76]

Notwithstanding its plain exterior, this clock cost George IV the sum of £1,000.[77] It was delivered on 19 September 1825. The clock is fitted with two independent but related movements, designed to prevent any inaccuracies caused by jolting. The dials are each signed, *Breguet et Fils/H.ger de la Marine Royale/N.º 3671*. The Breguets were in no doubt about the excellence of their regulator. Louis, the son, described it in a memorandum of 1824 as 'la plus grande recherche tant pour la main d'oeuvre que pour sa belle composition et peut être considéré comme un monument de l'art de l'horlogerie à cette époque de notre Siècle'.[78] Besides this memorandum, George IV received a pen-and-wash drawing of the clock.

Height, 80¼ in; width, 19½ in; depth, 11⅝ in.

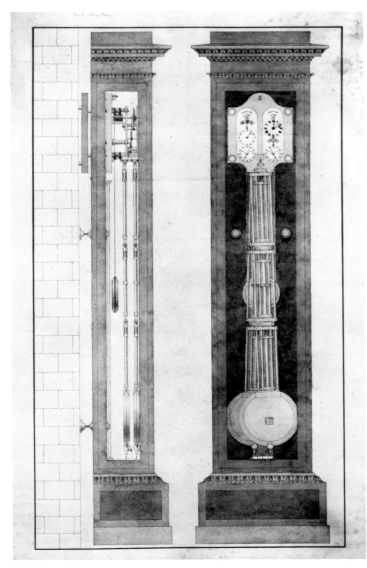

EXPLANATORY DRAWING OF BREGUET'S CLOCK

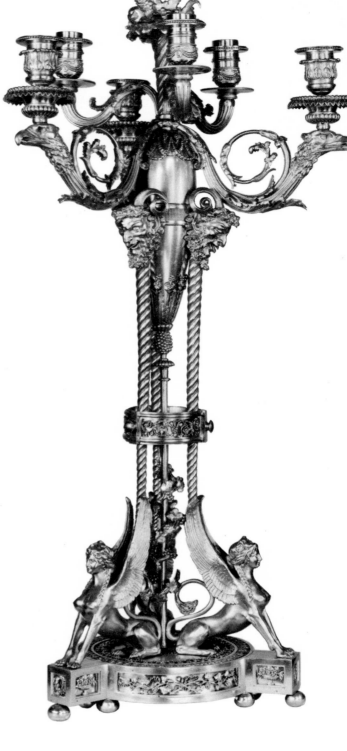

FRENCH BRONZE WORK

TRIPOD CANDELABRUM

One of four gilt bronze candelabra made in France in the late eighteenth century. Of four lights each, they are in the form of a black enamelled vase filled with fruit and flowers, which is supported on a tripod stand chased with goats' heads and hooves. Within the tripod the vase rests on a rod entwined with a serpent.

Though the date of their purchase by George IV is not known, it must have been before 21 June 1806, when Vulliamy submitted a bill for the repair and regilding of two of the four candelabra at a cost of £80.5.0.[79]

Height, 32⅛ in; *width,* 16 in.

CANDELABRUM, POSSIBLY BY GOUTHIERE

One of a pair of six-branch tripod candelabra in gilt bronze made in France in the late eighteenth century.

Though it is hazardous to make attributions where the provenance is not known, it is possible that these candelabra, which are very finely chased, may be by Pierre Gouthière (1732–1813/14), perhaps the most celebrated bronze manufacturer *(ciseleur-doreur)* of his time. They correspond to a model which has been described as almost certainly by Gouthière,[80] and which was delivered by the *marchand-mercier*, Dominique Daguerre, for Marie-Antoinette's use at Saint-Cloud.[81] The only important difference in design is in the substitution of the three sphinxes on the Buckingham Palace model for three goats.

Height, 30⅛ in; *width,* 14 in.

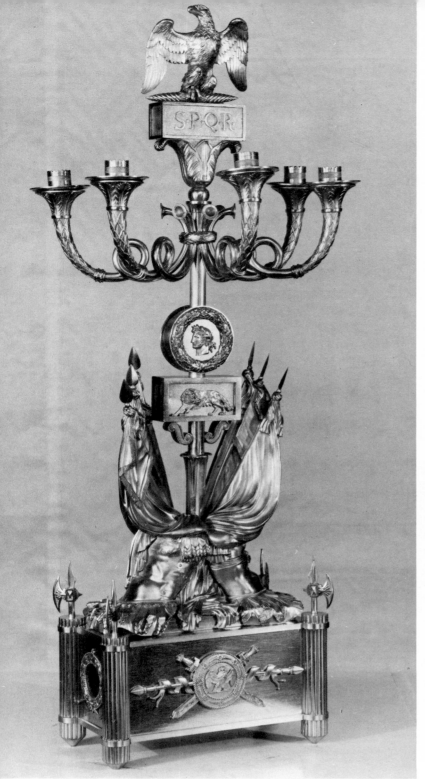

CANDELABRUM BY THOMIRE

One of a pair of candelabra made in France in the early nineteenth century by P-P. Thomire (1751–1843). Their design is of classical inspiration. The feet are in the form of Roman fasces and the candle-arms are shaped like trumpets.

As the Continental Blockade was proving injurious to French industry, Napoleon expressly authorised a few favoured manufacturers (including P-P. Thomire) to trade with the enemy. George IV eagerly took advantage of this dispensation. An important shipment from Thomire of clocks and candelabra (which included the pair illustrated) was received at Carlton House in July 1813, that is to say at the time that Wellington was driving the French back into France across the Pyrenees following the Battle of Vittoria.

Height, 32½ in; *width of base,* 10⅜ in; *depth of base,* 5½ in.

CANDELABRUM, POSSIBLY BY GALLE

One of a pair of five-light candelabra in gilt bronze made in France in the early nineteenth century, possibly by the Parisian bronze manufacturer, Galle.[82] Fitted with scrolled branches which issue out of a cornucopia terminating with a stag's and a boar's head respectively, they rest on a *verde antico* marble base mounted with a low-relief scene in gilt bronze. The unusual shape of these candelabra, though probably inspired by a contemporary engraving of the architect, C. Percier, derives ultimately from the classical drinking-vessel, the rhyton, which was in the form of a horn terminating in the head of an animal.[83]

Height, 38 in; *width of base,* 13½ in; *depth of base,* 6½ in.

FRENCH FAUN AND NYMPH CANDELABRA, ON STANDS, BY TATHAM & BAILEY

The candelabra of gilt and patinated bronze, which form a pair, are composed of a faun and a nymph each holding a cornucopia filled with grapes and vine leaves and fitted with branches for six lights.

These candelabra, together with another pair in the royal collection, were made in France in the late eighteenth century. Other versions are known, some dating from the nineteenth century. Their popularity in the eighteenth century is attested by an anonymous late eighteenth-century French drawing in the Musée des Arts Décoratifs, Paris (illustrated on page 194), in which the nymph candelabrum is represented in what is presumably an artist's impression for a proposed interior scheme.

The tripod stand, one of a set of four, is of beechwood carved and gilt, with applied ornaments in wood, also gilt. These stands were probably made by Tatham, Bailey & Saunders. They correspond to an entry in Jutsham's Carlton House ledger for June 1811 recording the receipt from Mr Tatham of '4 handsome Carved and Gilt Tripods with Crane Figures . . .'[84]

Candelabra: *height*, 44¾ in; *width*, 24½ in.
Stand: *height*, 52⅞ in; *width*, 27¾ in; *depth*, 24½ in.

CLOCK AND CANDELABRUM SUPPLIED BY LIGNEREUX

The clock-case is of yellow Siena marble and is mounted on one side with a figure of Apollo, in patinated bronze, holding a staff and a lyre and on the other with a flaming torch. The dial and movement, which are not original to the clock-case, were inserted by B. L. Vulliamy in 1820 (movement numbered 744).

A number of other versions of this model are known. One, in a red marble case, stands on the chimney-piece in the Royal Closet (page 56). The present one was probably part of a consignment of works of art bought by George IV in April 1803 from the Parisian furniture maker and dealer, M-E. Lignereux. Included in the same shipment were two five-light candelabra, each supported by a female Egyptian figure on a Siena marble base.[85] They can probably be identified as a pair now in the Billiard Room at Buckingham Palace (one illustrated).

Lignereux's shop in the rue Vivienne appears to have been thronged with English tourists visiting Paris during the brief interlude in the Napoleonic wars from 1802 and 1803. Some complained that his prices were too high, others enthused over the excellent quality of his stock. Bertie Greatheed, recording a visit on 2 March 1803, wrote: 'Nothing can be more beautiful nor more costly. Tables and Secretaries of yew, with gilt and Bronze ornaments for 1000 *Louis*. For 30 per Ct. advance he will deliver them to England. He says the chief sale is there. The bronze figures supporting candles, the lamps, the clocks, the china tables are all in the richest and best taste.'

Clock: *height,* 28⅛ in; *width,* 21 in; *depth,* 7⅛ in.
Candelabrum: *height,* 31 in; *width,* 11¾ in.

ENGLISH BRONZE WORK

WEEPING WOMEN CANDELABRUM BY VULLIAMY

The candelabra, of which this is one of a pair, are signed, *Vulliamy London AD 1811,* and were supplied to George IV for Carlton House. They are composed of three weeping female figures, in patinated bronze, standing back to back on a black marble base and supporting on their shoulders a gilt bronze vase containing branches for five lights.

Twenty-one craftsmen or firms were involved in their manufacture from September 1806 to 1811. Their work ranged from the initial supply of a wooden stand 'to model the fig upon' (the sculptor Smith was paid £36 for '3 Models of the Women in plaister') to the final mounting of the finished figures. The total cost to the Vulliamys came to £351.0.11, which B. L. Vulliamy passed on to George IV in 1815, together with an additional £69 for his own work–which seems to have been limited to designing the candelabra.[86]

ATLAS CANDELABRUM BY VULLIAMY

One of a pair of candelabra in the form of a figure of Atlas, in patinated bronze, supporting on his shoulders a vase with snake handles, which is fitted with three branches in gilt bronze. They were delivered to Carlton House by B. L. Vulliamy on 2 June 1814.[87]

Fifteen craftsmen and firms were involved in their manufacture over the period May 1812 to June 1814. Sold to George IV for £273, they cost £220.16.3 to make.[88]

The design for these candelabra may have been suggested to Vulliamy by an engraving of a clock, in the form of a celestial globe supported by Atlas, in Grolier de Servière, *Recueil d'ouvrages curieux de mathématique et de mécanique . . .* (Lyon, 1719). Vulliamy owned a copy of this work, which is now preserved in the Institution of Civil Engineers.

Height, 24¾ in; *diameter of base,* 8 in.

Height, 37⅛ in; *diameter of base,* 8 in.

CHINESE VASE MOUNTED BY VULLIAMY

One of four bottles of late eighteenth-, early nineteenth-century Chinese porcelain fitted with snake handles, which stand on a green marble pedestal enriched with gilt bronze mounts. The bottles were acquired by George IV and sent to the Vulliamys for mounting. In September 1814 they were returned, complete with pedestals, and were placed in the Blue Velvet Room at Carlton House. Two of them can be identified in the engraving of this room in Pyne's *Royal Residences*. The account of the manufacture of the pedestals and of the mounts for the bottles extends over more than six years, from February 1808 to September 1814.

Models for the mounts were made in wood, clay, wax and metal. A wooden pattern of one of the bottles was carved to try out the handles, as well as a 'Square wood peidestal to try the Effect'. When the mounts had been cast, chased and gilt, the bottles were sent to Robert Fogg, the porcelain dealer, to have holes drilled for the attachment of their bronzes.

The total cost of manufacture came to £1,136.2.3 and involved the work of thirty-one different firms or craftsmen. They were sold to George IV by B. L. Vulliamy for £1,680.[89]

Vase: *height,* 43¾ in; Base: *overall height,* 16¾ in; *width,* 17½ in; *depth,* 18½ in.

TRIPOD CANDELABRUM BY VULLIAMY

One of a pair of five-light tripod candelabra in gilt bronze. The account of the manufacture of these candelabra, which were invoiced to George IV on 31 December 1814, is contained among the Vulliamy papers in the Public Record Office.[90] Twelve craftsmen were involved in their manufacture, and were paid by B. L. Vulliamy the sum of £76.2.10 for their work. The candelabra were probably sold to George IV for £94.10.0.[91]

Height, 23½ in; *width,* 16¾ in.

TWO
FOUR-DIALLED
CLOCKS

CLOCK BY NORTON

A four-sided astronomical clock, of mahogany elaborately carved and mounted with open-work silver panels which incorporate the lion and unicorn, repeated on all four sides of the cresting, and confronted female sphinxes on the inset panels of the base.

The four dials, which are of white enamel, show respectively the time of day and solar time; a planetarium; the age and phases of the moon, and the tides at thirty-two points, mostly ports in the British Isles; the signs of the zodiac, the days of the week, the month and the year.

The issue of the *Gentleman's Magazine* for June 1765 provides a description of the four faces of the clock, and refers to its installation by Pinchbeck and Norton in the Queen's House (i.e. Buckingham House).[92] Though both Pinchbeck and Norton are mentioned, a notation in a Privy Purse bill-book makes it clear that it was Eardley Norton who actually built the clock. On 5 July 1765 he was paid the large sum of £1,042.[93] Unfortunately, the bill no longer survives. It might have included details of the clock-case, which in the quality of its carving is in no way inferior to the workmanship of the mechanism itself. Clifford Smith identifies this clock-case as the 'bracket for a clock' which John

Bradburn made for the King in 1766 at a cost of £38.15.0.[94]

If we examine the account in full[95] it appears doubtful whether the item supplied was in fact a clock-case. It seems more likely that it was a bracket in the usual sense of the word, i.e. a support for a clock to stand on, probably for the Eardley Norton clock itself. The bracket, if such it was, no longer exists. George III would have had it replaced by a stepped base. This change probably occurred when the clock was moved to the Octogon Library, where it can be seen in Pyne's engraving published on 1 February 1818 (page 102).

Though the name of the cabinet-maker who supplied the clock-case must still remain in doubt, the carving is of such high quality that, paradoxically, Clifford Smith was probably right in identifying it as the work of John Bradburn. The cost of the case may have been included in the figure of £1,042 paid to Eardley Norton–this would explain why no separate account has been found for it among the Lord Chamberlain's papers in the Public Records Office.

Height, $17\frac{1}{4}$ in; *width,* $9\frac{5}{8}$ in; *depth,* $10\frac{1}{8}$ in.

CLOCK BY PINCHBECK

The mechanism of this four-sided astronomical clock is by Christopher Pinchbeck (1710–83), assisted by John Merigeot and John Monk.[96] The astronomical works were modelled on those of the Eardley Norton clock (page 158).[97]

The four dials show, respectively, the time of day, with an extra hand for solar time; a planetarium, with a dial thermometer; the tides at forty-three points, mostly ports situated in the British Isles; and the signs of the zodiac and the sidereal time.

The clock-case, which is veneered in tortoise-shell, is enriched with finely chased gilt bronze mounts. It was designed by Sir William Chambers, assisted, it is said, by George III. Lady Mary Coke, who paid a visit to Mr Pinchback [sic] on 29 January 1768, comments in her journal: 'The case is magnificent, the execution extremely fine, & the design partly His Majesty's, & partly Mr. Chambers his Architect'.[98] A full-scale preliminary design by Chambers (here illustrated) is preserved in Sir John Soane's Museum.[99] This design, which measures $26\frac{1}{4}$ by 15 in, in pen and ink with green and grey wash, differs in certain details from the actual clock. For example, the silver decoration in the form of palm branches in the spandrels above the dial has been replaced by scroll-work. The rosettes flanking the urn below the dial are missing on the clock. The clock has been heightened by the addition of a drum below the dome. The case has also been enlarged from 15 to 16 in.[100] An interesting feature of the design is the urn draped with a heavy garland of oak leaves chased with acorns which stands below each of the dials. It is treated in the same spirit as the designs of J-C. Delafosse, whose first publication, *Nouvelle Iconologie Historique . . .*, appeared in Paris in 1768, the year that this clock was completed.

Height, $30\frac{5}{8}$ *in; width,* 16 *in; diameter of base,* $20\frac{1}{4}$ *in.*

FRENCH AND ENGLISH MANTEL CLOCKS

THE 'NEGRESS HEAD CLOCK' BY LEPINE

Known as the 'Negress Head Clock', this clock was acquired by George IV some time before December 1807, the date of a bill submitted by Vulliamy for its repair and partial regilding. It may have been purchased in 1790 (*see* note 101). The bust, which is in gilt and patinated bronze, contains the clock movement. It stands on a musical case of white marble and gilt bronze, which in turn rests on a plinth of white and black marble. The manner in which the time is indicated is not immediately apparent. Behind the negress's left eye is a drum marked with the hours in Roman figures and behind her right eye is another drum with the minutes calibrated in Arabic numerals in two-minute intervals. Ten minutes before the hour the eyelids slide away revealing the time; they close two minutes after the hour. The eyes can be opened at all other times by pulling the negress's right ear-ring. Her left ear-ring operates the sixteen-pipe organ which plays eight different tunes.

The movement is signed by J-A. Lépine[101] (1720–1814). Other versions are known, though they are not by Lépine. In two cases the movements are by J-B-A. Furet, who seems to have specialised in this type of clock; in 1784 he invited the public to come and admire one on view in his Paris shop.[102]

Height, 29¾ in; *width,* 16¹³⁄₁₆ in; *depth,* 9⅜ in.

CLOCK, ON SATINWOOD PEDESTAL, BY VULLIAMY

A clock and pedestal of oak veneered in satinwood, boxwood and tulipwood.[103] In a memorandum by B. L. Vulliamy dated 1 January 1835 he refers to this clock as having been specially made in 1790 by his father, Benjamin Vulliamy, for George III's use at Windsor Castle.[104]

The clock-cylinder, which is hung with laurel garlands in gilt bronze, rests on the top of a temple containing a Derby group in biscuit porcelain of 'Time clipping the wings of Cupid'. In addition to the grisaille painting of arabesques, garlands and swags on the pedestal and temple, mythological scenes are reproduced in three oval reserves on the pedestal. The theme of the centre one, 'Apollo in his chariot', is repeated on a number of other pedestals similar in character. It has been suggested on rather flimsy evidence that G. B. Cipriani, the Florentine artist who came to England in 1755, may have painted them.[105]

Though pedestals were supplied as supports for clocks by B. Vulliamy, in this case it is unlikely that the pedestal was specially designed for this clock. The Windsor guide-book for 1792 provides a description of the clock, when it was located in the Queen's Drawing Room, but not of the pedestal.

Clock: *height*, 32 in; *width*, $19\frac{11}{16}$ in; *depth*, $11\frac{3}{4}$ in.
Pedestal: *height*, $48\frac{3}{4}$ in; *width*, $23\frac{5}{8}$ in; *depth*, $13\frac{1}{8}$ in.

CLOCK BY VULLIAMY

A clock of white marble with gilt bronze ornaments mounted with three Derby biscuit porcelain figures which was made by Benjamin Vulliamy in 1788 for George IV.[106] The parchment resting on the reversed corinthian column records that it was *Design'd/for his/R.H. γ^e P./of WALE[S]*.[107]

In the published correspondence, dated 1788, between Vulliamy and William Duesbury of Derby, son, who took over the manufactory on his father's death in 1786, there are several references to biscuit figures which Vulliamy commissioned Duesbury to make for mounting on his clocks.[108] This innovation was evidently popular with Vulliamy's clients, as it was carried on into the nineteenth century. Vulliamy's Clock Book covering the years 1797–1806[109] contains a number of entries referring to Derby figures. The figures of boys, mounted as pairs, were sold to Vulliamy for a guinea the pair. A seated female figure accompanied by a boy cost, however, as much as £6.16.6.

Height, $18\frac{1}{4}$ in; *width*, $31\frac{1}{4}$ in; *depth*, $12\frac{3}{4}$ in.

CLOCK BY DE LA CROIX

The French eighteenth-century clock, which is of gilt bronze, is flanked by two standing female figures in patinated bronze, who are represented writing, one holding a parchment, the other an open book. The dial and movement are not original to the clock. They were inserted, *c.* 1851, by B. L. Vulliamy (movement numbered 1910). Probably also of nineteenth-century date is the base, chased with low-relief scenes in gilt bronze.

Exceptionally, the clock-case is signed by its bronze manufacturer, De La Croix, possibly Pierre Delacroix. When he was declared bankrupt in 1771 he had in his workshop a very large clock valued at 4,000 livres. Unfortunately its description is too imprecise to allow one to identify it with the Buckingham Palace clock.[110] In style the Buckingham Palace clock belongs to the third quarter of the eighteenth century. The treatment of the massive garlands of oak leaves and acorns suspended at the fore-corners from rams' heads is particularly characteristic of the beginnings of the *style Louis XVI*. Reflected in the mirror behind the clock are two seven-light candelabra by P-P. Thomire, which were acquired by George IV in July 1813.

Clock: *height,* 73¼ in; *width,* 48½ in; *depth,* 18⅝ in.

CANDELABRUM BY THOMIRE

The candelabrum, which is one of a pair, is in the full neo-classical idiom: a draped female figure in patinated bronze supporting on her head a basket containing twelve branches for lights; the basket rests on a cushion formed by a coiled garland chased with forget-me-nots and entwined with a ribbon.

The arms are not soldered to the body but are secured by screws. The circular wooden base does not form part of the candelabrum.

The candelabra, almost certainly by P-P. Thomire (1751–1843), were probably part of a consignment despatched by Thomire to Carlton House in July 1813.[111] They can be seen in an engraving of the Rose Satin Drawing Room published four years later (*see* pages 120–21), standing on the square pedestals (page 147), which also formed part of the same shipment and were supplied as stands for these candelabra.

Height, 47½ in; *width,* 23 in.

CLOCK IN THE LOUIS XVI STYLE

The gilt bronze clock made in France in the late eighteenth century rests on a white marble base. Its cylinder is flanked by two groups in patinated bronze and is crowned by an eagle straddling a garland of fruit and flowers.

In 1819 B. L. Vulliamy replaced the original French movement by his own, bearing the number 679.

The design of this clock can be related to a late eighteenth-century drawing (here illustrated) in the Metropolitan Museum of Art, New York. This drawing is thought to have formed part of a mail order catalogue of works of art on sale at the shop of the Parisian dealer, Dominique Daguerre, which he sent to Marie-Antoinette's brother-in-law and sister, Albert of Sachsen-Teschen and Maria-Christina, who were joint governors of the Low Countries up to 1792.[112]

Other clocks of this same model are known and it would therefore be hazardous to identify this model with the one offered to Marie-Antoinette's brother-in-law, even if they were absolutely identical, which they are not.

164   *Height,* 30 in; *width,* 28½ in; *depth,* 10⅞ in.

CLOCK BY LEPINE

A French late eighteenth-century clock of gilt bronze, which rests on a white marble base. Flanking the clock-cylinder, which is supported on a tall plinth, are two figures, the female one representing Study and the male one Philosophy.[113] The dial is signed by the Parisian clockmaker, J-A. Lépine (1720–1814).[114]

A number of versions of this clock are known, including two others in the royal collection. In the case of the model here illustrated, the height of the plinth supporting the clock-cylinder is twice that of the others. A drawing of the clock, c. 1827, which forms part of George IV's Pictorial Inventory (see illustration), reveals that it has been purposely heightened. The original marble base has been replaced by another one fitted with a different set of ornaments. The two bronze plaques, each chased with addorsed trumpeting satyr infants, which in the drawing are mounted on the base, are now fitted to the front and back of the metal cube added below the clock-cylinder.

These alterations, which were probably done prior to 1837, may have been carried out so as to make this clock match the one on the opposite page. Their height and the decoration of their bases correspond; furthermore, it is known that they were both located in the White Drawing Room at Buckingham Palace in the late nineteenth century.

Height, 28¼ in; width, 28⅛ in; depth, 9⅞ in.

165

ASTRONOMICAL CLOCK BY LEPINE

A late eighteenth-century French clock of white marble enriched with bronze mounts finely chased and gilt.

In a bill for its repair, dated 24 March 1808, Benjamin Vulliamy described this clock as 'a very Large Astronomical Equation Clock with three dials name Le Pine that shews the Rising and Setting of the Sun, the Moons Age, the Year, the days of the Month & Week, and the Signs of the Zodiac . . .'[115] Of particular beauty are the two smaller dials which are of hard-paste porcelain, probably of Sèvres porcelain, painted with jewel enamelling, and richly gilt. The one illustrated is painted with the signs of the zodiac. Both dials are signed, *Coteau*, who can probably be identified as the miniaturist Jean Coteau (c. 1738–after 1812), a native of Geneva living in Paris, who worked briefly for the Sèvres manufactory c. 1780–84.

According to an entry in *L'Avant-Coureur* dated 25 January

1762, painted porcelain dials made in the Meissen and Sèvres manufactories were in favour as early as 1762. However, the technique of jewel enamelling, as used on these two dials, is much later. It was perfected at the Sèvres manufactory by Parpette, a painter of flowers, and Coteau, and was first used on Sèvres porcelain about 1778.

The dial of a lyre-shaped clock in the museum at Sèvres,[116] but in enamel as opposed to porcelain, is painted with the signs of the zodiac of identical design. It is signed by Coteau and in addition is dated 1786.

The clock in the royal collection may have been one of those bought by George IV from Lépine in 1790 at a cost of £3,250, for which the sum of £2,850 was still owing in July 1799.[117]

Height, $25\frac{1}{2}$ in; *width,* 28 in; *depth,* $8\frac{1}{4}$ in.

THE 'OATH OF THE HORATII CLOCK'

This French Empire clock, which is of gilt bronze, rests on a *verde antico* marble base mounted on the front with low-relief figures also in gilt bronze. Its present dial and movement by B. L. Vulliamy (the latter numbered 678) were inserted in 1819 in replacement of the original French movement, which the English clockmaker had condemned as 'very bad'.

Known as the 'Oath of the Horatii Clock', the principal scene is adapted from a painting by Louis David, dated 1784. The three brothers face their father and vow mutual fidelity at the altar, before fighting the Curatii to determine the supremacy of Rome or of Alba. Two of the Horatii and the three Curatii were killed. In the scene on the base the surviving brother is being welcomed back by his father, while on the left are his two dying brothers; on the right his sister, the betrothed of one of the Curatii, turns away in anguish.

'THE OATH OF HORATII'
PAINTED BY LOUIS DAVID

'THE APOLLO CLOCK' BY THOMIRE

Clock-cases designed after classical paintings and sculptural groups were particularly popular in the early nineteenth century. John Scott confirms this when writing about the shops in the Palais Royal, which he much admired while visiting Paris in 1814. 'Nothing can be imagined more elegant and striking than their numerous collections of ornamental clock-cases: . . . modelled after the most favorite pictures and sculptures: . . .' In particular he remarked on the popularity of the Horatii and Curatii model inspired by David's painting.[118]

The Buckingham Palace model, however, predates Scott's visit by at least five years. It was purchased by George IV from a Mr Ricordon in January 1809.

Height, 26¾ in; width, 23½ in; depth, 8¼ in.

A clock by P-P. Thomire (1751–1843) showing Apollo driving his chariot drawn by four horses across the arch of Heaven, which is partly overhung with clouds. The arch, which rests on a griotte marble base, is of blued metal and is chased with four signs of the zodiac in gilt bronze (Pisces, Aries, Taurus and Aquarius). The dial is formed by the wheel of the chariot.

B. L. Vulliamy, in a memorandum dated August 1834, notes that 'The works of the Clock are good for nothing, & the case is very dirty. The case is well worth cleaning & new works [*sic*]'. His advice was followed. The present movement by Vulliamy, which replaces Thomire's, is numbered 1223 and was inserted in 1834.[119]

Height, 29½ in; width, 30½ in; depth, 10¼ in.

LACQUER WARE

The fashion for collecting small oriental lacquer objects reached its peak in France in the mid-eighteenth century.[120] Lacquer ware was prized for its rarity, for the brilliance and depth of its colours, for the smoothness of its surface, and, like porcelain, it was often mounted in gilt bronze.

The Jesuit missionary Le Comte, writing to the duchesse de Bouillon from Peking in 1685, praises lacquer for yet another of its properties: 'Worms do not easily breed in it, nay, and moisture scarce ever penetrates it, not so much as any Scent can fasten to it; if during meals there be any Grease or Portage spilt, if it be presently wiped with a wet Clout, one not only finds no remainders or signs of it, but does not so much as perceive the least smell'.

Lacquering was practised in China as early as the fourth or fifth century B.C. It was not, however, till the third century A.D. that the process became known in Japan. For the cheaper varieties the lacquer—which is a resin from the lac tree, *Rhus vernicifera*—was painted directly on the wood of the vessels. In other cases the wooden surface was first covered in hemp; very occasionally no wooden core was used at all. To achieve the lustre which was so much prized, the lacquer was applied in successive layers and after each application it was left to dry in a humid atmosphere and then polished. As many as thirty coats could be used. Embellishments in mother-of-pearl, gold and silver were sometimes added.

From the earliest times lacquer ware was regarded as a luxury and its possession as a sign of affluence. The complaint that 'nowadays the wealthy go in for [lacquer vessels with] silver rims and gilt handles' could have been made in the eighteenth century, almost with the bowls on pages 170 and 171 in mind; in fact it was made by a Chinese moralist writing in the first century B.C.

JAPANESE LACQUER BOWL

One of a pair of bulbous Japanese lacquer bowls of the early eighteenth century, fitted with gilt bronze mounts made in France in the mid-eighteenth century. The wooden bowls are lacquered on the inside and outside in imitation of aventurine. The raised decoration in gold lacquer studded with mother-of-pearl includes plants, trees, eddies and herons.[121]

Height, $11\frac{3}{4}$ in; *width,* 15 in.

JAPANESE LACQUER BOWL AND COVER

A Japanese lacquer bowl and cover of the early eighteenth century, fitted with gilt bronze mounts made in France in the mid-eighteenth century; of wood, lacquered on the outside in imitation of aventurine with stylised chrysanthemums in gold picked out alternately in black and gold, and on the inside in red lacquer.[122]

The elaborate gilt bronze mounts recall the shapes adopted by the manufacturers of tureens which were made in porcelain and silver in the middle of the eighteenth century.

Height, $11\frac{1}{4}$ in; *width,* $13\frac{3}{4}$ in.

JAPANESE LACQUER CABINET

One of a pair of identical cabinets, of which there are two further related ones. They are each constructed out of a conventional Japanese lacquer cabinet of rectangular shape. In their altered form they now have splayed sides, a white marble top and claw and ball feet chased with honeysuckle ornament. The same lacquer designs are repeated on a number of the panels, though reversed in relation one to the other, such as the birds which are lacquered on the inside of the doors.

All four cabinets stood in the Banqueting Room Gallery of the Pavilion at Brighton, where they can be seen in the engraving of this room published by John Nash on 26 July 1823.

Height, $36\frac{3}{4}$ in; *width,* $55\frac{3}{4}$ in; *depth,* $20\frac{3}{4}$ in.

CORNER-CUPBOARDS BY BAUMHAUER

One of a pair of corner-cupboards which bear the stamp, *JOSEPH,* between two fleurs-de-lis (probably the stamp of the Parisian *ébéniste* (cabinet-maker) Joseph Baumhauer, master before 1767–1772); of oak veneered in ebony and on the inside of the door in tulip-wood. Inset into the door on each piece is an oriental lacquer panel of a hunting scene. The top is of dove-grey marble. The two lacquer scenes originally formed a single panel. By joining them together, it is possible to reconstitute the deer-hunt. On the right-hand section are the huntsmen, one of whom has shot an arrow. On the other is the quarry, the rearmost deer having just received the arrow shot by the huntsmen in its hind-quarters, while the other deer watch from behind cover.

These two corner-cupboards, together with a chest of drawers

also stamped by the same cabinet-maker (now at Windsor Castle), were purchased for George IV by Sir Charles Long in Paris and reached Carlton House on 14 January 1825. The three pieces formerly belonged to the duchesse de Mazarin; they can be identified in the catalogue, drawn up by J-B-P. Lebrun, of her effects, which were put up for auction in Paris on 10–15 December 1781 (Lots 218 and 219).

Height, 37¼ in; *width,* 31½ in; *depth,* 21¼ in.

SECRETAIRE BY MOLITOR

One of a pair of secretaires of late eighteenth-century design. Of oak veneered in ebony and mounted with oriental lacquer panels in black and gold.[123] The two marble slabs are of brocatelle marble. Stamped by Bernard Molitor (master 1787) on the veneered surface of the forward edge of the drop-front next to the lock (here illustrated). It is rare to find on French furniture an *ébéniste*'s stamp so placed, though on the relatively few pieces of English furniture of the nineteenth century which were stamped by their cabinet-maker, this would be the rule rather than the exception.

In design these secretaires are identical to a pair in the Louvre, which were purchased by Louis XVIII from Molitor in 1820, but which were made much earlier, having been ordered by Marie-Antoinette in 1790 and completed three years later.[124]

Height, 57¼ in; *width,* 32¾ in; *depth,* 16 in.

CORNER-CUPBOARD BY SADDON

One of a pair of bow-fronted corner-cupboards stamped by a Parisian furniture maker, J. Saddon (fl. mid-eighteenth century);[125] of walnut decorated in black and gold European lacquer in the Chinese style. The mounts are of gilt bronze and the slab is of white marble.[126]

Height, 34¾ in; *width,* 30 in; *depth,* 21¼ in.

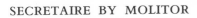

SEVRES GARNITURES AND VASES

LEFT: CABINET BY WEISWEILER, WITH GARNITURE

Standing on a late eighteenth-century French cabinet are three soft-paste Sèvres vases with a green ground. The centre vase, *c.* 1768, is among the most elegant productions of the Sèvres manufactory. It is painted in the reserve on the front with a camp scene in the manner of Morin and on the back with a military trophy. The vase is unmarked.[127] The flanking pair of vases dates from *c.* 1772.

The cabinet, which is stamped by the Parisian *ébéniste*, A.

Weisweiler (master 1778), is of oak veneered in ebony and *première-partie* Boulle marquetry (brass and pewter on tortoise-shell). It is inlaid with six *pietre dure* panels and enriched with gilt bronze mounts.[128] The slab is of brocatelle marble. Three doors give access to the inside of the cabinet.[129]

Centre vase: *height,* 17½ in; *width,* 10¼ in.
Cabinet: *height,* 39⅜ in; *width,* 59 1/16 in; *depth,* 19 in.

ABOVE: TABLE BY BELLANGE, WITH GARNITURE

One of a pair of side-tables supporting a *garniture* of soft-paste Sèvres porcelain. The centre vase, which is a very rare model, bears the date-letter T for 1772.[130] The table, which is of oak, rests on eight legs; the forward ones are of steel, mounted with gilt bronze heads emblematic of the four seasons and decorated with studs in cornelian and panels of lapis lazuli. The panels are inlaid with slabs of *verde antico* marble.

These tables, together with two others, smaller but similar in character, are by Alexandre-Louis Bellangé (1799–1863).[131] Bellangé was a distinguished member of a family of furniture

makers, who were active in Paris, mainly in the nineteenth century. The four pieces, which can be dated to *c.* 1823–24,[132] were purchased by the dealer, R. Fogg, for George IV at the Watson Taylor sale in 1825 for the sum of £1,490.[133] Originally intended for Windsor, they were brought to Buckingham Palace in 1834. It was probably at this stage that the larger pair, one of which is shown here, were slightly reduced in size to fit the space between the pillars.[134]

Centre vase: *height,* 18¼ in; *width,* 15¼ in.
Table: *height,* 46⅞ in; *width,* 99¾ in; *depth,* 29¼ in.

VASE AND COVER

One of a pair of vases and covers, *c.* 1780, which are unmarked. Of soft-paste Sèvres porcelain, green ground, the front reserves are painted with scenes of children at play.[135] In the reserves on the back are trophies. One is composed of produce of the land and harvesting implements and the other of toys (see detail). These consist of a doll, a violin and bow, a tennis racket, a kite, a bow and arrow, and a toy cart containing a garland of flowers. The choice of a trophy composed exclusively of toys is a charming conceit, which is in keeping with the scenes of children painted on the front.

Height, 13⅝ in; *width,* 7½ in.

FLOWER VASE PAINTED BY MORIN AND TANDART

A flower vase of soft-paste Sèvres porcelain with a turquoise blue ground.[136] In the front reserve is a genre scene of peasants drinking; sprays of flowers are painted on the sides; the back is plain.

This vase bears the date-letter H for 1760 and the marks of two painters—Morin, the painter of figures, who is known principally for his military and marine subjects, and Tandart *jeune,* who was presumably responsible for painting the flowers.

Height, 7¾ in; *width,* 9⅞ in.

FLOWER VASE ON SCROLLED FEET

The other flower vase, *c.* 1760, is unmarked.[137] It is of soft-paste Sèvres porcelain with a dark blue and green ground decorated in gold with marbled and trellis patterns. The genre scene on the front is identical to that on the turquoise vase. The same scene reappears on yet another flower vase, of still another shape, which bears the date-letter K for 1763 and the mark of Morin.[138]

Though it is possible that a painter working at Sèvres other than Morin was responsible for the panel on the unmarked flower vase in Buckingham Palace, the colouring and style of painting are so similar on all three that an attribution to Morin seems justified.

Height, 6¹³⁄₁₆ in; *width,* 10¹³⁄₁₆ in.

EGG-SHAPED VASE AND COVER

A vase and cover, of soft-paste Sèvres porcelain with a dark blue ground decorated with an overall *oeil-de-perdrix* pattern in gold. The cover is in the form of a French royal crown. Two biscuit porcelain plaques are mounted on the front and back of the vase, each chased with a profile head of Louis XV. The vase, which is unmarked, dates from about 1770.[139] The profile head is identical to that on a medal first struck in 1739 (here illustrated) to commemorate Louis XV's role as peacemaker between Austria and Russia on the one hand and Turkey on the other. This youthful head of the king by the medallist J-F. Marteau was evidently very popular.[140] It continued to be used on medals up to 1756 and on coins up to 1770, by which time the king was sixty years old.[141]

Other vases of this model were designed for use as a clock, the dial replacing the oval plaque on one side.[142]

Height, 14⅞ in; *width,* 8½ in.

VASE AND COVER
WITH MEDALLION HEADS

A vase and cover, *c.* 1770, of soft-paste Sèvres porcelain with a blue and white ground. The cover is mounted with medallion portraits in biscuit porcelain of Louis XV and the Empress Maria Theresa of Austria. It is unmarked.[143] As on the vase above, the portraits are almost certainly copied from medals. The medallion of Maria Theresa corresponds exactly to a profile head of the Empress on a medal struck *c.* 1760 by the Austrian medallist, Franz Würth,[144] and the medallion of Louis XV to a profile of the King on a medal struck by P-S-B. Duvivier in 1767 (here illustrated). This same portrait was later used by Duvivier on a medal issued in 1770 to commemorate the setting free of a number of debtors from prison, ordered by Louis XV to mark the marriage of the dauphin, the future Louis XVI, with Marie-Antoinette of Austria.

Perhaps this vase, with portraits of the French and Austrian sovereigns, was also commissioned in 1770 to honour this dynastic alliance.

Height, 13¾ in; *width,* 13 in.

DON QUIXOTE

One of four Gobelins tapestries (the one reproduced signed by the weaver, Neilson), which form part of a series of twenty-eight designs illustrating the exploits of Don Quixote. First mentioned in the Gobelins records in 1714, the series was repeatedly rewoven throughout the eighteenth century, sometimes with modified borders. The borders eclipse the scenes in importance and the designers of the former were paid correspondingly more than the artist, C. Coypel, who provided the cartoons for the scenes.

The Buckingham Palace tapestries reproduce the fifth set of border designs; their background, which simulates crimson damask with a figured pattern of flowers and foliage, is copied from a cartoon painted by M. Jacques in 1760.[145]

The panel illustrated represents 'The Princess begging Don Quixote to restore her to her Throne'. The subjects of the other tapestries are 'Sancho administering Justice', 'The awakening of Sancho and his Despair at the loss of his Ass', and 'Don Quixote cured by Wisdom of his Madness'.

Clifford Smith states that the Buckingham Palace pieces were woven by Neilson, but does not discuss their history.[146] By studying the detailed account of the different weavings of this series, it is possible to show that only two were woven on Neilson's low-warp looms, the other two coming from the high-warp workshops of the same manufactory.[147]

On 18 July 1788 Richard Cosway, the miniaturist, was presented by Louis XVI with four pieces from the Don Quixote series, as a gesture of thanks for the four tapestry cartoons by Giulio Romano of the history of Scipio which Cosway had given to the King for display in the Louvre. The records published by Fenaille reveal that the subjects, the borders and backgrounds of the tapestries received by Cosway are identical to the ones now in Buckingham Palace. Two were woven on J. Neilson's low-warp looms and two on the high-warp looms.

Cosway's biographer notes that the painter presented the tapestries given him by Louis XVI to the Prince of Wales (later George IV).[148] This gift was probably made shortly after their receipt by Cosway.[149]

Height, 11 ft 5 in; *width,* 10 ft 3 in.

TAPESTRIES FROM THE GOBELINS MANUFACTORY

JASON AND THE GOLDEN FLEECE

One of two Gobelins tapestries (this one dated 1780) from a series of seven designs after J-F. Detroy, which illustrate the story of Jason and the Golden Fleece as told in the seventh book of Ovid's *Metamorphosis*.[150] After ten years of marriage, Jason fell in love with Creusa and abandoned his wife, Medea. To avenge this injury, she killed Creusa, burnt Corinth – which is represented in flames in the background of the tapestry – murdered her two children by Jason – their bodies are draped over the front of her chariot – and drove her team of dragons to Athens. The yapping King Charles spaniel, which is frequently introduced into eighteenth-century engravings of boudoir trysts, seems strikingly out of place in this fearful scene of domestic retribution.

This tapestry and its companion were purchased for George IV by Sir Charles Long in Paris and reached Carlton House in January 1826.[151]

Height, 13 ft 7 in; *width,* 16 ft 8 in.

THE RAPE OF PROSERPINE

'The Rape of Proserpine', one of a series of four tapestries entitled *Les Amours des Dieux* which was woven at the Gobelins manufactory. The cartoon for this tapestry was painted by J-M. Vien in 1757, and the panel, begun in 1787 on the Gobelins looms of the weaver, Cozette *père*, was completed three years later.

Proserpine is represented with four companions bedecking with garlands a statue of her mother, Ceres. On the right Pluto, who is advancing rapidly in his chariot, is about to carry her off.[152] This panel and its companion (illustrated on page 180) were sold by the French government on 14 July 1797 to the *citoyen* Chapeau-Rouge, an army supplier established in Hamburg.

These tapestries were eventually acquired for George IV by Sir Charles Long in Paris and reached Carlton House on 9 January 1826.[153]

Height, 13 ft 4 in; *width*, 12 ft 7 in.

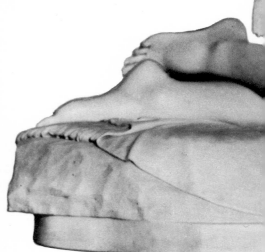

SCULPTURE

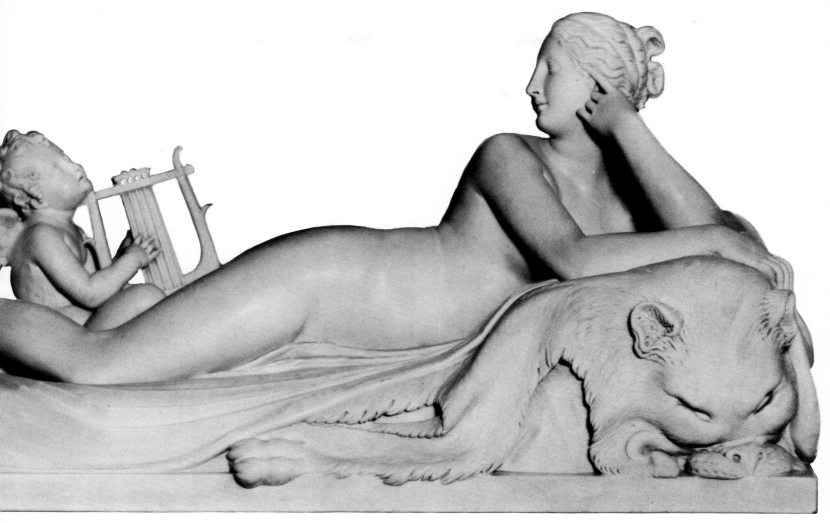

MARS AND VENUS BY CANOVA

A marble group of Mars and Venus by Antonio Canova (1757–1822). The spear above the raised hand of Mars is of wood. This group was commissioned by George IV following Canova's visit to England in 1815.[154] Writing to his friend Cicognara on 4 January 1817, Canova announced that he had finished modelling the group.[155] However, it was not despatched until two years after his death. On 10 April 1824 Jutsham recorded the receipt at Carlton House of 'Mars and Venus' and 'Dirce in a Sitting Attitude'. They were placed in the Conservatory by Richard Westmacott, who received the sum of £6.7.6 for unpacking and erecting the statues.[156] The Conservatory had been designed by Thomas Hopper in 1807 and was built partly in cast iron in 'that style of ancient English architecture denominated "the florid Gothic"'.[157] These naked neo-classical figures must have been strangely ill at ease illuminated by stained glass windows and in the company of 'Five Gothic Figures representing Old Kings',[158] which the firm of Coade & Sealy had sculpted, and which stood in niches. Two years later the Canova pieces were removed to Francis Chantrey's premises in Pimlico for storage. In correspondence dated 3 May 1822 in the Windsor archives mention is made of the sum of £1,000 disbursed 'in part payment of certain works which the Marquis Canova is executing for His Majesty'.[159] In August 1825 the price which was finally agreed for these two works was 5,000 gns.[160] Settlement was made in favour of Antonio Canova's half-brother, the Abbot Canova. The intermediary involved in these transactions was W. R. Hamilton, Minister at the Court of Naples from 1822 to 1825. In 1815 he had assisted Canova to recover for the Pope the works of art which Napoleon had confiscated from the Vatican, and in so doing had earned the venomous hatred of the French.[161]

Height (excluding spear), 83¾ in; width at base, 48½ in; depth at base, 25¼ in.

FOUNTAIN NYMPH BY CANOVA

Marble group of a reclining naiad and cherub, by Antonio Canova (1757–1822).

Described by Canova as a *Ninfa delle fontane*, the model was completed in October 1817 and the marble group in February 1818.[162] Water issues from the rock which serves as her pillow, and the nymph, awakened by the playing of a zither, half raises herself on her left elbow and turns her head towards the sound of the music.

It was commissioned by Lord Cawdor, who on Canova's evidence was so entranced by the *Venere vincitrice,* where Canova had represented Pauline Borghese reclining on a couch naked to the waist, that he wished to own a statue similar in style.[163] Nevertheless he agreed to relinquish his rights to it in favour of George IV.[162] It reached Carlton House on 12 June 1819.

Height, 32½ in; width, 72½ in; depth, 32 in.

BUSTS FROM THE TEMPLE OF MILITARY FAME

GEORGE III BY CHANTREY

A marble bust of George III inscribed on the back: *COPIED IN 1837, BY CHANTREY/FROM A BUST/ MADE IN 1771, BY BACON*. This bust was one of five by Sir Francis Chantrey which William IV commissioned for the Temple of Military Fame at Kew, built in 1837. The others were of the Duke of York (illustrated) after Joseph Nollekens, George IV (illustrated), William IV (illustrated) and the Duke of Wellington. Chantrey charged 100 gns for the Bacon and Nollekens copies, 150 gns for the bust of the Duke of Wellington and 200 gns for the other two.[164] Besides the five busts, the Temple contained nineteen tablets, which are still there, commemorating the dates and places of battles fought by British soldiers between 1760 and 1815. Though the King died in the year that the Temple was built, his plans were followed and the busts were installed. Frederick Scheer, in his guide-book to Kew, published in 1840, concludes his account of the Temple with a tribute to its founder: '. . . that which we behold is the index of a noble disposition, a grateful heart, a patriotic and pious mind! We like to honor the dead! We love those who honor them!'[165]

This fulsome tribute to the dead may not have endeared the writer to the Duke of Wellington, who had still twelve years of active life before him. The original bust of George III by J. Bacon to which the inscription refers was made *c.* 1771. It is reported that at the sittings Bacon took care not to offend the sensibilities of the King–he used a silver syringe to wet his clay instead of spouting water from his mouth.[166]

Height, 25½ in.

Three of the five busts commissioned by William IV in 1836 for the Temple of Military Fame at Kew. For further details, *see* opposite page.

GEORGE IV BY CHANTREY

(Opposite page.) A marble bust of George IV by Sir Francis Chantrey, signed and dated 1837.

Height, 27½ in.

DUKE OF YORK BY CHANTREY

(Above.) A marble bust of Frederick Augustus, Duke of York (1763–1827) by Sir Francis Chantrey. Signed and dated 1837. It is a copy of a bust by Joseph Nollekens dated 1813.
The Duke of York, younger brother of George IV, was Commander-in-Chief of the British Army from 1798 to 1809 and from 1811 to 1826. Though not successful as a commander in the field, his administrative reforms had the greatest influence on the subsequent history of the British Army.

Height, 22 in.

WILLIAM IV BY CHANTREY

(Right.) A marble bust of William IV by Sir Francis Chantrey, signed and dated 1837.

Height, 26½ in.

THE PRINCE CONSORT
BY WOLFF

A marble statue of the Prince Consort by E. Wolff, signed and dated 1846.[167] This is a replica of one by the same sculptor, now at Osborne, which was given by the Prince Consort to Queen Victoria on her twenty-third birthday, on 24 May 1842, though it was not completed till two years later.[168] The Prince Consort wears a suit of classical armour. As with the Gibson statue of Queen Victoria, emblems, which include the rose, the thistle and the shamrock, are chased on his attire.

When the original was completed it was put in the store at Windsor in Winchester Tower. Queen Victoria, who saw it there on 8 September 1844, found it '. . . very beautiful . . .' adding, however, 'but we know not yet where to place it'. In a later entry in her journal she gives the reason for the difficulty in finding a home for it '. . . Albert thinking the Greek armour, with bare legs & feet, looked too undressed to place in a room . . .'[169] It was eventually installed in a niche on top of the second staircase at Osborne on 15 August 1846.

This replica was given as a Christmas present to the Queen by the Prince Consort in 1849.[170]

Height, 75¼ in.

QUEEN VICTORIA
BY GIBSON

A marble statue of Queen Victoria, signed by J. Gibson.[171] It is a replica of one by the same sculptor, *c.* 1847, now at Osborne. The Queen is represented in classical attire holding in her right hand a wreath and in her left a parchment. The corners of her cloak are chased with a posy composed of the emblems of the British Isles, the rose, the thistle and the shamrock.

Writing about the original, Queen Victoria commented in her journal:[172] 'The attitude, drapery & everything is beautiful, like an Antique, but Albert is not quite satisfied with the likeness, though the figure is quite correct & gives the impression of youth & yet great dignity, as well as of the stature of a small person'.

This is probably the statue which was given by the Queen to the Prince Consort on 26 August 1849. The entry in her journal reads: 'This is almost the dearest & most blessed day to me in the whole year—the birth day of my beloved Husband, . . . Another present is a replica of my statue by Gibson . . .'

Height, 66½ in.

POTS-POURRIS AND PERFUME

The pot-pourri vase, unknown in France before the last quarter of the seventeenth century, was essentially an eighteenth-century phenomenon. Lazare Duvaux, the *marchand-mercier* (dealer), records in his day-book (1748–58) the delivery of numerous pots-pourris in porcelain, lacquer, silver and gold.

The receipts for their contents were as numerous as the vases. Ladies of fashion experimented in their composition, studying perfumes which they thought appropriate to their type of beauty. To obtaïn the finest fragrance, some of these essences were left to mature for as long as nine years.

MOUNTED CHINESE POT-POURRI VASE

A Chinese porcelain vase and cover, *c.* 1740, which has been elaborately mounted in gilt bronze in France in the mid-eighteenth century, so as to form a pot-pourri vase. The band separating the cover from the vase is pierced with eight 'eyes' to allow for the escape of the aromatic fumes.

Gabriel de Saint-Aubin illustrates one of a pair of similar covered urns fitted with gilt bronze mounts in his copy of the catalogue of the L-J. Gaignat sale of 1769 (Lot 95). Described as '. . . léger, délicat & peu commun . . .', the porcelain of these urns corresponds to that of the vase illustrated: 'fond céladon, avec animaux & arbustres en bas-relief blancs, lisérés d'un filet bleu'. There is, however, no indication either in the rough drawing or in the text that the bronze band separating the bowl from the cover on the Gaignat vases was pierced.

Height, $13\frac{1}{2}$ in; *width,* $12\frac{7}{8}$ in.

SEVRES POT-POURRI VASE IN THE FORM OF A SHIP

This pot-pourri vase, which is in the form of a ship, bears the date-letter F for 1758. It is of soft-paste Sèvres porcelain, with a blue and green ground and *oeil-de-perdrix* decoration in gold. The reserve on the front is painted with a genre scene and that on the back with sprays of flowers. The gilt bronze base probably dates from the nineteenth century.

This *vaisseau à mât* was purchased for George IV by François Benois in Paris in October 1817 at a cost of 2,500 francs. It may possibly have belonged previously to Louis XV.[173]

Height, $17\frac{15}{16}$ in; *width,* $14\frac{7}{8}$ in.

PERFUME BURNER

One of a pair of English perfume burners, *c.* 1800, in the form of a classical vase supported on a square base. Of oak, veneered in sycamore, mahogany, dyed walnut, satinwood and ebony. The gilt bronze mounts on each vase include four dolphins' heads and four male Egyptian heads, which are fitted above and below the tambour doors forming the body of the vase. The steps, visible in the photograph, can be folded back into the base.[174]

Scented pastilles were burnt in a metal container housed in the top of the vase. The fumes emitted through vents in the cresting in gilt bronze served to counteract the smell of burning candle grease.

Height, 70¼ in; *width,* 24¼ in; *depth,* 24¼ in.

LACQUER BOWL MOUNTED AS A POT-POURRI VASE

One of a pair of cylindrical Japanese lacquer vases of the early eighteenth century. Each jar is mounted as a pot-pourri vase;[175] an open-work band composed of a Vitruvian scroll in gilt bronze separates the cover from the bowl. This band, together with the other French mounts, dates from the second half of the eighteenth century. The stiff scrolled handles, pineapple finials and thick metallic bases threaded with laurel garlands and swags are similar in character to decorative designs by J. Beauvais and J-C. Delafosse published in the 1760's and 1770's.

The wooden bowl and cover, which are lacquered in imitation of aventurine in gold on a dark brown ground, are painted on the outside with peonies in raised gold lacquer.

Height, 13 in; *width,* 12¾ in.

SEVRES POT–POURRI VASE

A vase and cover of soft-paste Sèvres porcelain with a dark blue ground, partly decorated in gold with a marbled design. On the front reserve is a quay scene in the manner of Morin and on the reserve on the back are sprays of flowers. The vase, which is un-marked, must have been made about 1760.[176] The pierced shoul-ders and open-work cover indi-cate that it was intended for use as a pot-pourri vase.[177] The gilt bronze base is a later addition. Another vase of the same model in the royal collection is similarly pierced; a third in the Wallace Collection has no openings either in the shoulders of the vase or in the cover.[178]

Height, 18½ in; *width*, 11¼ in.

CHELSEA POT-POURRI VASE

One of a pair of soft-paste porcelain vases made at the Chelsea manufactory, *c.* 1760, which are marked on the underside with an anchor in gold. The neck and dome of the vase are pierced for use as a pot-pourri. On the front and back are figure scenes set in a sylvan setting.[179]

French influence is in evidence not only in the subjects chosen for the paintings, but also in the profusion of gold and in the use of the 'mazarin' blue on the handles and cover. However, unlike the practice at the Sèvres manufactory of painting the scenes in the reserves on a white ground separated from the principal ground colour of the vase by gilt bands or floral sprays also in tooled gold (cf. illustrations on pages 176 and 177), the ground colour on these vases, which is in gold, encroaches directly on to the scenes, forming a jagged edge.[180]

Height, 13⅛ in; *width,* 6½ in.

SPHINX PEDESTAL

One of a set of four (originally eight) pedestals of pine, carved and gilt. The eight pedestals can be identified in the illustration of the Throne Room at Carlton House published by W. H. Pyne (*see* illustration).

Clifford Smith assumed they were designed for Carlton House by the architect, Henry Holland.[181] There would be no reason to question this view were it not for the recent discovery of a French late eighteenth-century drawing of a pedestal (here illustrated) which is almost identical to the Buckingham Palace pieces. The only significant difference is in the treatment of the caryatids.

It is possible that this drawing, like the one of the clock (page 164), was executed for a catalogue, which a dealer such as Dominique Daguerre would have sent to his clients.[182]

In the actual construction of the pedestals there is nothing which proves that they must have been made in England rather than in

THE THRONE

France, or *vice versa*. It is conceivable, therefore, that they were both designed and manufactured in France and imported into England for use at Carlton House.

Height, 48¾ in; *width,* 23⅝ in; *depth,* 16 in.

ROOM, CARLTON HOUSE

Engraving published by Pyne, 1 October 1818

COUNCIL CHAIR

One of a pair of arm-chairs of pine and beechwood, carved and gilt, with backs shaped like Roman chariots. The front supports are composed of sphinxes, their wings forming the arm-rests.

Clifford Smith suggests that these chairs may be the '2 Very large Antique Elbow chairs' purchased by George IV from Tatham & Co. in 1813 for the sum of £587.12.0.[183] One of them can be seen in the engraving of the Throne Room at

Carlton House (see above).

Designers of furniture working in England in the Regency style were evidently fascinated by monumental seats of this shape. In 1799 C. H. Tatham published several sketches of marble seats which are variants of this design (one illustrated in reverse). Thomas Hope published similar designs in 1807.

Height, 42¾ in.; *width,* 37 in.; *depth,* 38 in.

SETTEE FROM THE BLUE DRAWING ROOM

One of a set of four settees, of walnut, carved and gilt. This settee resembles the one on the opposite page in general shape and in the choice of particular motifs, such as the lion's paw feet and the arm-rests supported on the heads of lions. According to Clifford Smith, however, the settees illustrated on this page were supplied eighteen years earlier than the others and were made by Tatham and Bailey. Though he may well be correct, it has not been possible so far to trace the documentary evidence on which he bases his attribution.[184]

Height, 42 in; *width,* 82 in; *depth,* 40 in.

SETTEE FROM THE GREEN DRAWING ROOM

A settee, forming part of a set which, according to Clifford Smith, was made by Morel & Seddon for Windsor Castle in 1828.[185]

Of mahogany, carved and gilt, the arms are in the form of lions' masks and the front legs terminate in lion's paw feet.

In the group by Winterhalter, painted in 1846 (illustrated on page 310), the Prince Consort and Queen Victoria can be seen seated on two chairs belonging to this set.

Height, 48¾ in; *width*, 91 in; *depth*, 42 in.

LEFT: BERGERE

One of a set of six *bergères,* of walnut, carved and gilt and decorated with applied ornaments, also gilt, which include anthemion motifs and scroll-work.

On the evidence of an entry in a Carlton House ledger dated 10 October 1812, Clifford Smith has identified this set as the one made by Morel and Hughes for George IV in 1812.[186] The description in this ledger[187] is, however, so perfunctory that it seems hazardous to assume on this evidence alone that the *bergères* here illustrated are the ones indicated in the records.[188]

Height, $37\frac{1}{2}$ in; *width,* $31\frac{1}{4}$ in; *depth,* $34\frac{1}{2}$ in.

REGENCY ARM–CHAIR

One of a pair of Regency arm-chairs, *c.* 1810, of beechwood lacquered in black and gold. The top of the back rail is painted with acanthus ornaments. The most striking features of this arm-chair are the boldly scrolled arm-rests, supported on legs carved with the head of a horned monster and terminating in lion's-paw feet.

This same monster, with its distinctive indented collar, appears in an engraving by Thomas Hope of a sideboard pedestal published in 1807.[189] The designer of the chair, whose name is not known, may well have used the Hope monster as his model.

Height, $33\frac{7}{8}$ in; *width,* 27 in; *depth,* $32\frac{1}{4}$ in.

THE RAPE
OF EUROPA

Zeus, captivated by the beauty of Europa, came to her on the seashore in the form of a bull. Finding the animal so tame, she and her attendants bedecked the bull with garlands, and greatly daring, she ventured to mount its back. The god then rushed into the sea and swam with her to Crete.

This theme was evidently a great favourite in France in the seventeenth and eighteenth centuries. It was treated on canvas by Claude Le Lorrain (illustrated on page 296), in tapestry at the Gobelins manufactory (opposite) and in gilt and patinated bronze by two Parisian clock manufacturers (as in the two examples here). The theme must also have appealed to George IV, as all these works of art were his purchases.

CLOCK BY OSMOND ON A MUSICAL CASE BY GOYER

On both clocks illustrated Europa is separated from her abductor by the cylinder containing the movement.

The appearance of the clock (upper left) of gilt and patinated bronze, has unfortunately suffered since it reached Carlton House on 23 February 1811. In 1817 B. L. Vulliamy obtained George IV's approval for the replacement of the original French dial and movement by his own (the Vulliamy movement is numbered 631).

Though we no longer know the name of the French horologist, we can still identify the bronze maker who was responsible for the clock-case. He adopted the practice, unusual for a bronze manufacturer, of signing his name, *OSMOND*–active in the third quarter of the eighteenth century–on the scrolled foot under the right-hand figure.

The bronzes on the green lacquer musical case which supports the clock are punched with the crowned C mark –they were probably made, therefore, sometime between 1745 and 1749.[190] The case itself bears the stamp of the Parisian *ébéniste*, F. Goyer (master 1740), who is known to have specialised in lacquered clock-cases.[191]

Clock: *height*, $18\frac{3}{4}$ in;
    width, $14\frac{9}{16}$ in; *depth*, $8\frac{5}{16}$ in.
Musical case: *height*, $8\frac{1}{4}$ in;
    width, $17\frac{7}{16}$ in; *depth*, $8\frac{15}{16}$ in.

CLOCK, POSSIBLY BY SAINT GERMAIN

Clock of patinated and gilt bronze made in France in the third quarter of the eighteenth century.

When purchased for George IV in April 1818,[192] the clock stood on a tortoiseshell musical case (now at Windsor). As with the Osmond clock, it too had its French movement and dial replaced by B. L. Vulliamy, the alterations being carried out in 1829.[193]

Though the clock-case is not signed by its bronze manufacturer, it is identical to one which bears the signature of J-J. de Saint Germain,[194] a noted Parisian *fondeur-ciseleur* who flourished in the third quarter of the eighteenth century. A clock of the same design is recorded in 1784 in the possession of Madame Victoire, Louis XV's fifth daughter. It formed part of the furnishings of her *Grand Cabinet* at Versailles, situated on the ground floor of the palace under the *Salon de la Guerre*.[195]

Height, 22$\frac{1}{2}$ in; *width,* 17$\frac{3}{4}$ in; *depth,* 7$\frac{3}{16}$ in.

GOBELINS TAPESTRY

'The Rape of Europa', one of a series of four tapestries entitled *Les Amours des Dieux* (*see* page 181) which were woven at the Gobelins manufactory. The cartoon for this tapestry was painted by J-B. Pierre in 1757. The tapestry itself, which forms part of the seventh set woven at the Gobelins, was completed in 1789.[196]

Height, 12 ft 3 in; *width,* 12 ft.

FRENCH CYLINDER- AND ROLL-TOP DESKS

CYLINDER-TOP DESK BY TEUNE

A late eighteenth-century French cylinder-top desk stamped by the Parisian *ébéniste*, F-G. Teuné (master, 1766); of oak and pine, veneered with a trellis pattern enclosing alternate squares of tulipwood and kingwood, and with gilt bronze mounts of conventional design. The cylinder-top is inlaid with an armorial trophy incorporating the

arms of Louis XVI's youngest brother, the comte d'Artois (who ascended the French throne in 1824 as Charles X). One of the collars of the three orders of chivalry encircling his arms is that of the Golden Fleece. As the comte d'Artois was only created a Knight of this order in September 1781, the desk must have been made after this date, probably for the comte d'Artois himself.[197] It is branded underneath with a cypher, CDT, which has been interpreted as the castle inventory mark of one of the comte d'Artois' residences, the Chateau du Temple. The desk was purchased for George IV by Sir William Knighton in Paris, and its receipt is recorded in Jutsham's day-book on 22 September 1828.

Compared with the Riesener roll-top desk (illustrated on pages 204–5) the marquetry and the bronzes of the Teuné desk are noticeably inferior in quality. The corner mount, composed of drapery threaded through two rings, is a stock mount to be found on a number of pieces of furniture made in the latter part of the eighteenth century. It was even recorded on furniture by artists, such as on a table in a portrait of an elderly lady, dated 1775, by Anne Vallayer-Coster (1744–1818).[198]

Height, $46\frac{7}{8}$ in; *width,* $50\frac{13}{16}$ in; *depth,* $28\frac{1}{8}$ in.

ROLL–TOP DESK BY RIESENER

A French roll-top desk, of the second half of the eighteenth century, made of oak veneered with purplewood and incorporating marquetry panels on a ground of harewood which include bouquets of flowers, a trophy of the arts, and a repeating fret design enclosing water-lilies. The centre drawer of the frieze pulls out to form a reading stand. A mechanical device mounted in the inside of the back panel ensures that the drawers of the lower stage are automatically locked when the roll-top is closed.

Though unstamped, this desk can be attributed to J-H. Riesener (master 1768–1806), perhaps the best known of all French furniture makers, who in 1774 succeeded to the post of court cabinet-maker to Louis XVI.[199] It is similar in shape and construction to a roll-top desk at Waddesdon Manor which is thought to have been made by Riesener for Louis XV's daughter, Madame Adélaïde. The Buckingham Palace piece could have been ordered by another of his daughters.[189] The beauty of this piece lies both in the quality of its marquetry and bronzes (see detail) as well as in its harmonious proportions. It is transitional in style. The cabriole legs and twisted candle-arms recall the *style Louis XV*, whereas the angular fret design in marquetry and the bronze panels mounted on the drawers in the frieze are characteristic of the *style Louis XVI*.

Height, $50\frac{3}{4}$ in; *width,* $54\frac{1}{4}$ in; *depth,* 32 in.

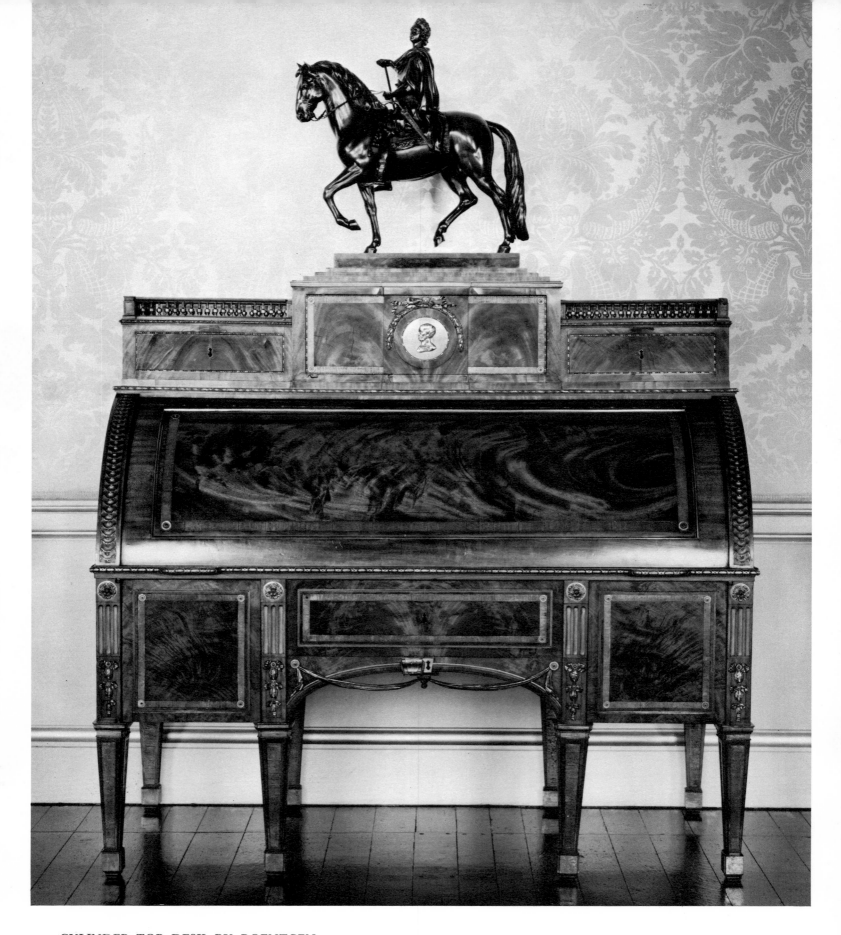

CYLINDER-TOP DESK BY ROENTGEN

A late eighteenth-century cylinder-top desk of monumental proportions; of oak veneered in mahogany and enriched with gilt bronze mounts; the drawers are in solid mahogany. A striking feature of this desk is its complicated mechanism. The superstructure pulls out and unfolds into a sloping reading stand flanked by compartments. Within the desk the architectural features—steps, columns and architraves—mask a nest of concealed drawers. In the lower stage the keyhole in the centre of the knee-hole section, which is normally hidden by the bronze motif in the form of a keystone, controls the two flanking doors which open to reveal two drawers on each side. Though unstamped, this desk is almost certainly by the German *ébéniste* David Roentgen (1743–1807). It corresponds in design and construction to a number of cylinder-top desks by this cabinet-maker, including one (now in the Hermitage Museum, Leningrad) which was made for Catherine II of Russia in 1786, and another (now in Versailles) which was presented to Louis XVI in 1785.[200]

Height, $57\frac{9}{16}$ *in; width,* $57\frac{15}{16}$ *in; depth,* $32\frac{3}{4}$ *in.*

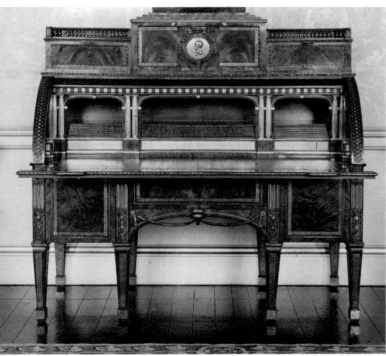

EQUESTRIAN STATUE OF LOUIS XV
AFTER BOUCHARDON

This bronze equestrian figure is a reduction of the bronze statue by E. Bouchardon completed by J-B. Pigalle which was unveiled in the Place Louis XV (now Place de la Concorde), Paris, in June 1763, the year following Bouchardon's death. The original was much admired by the public, though there were complaints that the horse should have been stepping out with his right fore-foot, not his left. The critics were silenced by C-N. Cochin, who defended Bouchardon, saying that the horse was represented in the act of walking and not as it was about to move off. If its critics had arrived a moment earlier they would have seen the horse with its right fore-foot raised. The statue was destroyed during the French Revolution. Seven reductions are known to have been cast in the 1760's by a pupil of Bouchardon, L-C. Vassé, and two others by J-B. Pigalle. These bronzes, of which the Buckingham Palace reduction is probably one of the Vassé survivors, were given away as presents to the King, Madame de Pompadour, and other public figures.[201]

Height, $23\frac{5}{8}$ *in; width,* $20\frac{15}{16}$ *in.*

CYLINDER-TOP DESK
BY JACOB

A French cylinder-top desk of the early nineteenth century. Of oak veneered in satinwood and purplewood; the drawers are in solid satinwood. The desk is mounted with ornaments in gilt bronze in the classical taste.

This piece of furniture was made by G-A. Jacob (1799–1870) whose stamp, incorporating his name and address, is punched on the underside.[202] G-A. Jacob belonged to a dynasty of furniture makers founded by his grandfather, Georges Jacob (cf. pages 215 and 216). He first studied architecture and worked as a pupil of C. Percier, and it was only in 1825, when his father, F-H-G. Jacob-Desmalter, retired that he took over the family furniture-making business.

This desk is of particular interest for two reasons. Firstly, it must represent one of the first pieces of furniture made in the family workshops after G-A. Jacob assumed control of the firm—its receipt at Carlton House was recorded by Jutsham on 8 April 1825.

Secondly, it serves to illustrate Jacob's debt to his former master, C. Percier. The bronze plaque on the cylinder-top, which represents a sacrifice to Vesta, the Roman goddess of the hearth, is copied from part of an engraving (here illustrated) of a chimney-piece designed by Percier and Fontaine and published in 1801.[203] This plaque may have been cast in the workshops of the bronze manufacturer, L-F. Feuchère.[204]

Height, 48½ in; *width,* 46 in; *depth,* 25½ in.

CABINET IN THE FRENCH TASTE

One of a pair of English marble-topped cabinets, *c.* 1760, of oak veneered in satinwood and rosewood, and mounted with elaborate gilt bronze mounts. The slab is of red griotte marble. The doors open to reveal shelves disposed in two tiers. A narrow drawer is housed immediately below the slab in the middle; the face of this drawer is in the form of a half circle and is mounted with a foliate cartouche in gilt bronze.

Though probably made in England, this cabinet betrays, in its serpentine shape, bowed panels and scrolled mounts, a strong French influence, and corresponds in style to furniture made in Paris in the 1740's. It is conceivable that the mounts were imported from France. A chest of drawers with identical fore-corner mounts was in fact described as French in a sale catalogue in 1964.[205]

Height, 36½ in; *width,* 62 in; *depth,* 25 in.

CHEST OF DRAWERS BY GATES

One of a pair of chests of drawers in the form of a half circle fitted with three drawers concealed behind two doors, which are flanked by shelves closed by two further doors. The frieze contains three further drawers; the centre one is covered with a slide for writing, the flanking ones swing open on hinges attached to the rear uprights. Made of oak and pine and veneered in satinwood, tulipwood and purplewood, with marquetry designs of vases and arabesques.

This pair of chests of drawers was made for George IV's apartments in Buckingham House. They are described in a bill dated 1781 submitted by William Gates, the cabinet-maker who succeeded John Bradburn in his post of cabinet-maker to the Great Wardrobe.[206] Gates, whose activities are recorded in the royal accounts between 1777 and 1790, seems to have been extensively patronised by George IV before the latter's move to Carlton House in 1783. Though typically English in style, the overall decoration in marquetry of vases and arabesques is ultimately of French inspiration.

Height, $35\frac{1}{4}$ in; *width,* 45 in; *depth,* 21 in.

ITALIAN EMBROIDERY PANEL

The embroidery panel, which is of Italian workmanship of the mid-seventeenth century, represents the Annunciation within a border composed of arabesques, baskets of flowers and, at the corners, biblical scenes contained in roundels. It is of linen cloth embroidered with long and short stitches and French knots with couched lines.

This panel is one of five—the four others are now at Hampton Court—which Lord Yarmouth bought for George IV at a sale held in London on 6 June 1815.[207]

Height, 12 ft 2½ in; *width,* 10 ft 6 in.

CHEST OF DRAWERS, POSSIBLY BY LANGLOIS

Below the panel is one of four bow-fronted chests of drawers, made in England, *c.* 1763,[208] of oak and pine veneered with rosewood and enriched with scrolled and foliate gilt bronze mounts. The inlay of the top, which incorporates in the centre a basket of flowers, is of engraved brass.

This chest of drawers with its bowed front, scrolled corners and foliate mounts, is clearly inspired by French furniture of the Louis XV style. It has recently been suggested on stylistic grounds that these chests of drawers may be by Peter Langlois.[209]

The four chests of drawers were also bought by Lord Yarmouth for George IV, at a sale held in London in 1818.[210]

Height, 33½ in; *width,* 59¾ in; *depth,* 26¾ in.

FRENCH
AND
ENGLISH
CHAIRS

ARM-CHAIR BY GOURDIN

One of a set of eleven (originally twelve) arm-chairs made of beechwood carved with stylised foliage and flowers. The gilding and the upholstery are modern. Stamped by the Parisian *menuisier* (joiner) J-B. Gourdin (master 1748), this arm-chair with its cabriole legs and serpentine-shaped back is typical of the furniture produced in the Louis XV style in the middle years of the eighteenth century.

It was during this period that much greater demands were being made than previously on furniture makers to supply pieces of furniture which were both useful and comfortable. The arm-chair had to be shaped to fit the human frame to the greater ease of the sitter. In the drawing by L-C. de Carmontelle (1717-1806) (here illustrated), the comte de Genlis has adopted just the sort of relaxed pose for which the Gourdin chair was designed.[211]

Height, 34¾ in; *width,* 26¼ in; *depth,* 24¾ in.

A CORNER OF THE MUSIC ROOM

On the chimney-piece are examples of soft-paste Sèvres porcelain flanked by two late eighteenth-century French candelabra. The arm-chair and settee are also French, of the late eighteenth century.

The gilt bronze candelabra, which form part of a set of eight, are of six lights each. Composed of a blue enamelled vase, they are supported on tripod legs chased with eagles, heads and goats, feet and crowned by a blazing torch. They can be identified in the engraving of the Throne Room at Carlton House, published by W. H. Pyne, 1 October 1818 (pages 194–95). The exact date of their purchase by George IV is, however, not known. On the evidence of bills for repairs, he must have acquired the set at least ten years previously.[212]

The arm-chair, which forms part of a set of thirty, is of beechwood carved and gilt.

They are stamped by Georges Jacob (master 1765–1814), who was perhaps the most famous Parisian *menuisier* (joiner) working in the latter half of the eigh-

teenth century. Like the arm-chair on page 216, this set of furniture must have been supplied by the expatriate French dealer, Dominique Daguerre (died 1796), who was employed by George IV at Carlton House from 1787. A label, in ink, which is still pasted to the underside of a number of the seat frames, partially confirms this. It reads: *Monsieur Daguerre/fauteuil courant pour le Sallon.*

Candelabrum: *height,* 58 in; *width,* 22 in.
Arm-chair: *height,* $35\frac{1}{8}$ in; *width,* $24\frac{3}{8}$ in; *depth,* $24\frac{3}{4}$ in.

The settees, of which there are four, are also by Georges Jacob, and also bear a similar label, indicating in this case that they were supplied by Daguerre for a drawing-room.

Settees: *height,* 44 in; *width,* 72 in; *depth,* 31 in.

215

ARM–CHAIR BY JACOB

One of four arm-chairs, of beech-wood carved and gilt, which are stamped by Georges Jacob (master 1765–1814). They each bear a label pasted to the underneath of the seat frames (here illustrated) which indicates that they were purchased from the French dealer, Dominique Daguerre, and were intended for use in a bedroom at Carlton House.[213]

Height, 42¼ in; *width,* 28½ in; *depth,* 28½ in.

SCROLLED–BACK CHAIR

A scroll-backed hall chair, of mahogany, partly gilt, which forms part of a set of ten chairs made *c.* 1790 for the Entrance Hall at Carlton House. In Pyne's engraving of this Entrance, published on 1 March 1819, they are shown aligned along the walls. Queen Victoria's cipher is a later addition. It has been suggested that these chairs may have been designed by Henry Holland.[214] They are certainly examples of the austere neo-classical style of the late eighteenth century, of which Holland was the most notable protagonist in England. The rosettes above the legs are probably inspired by similar motifs on chairs of the Louis XVI style such as on the arm-chair illustrated above.

Height, 37½ in; *width,* 20 in; *depth,* 22 in.

CHAIR, PROBABLY BY HERVE

One of a set of twelve mahogany chairs, carved and partly gilt, probably made in England, *c.* 1790, for Carlton House. Though the coiled snakes in the open-work back and those entwined round the legs belong to the English rather more than to the French repertoire of ornament of this period, other details may well have been inspired by French models, such as the male mask flanked by arabesques on the cross-piece of the chair back, and more particularly the square plinths of the seat rails above the legs, which are carved with rosettes.

It is possible they were the 'twelve Maho.. Chair frames, a La truce' which Francis Hervé supplied in 1792 for the ground floor Dining Room at Carlton House,[215] and which were sent back to him for repair three years later.[216]

Height, $37\frac{3}{8}$ in; *width,* $18\frac{5}{8}$ in; *depth,* $19\frac{7}{16}$ in.

CHAIR BY BAILEY & SAUNDERS

A chair, of beechwood, lacquered in imitation of ebony and decorated with applied gilt fretwork ornaments in satinwood.

Thirty-six chairs of this design, together with two arm-chairs, were supplied in 1817 by the firm of Bailey & Saunders for the Banqueting Room at Brighton Pavilion at a total cost of £669.12.0.[217]

The beauty of this chair owes much to the basic simplicity of its design and decoration—in sharp contrast with, for example, the arm-chairs made in 1817 for the Music Room at Brighton (page 128).

Height, $35\frac{1}{4}$ in; *width,* $21\frac{3}{8}$ in; *depth,* $21\frac{1}{4}$ in.

1 R. W. Symonds, *Thomas Tompion, His Life and Work* (1951), pp.295–96.

2 Symonds, *loc. cit.*

3 Clifford Smith, *op. cit.*, p.241. He does not, however, provide any documentary evidence in support of this.

4 Of the three other tables, one is probably in the Art Institute of Chicago (information kindly supplied by Allen Wardwell); the whereabouts of the other two is not known.

5 Clifford Smith, *op. cit.*, p.241.

6 Clifford Smith, *op. cit.*, pp.148–49.

7 P.R.O., L.C.9/307, 21, Quarter to Lady Day 1762. 'For an Exceeding fine Mohogany Secretary with Drawers, & a Writing Drawer, a Sett of Shelves at Top with a Crown Carv*d.* at Top & the Side & Back [*sic*] all handsome Cuttwork 71–0–0'. Quoted by Clifford Smith, *op. cit.*, p.278.

8 P.R.O., L.C.9/314, 61, Quarter to Midsummer 1767. 'For a Drawing of the Following Case, and Attending at Richmond to Shew Ditto for Her Majestys Aprobation 1–10–0'.

9 'For a Neat Mahogany Glass Case to stand on the Top of Her Majesty's Secretary with Neat frett Work Doors in front, and Ends, and 8 Squares of plate Glass to Ditto, 2 Neat Locks, and a Dutch bowd Key &c Compleat to the Drawing above 24–10–0'. I should like to acknowledge my indebtedness to Derek Shrub, who, in the course of a conversation, first put forward this suggestion.

10 P.R.O., L.C.9/310, 8, Quarter to Xmas 1763. Quoted by Clifford Smith, *op. cit.*, p.78. The compartments referred to in the accounts no longer exist.

11 P.R.O., L.C.9/308, 8, Quarter to Xmas 1762. 'For a very handsome Mohogany Bookcase with plate Glass Doors the upper part & Wood Doors at Bottom. a Pedement Head with Pilasters & Trusses the whole very handsomely Carv'd, to match the Cabinet in the Queen's Bow Closet at S*t* James's, one side of this is all in one Door that opens from Top to bottom and Serves for the Door that goes into the Water Closet within the Bed Chamber 107–14–0'.

12 Derek Shrub, 'The Vile Problem', *Victoria and Albert Museum Bulletin* (October 1965), pp.26–35.

13 James Parker, 'A Regency Sewing and Writing Table by Morgan and Sanders', *Metropolitan Museum of Art Bulletin* (November 1963), pp. 125–32.

14 Horace Walpole, *Letters*, ed. P. Cunningham, Vol. IV (1857), p.58. I am indebted to Oliver Millar for kindly bringing this to my attention.

15 P.R.O., L.C.9/309, 35, Quarter to Midsummer 1763. Quoted by Clifford Smith, *op. cit.*, p.247.

16 Margaret Jourdain, in *Country Life*, 26 April 1930, pp.611–13.

17 Clifford Musgrave, *Adam and Hepplewhite . . .* (1966), pp.103–4.

18 James Parker, in *Decorative Art from the Samuel H. Kress Collection at the Metropolitan Museum of Art* (1964), pp.40–42.

19 Clifford Smith, *op. cit.*, pp.218–19.

20 Pl. 31, published 6 October 1793; Pl. 32, published 1 November 1793.

21 For a detailed discussion of the furnishings of the Chinese Drawing Room, *see* G. de Bellaigue, 'The Furnishings of the Chinese Drawing Room, Carlton House', *Burlington Magazine*, Vol. CIX (September 1967), pp.518–28.

22 Windsor, Royal Archives: Georgian Papers 25338. Invoice dated 5 June 1811; the alteration and repairs came to £47.7.6.

23 A clock related in design is in the Musée Nissim de Camondo, Paris (No. 182 of the museum's catalogue).

24 *Burlington Magazine, art. cit.*, p.523, note 25.

25 Other pieces of porcelain similarly decorated are in the Bowes Museum, County Durham, the Metropolitan Museum of Art, New York, and the Czartoryski Museum, Cracow. Some of the pieces in the Metropolitan are marked with the same initials, *GI*.

26 Clifford Smith, *op. cit.*, p.221.

27 Clifford Musgrave, *Regency Furniture 1800–30* (1961), pp.30–31.

28 Dorothy Stroud, *Henry Holland, His Life and Architecture* (1966), pp.81–82.

29 For a detailed discussion of the evidence, *see Burlington Magazine, art. cit.*, p.524.

30 P.R.O., H.O.73/20. Hervé's bill came to £239.8.0 and included the cost of separate models for the three types of chair. For a full discussion of this set of furniture, *see Burlington Magazine, art. cit.*, pp.520–23.

31 The initials *AL*, *IS* and *BP* which are stamped on the inside of the frames of some of the seats are probably the initials of the craftsmen who actually made the pieces. Their appearance on other chairs, hitherto unattributed to any joiner, would

be *prima facie* evidence that they too were made in the Hervé workshop.

32 Windsor, Royal Archives: Georgian Papers, 34223, 34224. Quoted by Henry D. Roberts, *A History of the Royal Pavilion Brighton . . .* (1939), pp.134–35, 146–47.

33 E. W. Brayley, *Illustrations of Her Majesty's Palace at Brighton* (1838), p.8.

34 Clifford Musgrave, *Royal Pavilion . . .* (1959), p.108.

35 Roberts, *op. cit.*, pp.134–35.

36 Brayley, *op. cit.*, p.8.

37 The only recorded clockmaker of that name was a Claude Ragot, working in Paris, *c.* 1785–90. If the movement was by him, it must have replaced an earlier one contemporary with the clock-case, which dates from *c.* 1730–40.

38 According to the account of the furnishing of the Music Room published by Roberts (*op. cit.*, pp.134–35), B. L. Vulliamy received £550 for the 'Rock Clock'. It is difficult to account for this figure – which is clearly more than Vulliamy would have been paid for replacing the original movement – unless he also served as intermediary in the purchase of the clock from France.

39 Though now eight in all, it appears that there were originally only seven (Roberts, *op. cit.*, p.148). Roberts is probably correct when he records that the largest was later divided into two. Of the eight at Buckingham Palace, four are 88 in. long, one 93 in., and the remaining three between 63 in. and 65 in. long.

40 The inscriptions are as follows: (1) engraved on a brass plate above the keyboard: *PATENT SOS-TENENTE GRAND/I.H.R. Mott I.C. Mott & Comp/95 PALL MALL LONDON/Makers To His Majesty*; (2) in gold lettering on the inside: '*I. H.R. MOTT/MAKER TO HER MAJESTY/ and to/THE PRINCIPAL ROYAL FAMILIES OF EUROP,/76, STRAND/LONDON*'. This second inscription may have been added during Queen Victoria's reign, when the piano was re-turned for possible repairs or alterations.

41 A. Feulner, *Das Residenzmuseum in München* (Munich, 1922), p.27. Its dial is signed, *PIERRE LE ROY DE LA/SOCIÉTÉ DES ARTS APARIS*. The bronze mounts differ, however, in detail from those of the Buckingham Palace clock, and are not from the same casting.

42 V. Malamani, *Canova* (Milan, 1911), p.39.

43 Letter from W. R. Hamilton to Sir Charles Long, dated 12 August 1825. Published A. Aspinall, *Letters of George IV*, Vol. III (1938), pp.123–24.

44 Clifford Smith, *op. cit.*, p.160.

45 'Four large Magnificent Tripod Candelabres Carved & Gilt throughout, with Scroll Branches for 9 Lights Each and Pine Apple Tops each on a Circular Column, supported by 3 Lions, Tri-angular Plinths & fluted Blocks'.

46 There is evidence that they were originally caned. The stamp, *G. JACKSON*, has been found on the frames of two of the chairs, and the initials *CS, P.P* on one other. These may be repairers' marks.

47 P.R.O., L.C.9/367. Quoted by Clifford Smith, *op. cit.*, p.170.

48 Queen's Gallery Exhibition, *George IV and the Arts of France* (1966), No. 19.

49 *Livre-Journal de Lazare Duvaux . . . 1748–58,* ed. L. Courajod (Paris, 1873), Vol. II, No. 1213.

50 Queen's Gallery Exhibition, *op. cit.*, No. 21.

51 Queen's Gallery Exhibition, *op. cit.*, No. 14.

52 Queen's Gallery Exhibition, *op. cit.*, No. 15.

53 Queen's Gallery Exhibition, *op. cit.*, No. 30.

54 Queen's Gallery Exhibition, *op. cit.*, Nos. 31, 32.

55 H. Huth, *Abraham und David Roentgen . . .* (Berlin, 1928), Pl. 21.

56 For a detailed discussion of the *pietre dure* plaques, *see* Å. Setterwall in *Burlington Magazine,* Vol. CI (December 1959), pp.425–35.

57 Windsor, Royal Archives: Georgian Papers, 26423.

58 Laking, *Sèvres Porcelain of Buckingham Palace and Windsor Castle* (1907), No. 108.

59 Laking, *op. cit.*, No. 85. Known in the eighteenth century as *Vase antique ferré (dit de Fontenoy)* (A. Troude, *Choix de Modèles de La Manufacture Nationale de Porcelaines de Sèvres* (Paris, 1897), Pl. 104).

60 Lord Gwydir's sale at Christie's, 21 May 1829, Lot 54. Purchased by the dealer, Baldock, for George IV, for the sum of £263.11.0.

61 Queen's Gallery Exhibition, *op. cit.*, No. 27.

62 *See* Simone Lanne, in *Gazette des Beaux-Arts* (July–December 1934), pp.283–85, and Serge Grandjean, in *Connoisseur* (April 1959), pp. 151–53.

63 Queen's Gallery Exhibition, *op. cit.*, No. 38. For a discussion of the *pietre dure* panels, *see* Å. Setter-well in *Burlington Magazine, art. cit.* (1959).

64 Laking, *op. cit.*, No. 118.

65 Lord Gwydir's sale at Christie's, 21 May 1829, Lot 52. Purchased by the dealer, Baldock, for George IV, for the sum of £163.16.0.

66 Laking, *op. cit.*, No. 88.

67 I am indebted to Mr. del Giudice for first drawing my attention to this connection.

68 Finials, probably in the form of brass vases, would originally have been fitted to the corner blocks of the cresting. The cherub which is clumsily attached to the top may have replaced an earlier ornament.

69 R. W. Symonds, *op. cit.,* pp.269–70.

70 Clifford Smith, *op. cit.,* pp.233, 250–51.

71 The dials are signed *'Alex Cumming/London'* and *'Alexander Cumming London'*.

72 Windsor, Royal Archives: Georgian Papers, 17132.

73 Clifford Smith, *op. cit.,* pp.265–66.

74 Sale held in Phillips's auction rooms, 15 June 1816, Lot 467. Bought by Lord Yarmouth for George IV for £262.10.0.

75 Though the work was carried out in 1821, the bill was not submitted till 31 December 1825.

76 For a detailed account of the workings of this clock, *see* Donald de Carle in *Horological Journal* (December 1946).

77 Windsor, Royal Archives: Georgian Papers, 26145. The figure of £1,115 quoted by Clifford Smith (*op. cit.,* p.261) includes the price of a watch invoiced in the same bill.

78 Memorandum dated 17 December 1824 preserved in the Royal Archives, Windsor.

79 Windsor, Royal Archives: Georgian Papers, 25202. *See also* 25235.

80 Jacques Robiquet, *Vie et Oeuvre de Pierre Gouthière* (Paris, 1920–21), p.188, Pl.XXVI.

81 Information recorded on the label to a pair displayed in the Louvre.

82 Galle, whose address in 1819 was given as 1 rue Colbert and 9 rue Vivienne, was one of the principal exhibitors to the exhibition of industrial arts held in Paris in that year. He displayed a table decoration which included a pair of cornucopia each terminating in a stag's head; they were identical in design to the stag's-head candelabrum now in Buckingham Palace. (L-S. Le Normand and J-G-V. de Moléon, *Description des expositions des produits de l'Industrie française depuis leur origine jusqu'à celle de 1819* (Paris, 1819), Vol. II, pp. 221–22, Pl. 20.)

83 Purchased by George IV from a Mr Courvoisier, they reached Carlton House on 21 April 1814.

84 Clifford Smith (*op. cit.,* p.156, note 2) quotes a bill from Tatham & Co. for some 'Very large elegant tripods superbly carved and double gilt, to design' supplied to George IV in 1811 at a cost of £143 each. This bill may possibly refer to these stands. Their design could have been suggested by Plate 26 of G. B. Piranesi, *Vasi, candelabri* . . . (Rome, 1778). The candelabrum in the engraving incorporates the same motif of three cranes round a central shaft, as well as the unusual feature of the twin claws which compose each of the feet supporting the base. The cranes, but not the twin claws, appear in a number of drawings and engravings of candelabra by C. H. Tatham, brother of the furniture maker, who, in partnership with Bailey, probably made the stands.

85 Lignereux's bill in the Royal Archives, Windsor (Georgian Papers, 25142), is dated 28 April 1803. The descriptions of the clock and candelabra are as follows:
'Une pendule à une figure dite l'Apollon en bronze couleur antique avec divers ornemens tant en bronze doré aumat qu'en couleur antique marbre jaune de sienne... £85 Sterl.
'Une paire de girandole avec figure de femme Egyptienne en bronze Couleur antique portant un groupe de Cinq lumieres en bronze doré aumat pied en marbre jaune de sienne... £70'.

86 P.R.O., Vulliamy Papers, C.104/57, Ornament Book [No. 4].

87 P.R.O., Vulliamy Papers, C.104/57, Ornament Book [No. 4].

88 Another pair is in the royal collection. A third pair is in the Victoria and Albert Museum, on loan from the Earl of Harewood.

89 P.R.O., Vulliamy Papers, C.104/57, Ornament Books [Nos. 1 and 4].

90 P.R.O., Vulliamy Papers, C.104/57, Ornament Book [No. 4].

91 P.R.O., Vulliamy Papers, C.104/57, Ledger, p.368.

92 *Gentleman's Magazine* (June 1765), p.296.

93 Windsor, Royal Archives: Georgian Papers, 17137. 'To Paid M . Pinchbeck for a Clock made by M.: Eardley Norton as p : Bill £1042-0-0'.

94 P.R.O., L.C.9/313, 64, Quarter ending Midsummer 1766. Quoted in part by Clifford Smith, *op. cit.,* pp.254–55. If this account did refer to the clock-case, one may well ask why the cabinetmaker's bill should have been submitted almost a year after the clockmaker's.

95 'For a very rich Antique carved & burnish'd gilt Bracket for a Clock in His Majesty's Dressing Room, the Front part made to Slide off the top part, and made to turn round to shew all the different Sides of the Clock with a Center Pin, & Brass Rollers, the whole Carving neatly pierced thro', & the Face of the inside Case which holds the Key is lined with blue Lustring to appear thro' the Carving & top Cornice very richly Carved with a neat Mosaick work Border round Dᵒ. for the Clock to stand in, and the Flowers pierced thro' and the Ground pannelled, and inriched with a small Ogee, the Front part & the sides of the Bracket is inrich'd with an Antique Foilage Leaf which Spreads at each End to support a Demi

Lyon & Unicorn, the whole very rich and compleatly finished'. As constituted today, the whole of the top of the clock-case lifts off; access to the inside is through one of the panels of the base, which is hinged to form a door. The clock, which has no attached base panel, rests on a wooden plinth which appears to be later in date.

96 The planetarium dial is signed: *C. PINCH-BECK/SUSCEPIT/I. MERIGEOT. I. MONK/ PERFECERUNT.*

97 Clifford Smith, *op. cit.*, p.161.

98 *Letters and Journals*, ed. J. A. Home, Vol. II (1889), p.181.

99 I am grateful to John Harris for kindly drawing my attention to this drawing.

100 A notation in pencil on the drawing, '$\frac{1}{4}$ of a diameter Wider', shows that the case was considered too narrow.

101 According to a note by B. L. Vulliamy in 1846, the clock movement is signed by Lépine on a part which is not normally visible and is numbered (? dated) 1790. It has not been possible to check this. The movement to the musical case is signed on the right, *L^e pine h^{er} du Roy AParis N° 4195*. This clock may have been purchased by George IV in 1790 (see note 117).

102 James Parker, in the Kress Collection Catalogue, *op. cit.*, pp.268–72.

103 Signed on the back, *Vulliamy London*, within an engraved floral wreath.

104 A description of this clock (without the pedestal) is given in the 1792 guide book to Windsor. At that time the clock was in the Queen's Drawing Room.

105 Clifford Smith, *op. cit.*, p.256.

106 Clifford Smith, *op. cit.*, pp.170–71.

107 It is engraved on the front: *Vulliamy/London 170*; the movement is signed within a floral wreath: *Vulliamy London*.

108 William Bemrose, *Bow, Chelsea and Derby Porcelain . . .* (1898). I am grateful to John Mallet for drawing my attention to these entries.

109 Preserved in the British Horological Institute.

110 His balance sheet, preserved in the Archives de la Seine in Paris (D^{4}B^6, carton 40, dossier 2213), is dated 6 February 1771. Among his creditors were the clockmakers Courvoisier and Gille and the bronze founders and chasers, Grimpel, Beaucour, Michel, Forestier, Osmond and Vapu. His stock, valued at 9,000 livres, included 'une très grande Pendule de valleur de plus de 4,000 livres . . .'

111 Their description in Jutsham's ledger differs in two respects: they are described as 51 in. in height, not 47$\frac{1}{2}$ in., and as fifteen-branch not twelve-branch candelabra. The difference in height is,

however, so small that it may be due to an error in measuring on Jutsham's part; secondly an examination of the candelabra themselves reveals in each case that they were originally fitted with two, probably three, additional candle-arms. For a reference to George IV's purchases from Thomire, *see* p.153.

112 James Parker, in the Kress Collection Catalogue, *op. cit.*, p.130.

113 After two models, *Le Philosophe* and *L'Etude*, supplied by the sculptor L-S. Boizot in 1780 for reproduction in biscuit porcelain at the Sèvres manufactory (E. Bourgeois, G. Lechevallier-Chevignard, *Le Biscuit de Sèvres* (Paris, 1908), Vol. I, Nos. 283, 503).

114 Dial signed: *Lepine/h^{ger}. Du Roi/PLACE DES VICTOIRES, N° 12*. Movement inscribed: *Lepine h^{ger} du Roy AParis/N° 4149*. This clock may have been acquired by George IV in 1790 (*see* note 117).

115 The centre dial is signed: '*Lépine/H.^{GER} DU ROI/Place des Victoires, N° 12*'; its movement is inscribed: *Lepine horloger du Roi, Paris N° 4175*. The dial also bears the partly effaced signature of its manufacturer, *B[?]CHON*. I am grateful to Theodore Dell for pointing this out to me.

116 I am indebted to Mademoiselle Brunet for kindly drawing my attention to this lyre-shaped clock.

117 Claim by Messrs. Boyd, Hoare & Co., dated 19 July 1799, which was laid before the Commissioners appointed in 1795 to inquire into George IV's debts (P.R.O., H.O. 73/32). Though this claim refers only to a single clock, earlier correspondance in November 1796 mentions the purchase from Lépine in 1790 of several clocks for the same amount. In view of the large sum involved, there must have been a number of clocks in this sale to George IV. The bill for the repair of 'une grande Pandulle astronomique de Lépine' submitted by the clockmaker J-P. De Belly on 12 February 1794 probably also refers to this clock (P.R.O., H.O. 73/18).

118 John Scott, *A Visit to Paris in 1814 . . .* (1816), pp.121–22.

119 The clock was purchased by George IV in May 1810 from a Mr Boileau. An identical clock was Lot 69 in the sale of the property of the French bronze sculptor, L-F. Feuchère, on 19 January 1829. The catalogue entry records that clocks of this model, made in the Thomire workshops, were selling at 1,500 francs. In the event, the Feuchère clock fetched 310 francs. (I am indebted to Francis Watson for kindly drawing my attention to this sale.)

120 For a detailed account of the taste for Japanese lacquer in eighteenth-century France, *see* F. J. B. Watson, in *Gazette des Beaux-Arts* (February 1963), pp.101–27.

121 Purchased by George IV, they formerly stood on cabinets flanking the chimney-piece in the Library at Brighton Pavilion.

122 This bowl may be the one purchased for George IV by F. Benois from the Parisian dealer, Rocheux, which is described in his bill dated 9 November 1816 as: '1 Beau Vase de laque fond avanturine a rosas(? tres) avec son Couvercle le tout Montés en bronze doré . . . 400 [francs]'. (Windsor, Royal Archives: Georgian Papers, 26423.)

123 Purchased for George IV in Paris, December 1816, by Mr Watier (probably John Watier, at the time Clerk Comptroller of the Kitchen at Carlton House), they were sent to Brighton in the following year.

124 Archives Nationales, o³2104 and o³1891. I am indebted to Francis Watson for drawing my attention to these documents.

125 It is not clear whether Saddon was an *ébéniste* (cabinet-maker) or a *menuisier* (joiner). His stamp has been found elsewhere on furniture normally made by *menuisiers* (see P. Verlet, *Les Meubles du XVIIIe Siècle*, Vol. I: *Menuiserie* (Paris, 1956).

126 Other corner-cupboards of the same design are in private collections in Paris and Brussels. Two of these are stamped by the *ébéniste*, B. Péridiez (master before 1738).

127 Laking, *op. cit.*, No. 84. The shape of this vase was known in the eighteenth century in France as *Vase fil et ruban*.

128 For information on *pietra dura*, see note 56.

129 The date of acquisition of this cabinet by George IV is not known, though it must have been before 16 September 1807, when Vulliamy submitted a bill for the repair and regilding of its bronzes (Windsor, Royal Archives: Georgian Papers, 25247).

130 Laking, *op. cit.*, No. 130.

131 The tables are stamped: *BELLANGE N°. 33/ RUE DES MARAIS Fᴮ Sᴵ MARTIN A PARIS.*

132 Denise Ledoux-Lebard, *Les Ebénistes Parisiens du XIXᵉ siècle* . . . (Paris, 1965), p.36.

133 Watson Taylor sale at Christie's, 28 May 1825, Lots 82, 83, 85, 86.

134 At the Watson Taylor sale their total width is given as 9 feet, whereas today they measure 8 ft 3¾ in.

135 Laking, *op. cit.*, No. 189. The shape of these vases is a variant of the one described as '*Vase Pâris Garni*' (Troude, *op. cit.*, Pl. 117).

136 Laking, *op. cit.*, No. 27. According to Troude (*op. cit.*, Pl. 130), this type of vase was known in the eighteenth century as '*Caisse à Fleurs A*'.

137 Laking, *op. cit.*, No. 34. This vase corresponds in shape to the outline drawing of a model of a vase, represented in two sizes, which is preserved in the archives of the Sèvres manufactory. The drawing is inscribed: *Caise à La Mhon sezonde et 3ᵉᵐᵉ grandeur fait au Mois daoust 1759.* (I am indebted to Mademoiselle Brunet for kindly bringing this to my attention).

138 This vase was examined when in the possession of the Antique Porcelain Company, London.

139 These vases were probably known in the eighteenth century as *vaze à médaillon du Roy*. Three, so named, were sold to Madame du Barry in 1768, one for 504 livres and two others for 432 livres each (P. Verlet, *Sèvres* (Paris, 1953), p.214).

140 It was reproduced in camaïeu on a Sèvres inkstand of about 1765, now in the Wallace Collection (illus. P. Verlet, *op. cit.*, Pl. 56).

141 The medal was also engraved. The engraving was first published in the May 1741 issue of the *Mercure de France.*

142 There is one in the royal collection (Laking, *op. cit.*, No. 66) and another in the Wallace Collection.

143 Laking, *op. cit.*, No. 98. The model of this vase is reproduced by Troude (*op. cit.*, Pl. 110), but without the handles or the ribboned foliate decoration of the centre band. There are also differences in the foot of the vase, and the medallions on the cover are left blank. According to Troude, this model was known in the eighteenth century as *Vase ovale Mercure.*

144 Karl Domanig, *Porträtmedaillen des Erzhauses Osterreich* . . . (Vienna, 1896), Pl. XLII, No. 284.

145 Up to 1760 the sets had been woven exclusively on the high-warp loom. Neilson, after making various improvements in the technique of low-warp weaving at the Gobelins, obtained permission to produce tapestries from the Don Quixote series on his improved looms. His pink damask background proved so popular that in 1763 the high-warp loom workshops of Audran and Cozette began a further set using the same background and the same borders.

146 Clifford Smith, *op. cit.*, p.173.

147 M. Fenaille, *Etat Général des Tapisseries de la Manufacture des Gobelins . . .*, Vol. III (Paris, 1904), pp.157–282.

148 G. C. Williamson, *Richard Cosway* . . . (1897), p.35.

149 The first reference to these tapestries in the Royal Archives is dated 27 August 1827. However, among the Carlton House papers in the Public Record Office (H.O. 73/32) there are two estimates by Henry Holland and Dominique Daguerre dated September 1794 which refer to tapestries to be fitted to the 'Princesses Private Drawing room' (Princess Caroline of Brunswick-Wolfenbüttel, whom George IV married on 8 April 1795). In Daguerre's estimate provision is

made for a set of 'Crimson Damask Window Curtains'. As was the custom at Carlton House, the curtains almost certainly were intended to match the other hangings in the room. There were no other Gobelins tapestries in the royal collection at that time with a crimson damask background, so the ones in question may well have been the four from the Don Quixote series.

150 Signed on the left: *De Troy a Rome 1746*, and on the right *COZETTE: 1780*. The inscription reads: *MEDEE/POIGNARDE LES DEUX FILS/QUELLE AVOIT EUS DE JASON/EMBRASE CORINTHE/ET SE RETIRE A/ ATHENES.*

151 For their earlier history, *see* M. Fenaille, *op. cit.,* Vol. IV (1907), pp.99–138.

152 The tapestry is signed: *jos. m. vien. 1757.*

153 M. Fenaille, *op. cit.,* Vol. IV, p.217.

154 V. Malamani, *Canova* (Milan, 1911), p.213.

155 Malamani, *op. cit.,* pp.229–30.

156 Windsor, Royal Archives: Georgian Papers, 26733.

157 Pyne, *op. cit.,* Vol. III: *The History of Carlton House* (1819), p.84.

158 Entry dated February 1811 in the Carlton House Receipts' Ledger kept by Benjamin Jutsham.

159 Windsor, Royal Archives: Georgian Papers, 27631–32.

160 A. Aspinall, *Letters of King George IV, op. cit.,* pp.123–24.

161 Cecil Gould, *Trophy of Conquest* (1965), p.120.

162 I am indebted to Hugh Honour for this detailed information.

163 V. Malamani, *op. cit.,* p.231.

164 Sir F. Chantrey's MS. ledger preserved in the Royal Academy Library.

165 Frederick Scheer, *Kew and its Gardens* (1840), p.46.

166 Margaret Whinney, *Sculpture in Britain 1530–1830* (1964), p.270, note 7.

167 Signed on the base: *E. WOLFF. FC/ROMAE. 1846.*

168 The statue at Osborne is signed and dated: *E. WOLFF. FC. ROMAE. 1844.*

169 Queen Victoria's Journal, 1 September 1846.

170 *Catalogue of the Paintings, Sculpture and other Works of Art at Osborne . . .* (1876), p.152. The date here indicated, 1844, must be a mistake, unless yet another replica was commissioned, which seems unlikely, as there are no records of a third statue.

171 Signed on the back of the base: *OPVS IOANNIS GEBSON' ROMAE.*

172 Entry dated 26 June 1847.

173 An entry dated December 1759 in the register of sales of the Sèvres manufactory records the sale to Louis XV for 960 livres of: '1 Pot poury Vaisseau Saffre et Verd Teniere' (information kindly supplied by Svend Eriksen).

174 Acquired in 1924 by H.M. Queen Mary.

175 For a note on pots-pourris, *see* page 188.

176 Laking, *op. cit.,* No. 35. This model was known in the eighteenth century as *Vase Boileau* (Troude, *op. cit.,* Pl. 89).

177 For a note on pots-pourris, *see* p.188.

178 Illustrated, P. Verlet, *op. cit.,* Pl. 33.

179 A pair of vases of identical shape, but of a claret ground colour, are in the Judge Untermyer Collection (Yvonne Hackenbroch, *Chelsea and other English Porcelain . . . in the Irwin Untermyer Collection* (Cambridge, Mass., 1957), Fig. 68).

180 Though Clifford Smith (*op. cit.,* p.205) states that these vases were purchased by George IV at Christie's at the sale of Queen Charlotte's collection on 11 May 1819, it has not been possible to identify them in the sale catalogue.

181 Clifford Smith, *op. cit.,* p.141.

182 For a discussion of Henry Holland's and Dominique Daguerre's work at Carlton House, *see* Dorothy Stroud, *Henry Holland . . .* (1966).

183 P.R.O., L.C.9/367. Quoted by Clifford Smith, *op. cit.,* p.148.

184 Clifford Smith, *op. cit.,* Pl. 177. Though he may well be correct, it is not clear on what documentary evidence he bases his attribution, as he fails to indicate his sources.

185 Clifford Smith, *op. cit.,* p.141.

186 Clifford Smith, *op. cit.,* p.165, note 2.

187 P.R.O., L.C.9/367. '6 Large Elegant Bergère Chairs, carved chimeres at £158.12 each'.

188 On the underside of the back stretcher the letter *M* (?W) is stamped on three of the *bergères,* and the letter *H* on the other three. It is tempting to conclude that they are initials of the makers, Morel and Hughes. Before, however, this suggestion can be advanced with any degree of certainty, other documented pieces by Morel and Hughes will have to be examined for similar marks.

189 Thomas Hope, *Household Furniture and Interior Decoration* (1807), Pl. 24, No. 6.

190 For a note on crowned Cs, *see* p.138.

191 Queen's Gallery Exhibition, *op. cit.,* No. 20.

192 Sale held in Squibb's auction rooms on 24 April 1818, Lot 80. Purchased for George IV by Lord Yarmouth at a cost of £125. (Information quoted by Jutsham.)

193 Present Vulliamy movement numbered 1040.

194 Sale held in Sotheby's auction rooms on 25 June 1965 (Lot 77).

195 Archives Nationales, o¹3510.

196 M. Fenaille, *op. cit.,* Vol. IV (1907), pp.189–223.

197 For a full discussion of the history of this desk, *see* F. J. B. Watson, in *The Connoisseur Coronation Book* (1953), pp.68–69.

198 Bowes Museum, Cat. No. 329.

199 Purchased by George IV at the Watson Taylor sale at Christie's, 28 May 1825, Lot 49, for £107.2.0; it was described at the time as having belonged to Louis XVI.

200 The Buckingham Palace desk was bought for George IV in Paris by F. Benois at a cost of £275, and reached Carlton House on 12 May 1820 (Windsor, Royal Archives: Georgian Papers, 25366).

201 For further details about these reductions, *see* Queen's Gallery Exhibition, *op. cit.,* No. 8.

202 [*A. JAC*]*OB F*ˢ *& C*ᴵᴱ *R. DE BONDY 30.*

203 C. Percier, P-F-L. Fontaine, *Recueil de Décorations intérieures . . .* (Paris, 1801).

204 At a sale of his stock held in Paris on 19 January 1829 in the year after his death, Lot 420 comprised 'Onze bas-reliefs très-bien fondus, non réparés, Sacrifice à Vesta'.

205 Kenure Park Sale, Dublin, 21–24 September 1964, Lot 304. The cabinets in Buckingham Palace may be by Peter Langlois (Theodore Dell, 'A Langlois commode', *Victoria and Albert Museum Bulletin* (April 1968), pp.65–70).

206 P.R.O., L.C.9/328, 25, Quarter to 5 April 1781. Quoted by Clifford Smith, *op. cit.,* p.92. The description in the account differs in one respect from the chest of drawers illustrated on p.211; it lists a total of seven drawers, whereas the piece of furniture contains only six.

207 Sale held at Oxenham's auction rooms, 6 June 1815, Lots 50–54.

208 Roughly scratched on the inlaid baskets of the top of three of the pieces are partly legible names and dates: on the chest of drawers illustrated, *M. Dutton*; on another, [?] *Focan*; on a third, *F. M. Le S* [?] *1763*. These names are not those of any known cabinet-makers working in London at this period. It is conceivable that they are the names of the craftsmen who executed the brass decoration of the tops, though if this is the case it is difficult to account for the slipshod way they have signed their work in contrast with the accomplished engraving of the flowers themselves.

209 Anthony Coleridge, 'Pierre Langlois his Oeuvre and some recent Discoveries', *Gazette des Beaux-Arts,* Vol. LXX (September 1967), p.160.

210 Sale held at Squibb's auction rooms, 20 April 1818 and following day, Lots 86 of third day and 83 of fifth day. Bought by Lord Yarmouth for £243.12.0.

211 Sir Anthony Blunt, *The French Drawings . . . at Windsor Castle* (1945), No. 315.

212 On 30 August 1808 Vulliamy submitted a bill for the repair and regilding of two of the candelabra at a cost of £220.10.0 (the repairs came to £31.10.0 and the regilding to £189). Subsequently three further pairs were similarly repaired and regilt for the same cost, as recorded in bills dated 25 and 26 September 1809 and 21 April 1810 (Windsor, Royal Archives: Georgian Papers, 25263, 25303, 25315). An earlier bill, dated 22 December 1806, refers to the supply of stands for three of the 'Large Tripod Candelabra'. This is possibly a reference to three of the above (P.R.O., Vulliamy Papers, C.104/58, Book 32).

213 The date of their purchase by George IV is not known, though it is probable that he acquired them about 1787. They are reproduced in an engraving of the Anteroom at Carlton House published by W. H. Pyne on 1 October 1818.

214 Clifford Smith, *op. cit.,* p.197.

215 Bill dated 2 February 1792 (P.R.O., H.O. 73/20).

216 On 5 May 1795 Francis Hervé submitted a bill for the repair of a set of lyre-backed chairs from the ground-floor Dining Room. The work involved the replacement of a back foot, a front foot and twenty-six rosettes. The price charged was £1.18.1 (P.R.O., H.O. 73/20).

217 Roberts, *op. cit.,* pp.146–47.

ACKNOWLEDGEMENTS

The service of Chelsea porcelain (pages 116–17) is reproduced by Gracious Permission of H.M. Queen Elizabeth The Queen Mother.

The drawing of the sideboard (page 142) is reproduced by courtesy of the Musée des Arts Décoratifs, Paris.

The drawing of the French clock (page 151) is reproduced by courtesy of the Metropolitan Museum of Art, New York.

Sir William Chambers' astronomical clock–case design (page 159)–is reproduced by courtesy of the Trustees of Sir John Soane's Museum.

The painting of 'The Oath of the Horatii' (page 168) is reproduced by courtesy of the Musée du Louvre, Paris.

The medal of Louis XV (page 178, left) is reproduced by courtesy of the Trustees of the British Museum; the medal of Louis XV (page 178, right) is by courtesy of the Manufacture Nationale de Porcelaine de Sèvres.

The drawing of the pedestal and candelabrum (page 194) is reproduced by courtesy of the Musée des Arts Décoratifs, Paris.

The Paintings

OLIVER MILLAR

The photographs of the paintings have been supplied by
A. C. Cooper Ltd, John R. Freeman & Co. Ltd,
the National Gallery, Photo Studios Ltd, and Mr Douglas Smith.

JOHANN ZOFFANY THE PRINCE OF WALES AND HIS BROTHER FREDERICK

QUEEN CHARLOTTE WITH THE PRINCE OF WALES
AND PRINCE FREDERICK

ON 23 SEPTEMBER 1674 John Evelyn went to see the havoc wrought by the fire at Goring House: 'with exceeding losse of hangings, plate, rare pictures and Cabinets, in a word, nothing almost was saved, of the best & most princely furniture that any subject had in England'. Nevertheless, by the time that he went with his son to dine with Lord Arlington just over two years later, on 16 November 1676, Evelyn found him surrounded once again by some very good pictures, by Palma, Van Dyck and Sebastiano del Piombo: 'but rare pieces indeede'.[1]

Arlington's possessions passed to his only child Isabella, who was married to the 1st Duke of Grafton, and thus to their descendants. None of his pictures seemed to have been acquired by John Sheffield who set himself to build up a large collection of pictures. His own statement of the money he had spent on Buckingham House[2] includes sums for decorative painting: £19 for 'Painting yᵉ Hall Stone Colour wᵗʰ Marbled Picture-frames'; a total of £46 for work in the Little Parlour ('Indian Painting all round it', 'Fitting Pictures over Doors', carved picture frames above the glasses over the chimney-pieces and plain ones over the doors); £76 for work, which included picture-frames, on the second storey; and £20 and £240 respectively for painting on this storey and in the Saloon. These amounts did not include the money paid for the 'Round Picture on yᵉ Roof' of the Saloon or the £400 paid by Buckingham to Louis Laguerre for painting the Stone Staircase. Special sums were also allocated to pictures. The three pictures set over the doors on the first storey cost the Duke £50; he paid £164 for the pictures in the Hall; and the pictures in the Saloon and the Picture Closet cost him in all £5,060.

In a charming letter to the Duke of Shrewsbury, another of the *magnifici* of the age, Buckingham describes his day: 'walk . . . in a *Salon* filled with pictures, some good, but none disagreeable; there also, in a row above them, I have so many portraits of famous persons in several kinds, as are enough to excite ambition in any man less lazy, or less at ease, than myself'. In this room, the Duke would read, write or look 'into the pleasantest park in the world'. At other times of the day he would be found in the Hall, 'the walls of it covered with a sett of pictures done in the school of RAPHAEL', or in the Parlour next door, embellished with a *bufette* partly decorated by Sebastiano Ricci. If he climbed the staircase, painted by Laguerre with the story of Dido, he would come into the little 'closet of original pictures, which yet are not so entertaining as the delightful prospect from the windows', and then into the Saloon with Orazio Gentileschi's

[1] *Diary*, ed. E. S. de Beer (1955), Vol. IV, pp.44, 102. The pictures by Van Dyck included the *Self-portrait* which is now in the Metropolitan Museum of Art, New York; the Sebastiano, which was then attributed to Raphael, was the superb *Cardinal Carondolet with his Secretaries,* formerly in the Arundel, and now in the Thyssen-Bornemisza collection.
[2] MS. in University of London Library.

Apollo and the Muses (originally painted for an earlier Duke of Buckingham at York House) set into the ceiling: 'The rest of the room is adorned with paintings relating to Arts and Sciences; and underneath divers original pictures hang all in good lights, by the help of an upper row of windows, which drown the glaring'.[1]

It is possible to reconstruct in a little more detail the disposition of the pictures at Buckingham House in the early years of the eighteenth century. In a volume of papers dealing with the Duke's estate[2] there is 'An Account of the paintings and pictures at Buckingham House', with an inventory annexed, and two copies of an inventory of the paintings drawn up in 1746.

The pictures in the Hall, which the Duke had described as painted in the school of Raphael, are probably those which in the 'Account' are described as eight Old Testament scenes, set in the panelling between pilasters. Laguerre's treatment of the story of Dido on a staircase is described in detail in the same source: a valuable commentary to set beside Stephanoff's water-colour.[3] On the newel of the staircase stood Giovanni da Bologna's *Cain and Abel* (now in the Victoria and Albert Museum), which the Duke had acquired from the widow of the 2nd (Villiers) Duke of Buckingham; with it he had probably bought the Gentileschi ceiling for his Saloon. To this circular canvas, said to be eighteen feet in diameter, 'all the rest of the painting in this room has relation': an interesting iconographical scheme designed by the Duke to celebrate Learning and the Arts. The 'Account' makes it clear that the Duke's 'portraits of famous persons' were not separate canvases. 'The space of 15 ffoot beneath the roof is filled with the portraitures of some persons most famous in their sev¹. kinds, as big as the Life and copied from their Statues Medals or Pictures. All these Pictures appear standing behind Ballisters round the Salon'.

Unfortunately the descriptions of the pictures in the three inventories are very brief and almost no measurements are provided; but the inventories provide a very clear impression of how the collection of an eighteenth-century grandee was arranged.[4] The family portraits were hung in the Japan Drawing Room and Crimson and Gold Damask Bedchambers. In the Great Parlour were more contemporary family portraits, portraits of Sir Robert Sheffield and Edmund, Lord Sheffield, and, over the fireplace, the version which is now at Parham Park in Sussex of the full-length of the Earl of Surrey, attributed to Guillim Stretes.[5] In Mr Phipps's Dressing Room were full-lengths of the Duchess of Richmond and of Lord Normanby and Lady Harriet Sheffield as children and a portrait of the Duke with his secretary. In the Vestibule the Duke had hung his royal portraits: a full-length of Queen Anne, Catherine of Braganza and 'Queen Mary' (presumably Mary of Modena or Mary II) over the doors and 'The Royal ffamily after Van Dyke'. In the 'Corner Room towards the Garden' were full-lengths by Kneller of the Duchess of Portland and her sister. In the Great Hall the Duke had placed the large picture, now in the National Maritime Museum at Greenwich, of the *Royal Catherine*, the vessel he had commanded as a young man in the Second Dutch War.

[1] *A Letter to the D . . . of Sh . . .* is printed in the Duke's *Works*, second ed. (1729), Vol. II, pp.253–64.
[2] Preserved in the office of the Surveyor of the Queen's Pictures.
[3] Published in 1818, in Vol. II (1819) of Pyne's *History of the Royal Residences, Buckingham Palace*, p.5.
[4] A number of the pictures can be traced in Sir Berkeley Sheffield's sale at Christie's, 16 July 1943.
[5] Royal Academy, *Holbein and other Masters*, 1950–51 (51).

In the Great Dining Room there hung appropriately, with other pictures, a *Boar Hunt* by Snyders. The Japan Drawing Room contained the *Adoration of the Kings* by Luca Giordano, which the antiquarian George Vertue greatly admired: 'a Fine large picture . . . bigger than the life. a noble composition strongly painted bravely colour'd. & highly finisht. This picture surpasseth all that I have seen of this master';[1] a *Virgin with Angels in the Clouds* by the same master hung in the Crimson Damask Bedchamber near to a *Peacock and other Birds* by Hondecoeter. The finest small pictures were hung, presumably very close together, in the Picture Closet. In the same closet were the limnings and small pictures. Miscellaneous works of art, pictures, prints and drawings, were placed in the Little Green Damask Bedchamber.

The pictures in the Saloon, 'some good, but none disagreeable', were presumably larger and would perhaps have been regarded as the cream of the collection. The attributions range from Bellini, Giorgione, Leonardo, Titian, the two Palmas, Giulio Romano, Salviati and Correggio, to Guercino, Caravaggio, Salvator Rosa, Castiglione and the Carracci. Van Dyck's *Endymion Porter and Family*, now in the possession of Mrs Gervas Huxley,[2] was praised by Vertue, who was warmer in praise of 'St Sebastian tyed to a tree' by the same artist: 'a Glorious picture . . . at lenght & alle naked . . . a jewell of inestimable Value'.[3] He also noted the picture of 'A naked Lady and son' by Lely, identifying it as the portrait of Nell Gwynn with her son, specially painted for Charles II and taken from Whitehall by the Duke of Buckingham at the Revolution.[4]

When Charles Sheffield sold Buckingham House to George III in 1762, none of the pictures were included in the purchase. The King's workmen took possession of the house on 9 May 1762 and the King himself lay there a fortnight later. It became an urgent matter to find pictures worthy of the new palace. The King could draw on two sources: the pictures that had been collected by his father Frederick, Prince of Wales, and the collection that he had inherited with the Crown on the death of his grandfather, George II, in 1760. It is possible that he did not get possession of all his father's pictures until the death of his mother Augusta, Princess of Wales, in 1772. His father's tastes were typical of his period: for Flemish, Dutch and, above all, Italian painting of the seventeenth century. He had been the first of the new dynasty to show enthusiasm, and no little discernment, in the patronage of artists and in the acquisition of works of art. George III ultimately inherited from the Prince fine paintings by Guido Reni, Pietro da Cortona, Maratti, Albano, Chiari, Lauri and Cagnacci and good examples of Teniers, Jan Bruegel and Gaspar Poussin. Prince Frederick's most important purchases had been, however, two magnificent Van Dycks and the superb pair of landscapes, *Winter* and *Summer*, by Rubens.[5]

[1]*Notebooks,* Vol. I, *Walpole Society,* Vol. XVIII (1930), p.97.

[2]Exhibited at Nottingham, *Paintings and Drawings by Van Dyck,* 1960 (11). In the earliest inventory of the pictures at Buckingham House, attached to the 'Account', a Van Dyck of the Countess of Clanbrassil is listed; it does not appear in the later inventories and may be the portrait in the Frick Collection, New York.

[3]*Notebooks,* loc. cit. In the volume of MS. relating to Buckingham House is an attestation by Vertue, dated 25 February 1747/8, concerning some of the drawings in the collection.

[4]In James II's catalogue it had been described as 'By Danckers [and] Sr Peter Lely. Being the Slideing Peice before Madam Gwynn's Picture naked with a Cupid' (British Museum, Harl. MS., 1890, f.55v.; Bathoe's ed. of James II's catalogue (1758), No. 305).

[5]All the pictures in this brief account of Prince Frederick's tastes are still in the royal collection.

The inherited royal collection of paintings was, in 1760, hanging at St James's Palace, Kensington, Windsor and Hampton Court and there was a large store at Somerset House. Although the collection had never recovered from the blow it had suffered when so many of the finest pictures were sold after the execution of Charles I in 1649, it was a big collection (well over a thousand pictures) and contained some very fine pictures indeed. By 25 May 1762 Walpole was writing to George Montagu: 'the King and his wife are settled for good at Buckingham House, and are stripping the other palaces to furnish it. In short, they have already fetched pictures from Hampton Court, which indicates their never living there'.[1] But the young King and his consort, for whom Buckingham House had been bought and was being so handsomely fitted up, were not content with bringing there the best pictures from other palaces: 'large commissions were sent to Italy for the purchase of paintings, antiques, and other curious articles to enrich this favourite mansion'.[2] Pictures were bought in Italy in the early part of the new reign to hang in Buckingham House. Richard Dalton, the Surveyor of the King's Pictures, was especially active in Rome and Bologna in the 1760's and early 1770's.

The greatest contribution made by George III to the shape and riches of the royal collection was his purchase in 1762 of the collection of Consul Joseph Smith. And it is almost certain that this great cache – of drawings, coins, medals, cameos, prints and books as well as pictures – was destined to embellish Buckingham House;[3] and that George III's activities as a collector of pictures were inspired by the purely practical need to furnish his new house. Smith had been British Consul in Venice since 1744 and had been trading there as a merchant since 1709. The King may have been contemplating before his accession the purchase of Smith's library; by 13 November 1762 the transactions were completed and the collection was in the King's hands: 'I don't think the pictures are worth much' wrote the traveller, Lord Northampton, on that date, 'there being very few capital peices'.

Modern opinion would hardly endorse Lord Northampton's opinion. Apart from its earlier Italian, Flemish and Dutch pictures, which include Vermeer's *Music Lesson* (page 244), the collection was especially rich in those Venetian painters with whom Smith had been so long associated: the Ricci, Rosalba Carriera, Francesco Zuccarelli and, above all, Canaletto. Although Smith's pictures by these painters are now chiefly at Windsor, there are at Buckingham Palace fine examples of their work from his collection. Zuccarelli's large upright landscapes, painted in the early 1740's, were probably designed to hang in, or be fitted into the panelling of, one of Smith's reception rooms. The fanciful views of famous English Palladian buildings (e.g., page 245) were painted by Zuccarelli in collaboration with Antonio Visentini in 1746 and reflect Smith's interest in Palladian architecture. George III, who admired the Burlingtonian school, would have shared his tastes; he placed these views in the Hall at Buckingham House.

Although the majority of Canaletto's paintings in the royal collection hang at Windsor, there

[1]*Correspondence*, ed. W. S. Lewis, Vol. X (1941), p.33.
[2]J. Watkins, *Memoirs of . . . Sophia-Charlotte, Queen of Great Britain* (1819), p.178.
[3]The best account of Smith's collection and its purchase by George III is to be found in M. Levey, *The Later Italian Pictures in the Collection of Her Majesty the Queen* (1964), pp.28–35.

is at Buckingham Palace a representative cross-section of his work. There are two from the set of five large views of Rome, painted by him in 1742 (e.g., page 248). It is assumed, not that Canaletto himself revisited Rome at this date, but that his nephew Bernardo Bellotto may have brought back from Rome to Venice work that influenced the older painter.[1] Far more striking are the two large canvases (e.g., page 249) from the great series of the artist's early views of his native city, which can be dated in the late 1720's: extremely broad and vigorous in handling and with a sense of water and flickering sunshine, and a feeling for the intensely picturesque quality of the city and its people, that Canaletto never again indulged so richly.

The pictures at Buckingham House in the earlier part of George III's reign must have been a magnificent embellishment of his new residence. We can gain from a number of sources a clear impression of the most important rooms.[2] The Hall, for example, was hung, as one can see in one of the views in Pyne's *Royal Residences,* with some of Consul Smith's largest views of Rome and Venice by Canaletto and with the concoctions by Visentini and Zuccarelli: 'These Canallettis', wrote Walpole, 'are bolder, stronger & far superior to his common Works'. The Passage Room contained at one time the fine portrait of a man by Frans Hals (page 247), the group of the Gerbier Family, begun by Rubens and now at Windsor, the two fine female full-lengths by Van Dyck which are also now at Windsor, and the group of the Five Children of Charles I which the King had bought in 1765.[3] In the 'Japan Room' the King had placed the two large royal subjects by Van Dyck, the equestrian portrait of Charles I (page 250) and the 'Great Piece' of Charles I, his consort and their two eldest children (page 251). More huge seventeenth-century pictures, including Van Dyck's 'St Martin' and Pietro da Cortona's 'Augustus and the Sibyl', were placed in the Drawing Room. A number of the smaller pictures, French, Flemish and Italian, hung in the King's Dressing Room, and the Closet and the great Library were hung principally with pictures bought by the King's father or by the King himself with the Smith collection. And late in 1763, or early in 1764, Raphael's Cartoons were brought from Hampton Court to hang, but not for long, 'in the great room, . . . on light green Damask'.[4]

The 'Warm Room' was devoted to the classical and heroic subjects by the American Benjamin West, which now hang in Kensington Palace. One of the Closets was filled with the famous series of oval portraits, of the King and Queen and thirteen of their children, which Gainsborough had painted at Windsor in the autumn of 1782. The Bedchamber was hung with portraits of the

[1] M. Levey, *op. cit.,* Nos. 368–73. For a particularly sensitive analysis of Canaletto's work for Smith the reader is also referred to Mr Levey's *Canaletto Paintings in the Collection of Her Majesty the Queen* (1964).

[2] There are two inventories, preserved in the office of the Surveyor of the Queen's Pictures, of pictures at Buckingham House; one was probably drawn up *c.* 1790–5; the other, dated 1819 on the cover, was composed after Queen Charlotte's death on 17 November 1818 and was probably drawn up under the direction of Benjamin West, who was Surveyor of Pictures until his death in 1820. Horace Walpole's valuable notes on the pictures he saw on a visit to Buckingham House on 25 June (?1783) are printed in Vol. XVI of the *Walpole Society* (1928), pp.78–80. Pyne's *Royal Residences* of 1819 includes (Vol. II) a description of the house and some most valuable coloured views of some of the rooms. In the Royal Library is a set of drawings to scale which indicate the arrangement of the pictures on the walls of some of the rooms early in the reign of George III. The removals of pictures from Buckingham House in 1804–5 are recorded in a volume in the Surveyor's Office.

[3] For these three Van Dycks, see Millar, Nos. 154, 158, 152; the fine early male portrait by Van Dyck (ibid., No. 160) was also in Buckingham House at this date.

[4] Public Record Office, A.O.I., 420, 201; Walpole, *loc. cit.*

Queen's relations and friends: by Angelica Kauffmann, Opie, Zoffany, Cotes and Gainsborough (page 254). Two well-known pictures by Zoffany (*c.* 1765) give us a clearer impression than any inventory or written account of the distinguished new interiors at Buckingham House. In one (page 226) the little Prince of Wales and his brother Frederick are seen in one of the Drawing Rooms with suitable (and identifiable) pictures by Van Dyck and Maratti hanging on the walls. In the other (page 226) the boys are seen in their mother's Dressing Room; there is a tantalising glimpse of the new Smith pictures in the background.

According to Walpole, the King had intended to hang in the Dining Room portraits of all his brothers and sisters; 'but on the marriages of the Dukes of Cumberland & Gloucester they were stopped'. There are still, however, at Buckingham Palace, two portraits which probably formed part of this scheme: Dance's portrait of the King's eldest brother, the Duke of York (page 254) and the double portrait by Francis Cotes of his sisters, Louisa Anne and Caroline Matilda (page 255). There is also in the Palace a very fine series of royal full-lengths from the age of George III. Van Loo's portraits (page 253) of the King's parents, Frederick, Prince of Wales, and Augusta of Saxe-Gotha, painted in 1742, mark an important stage in the development of the English State Portrait. In quality, character and design they are extremely French. Van Loo had worked in Paris and it is under this lively French influence that the State Portrait in this country developed from the rigid and stereotyped patterns thrown off for it by Sir Godfrey Kneller. In colour, and in the elaborate rococo settings, Van Loo's portraits have affinities with Nattier. This influence is felt even more strongly in the next pair of State Portraits (page 252), those painted for George III and Queen Charlotte by the Scots painter Allan Ramsay. Grander than Van Loo's portraits, Ramsay's portraits have a sophisticated and very French richness of tone and the magnificence of robes and background do not swamp the rather *gauche* charm that Ramsay recognised in the sitters. Ramsay's are perhaps the finest and most satisfying of all English State Portraits, within the formal context of this *genre*; they also represent the climax of the development of the *genre* from the point when it was given a new lease of life by Van Dyck in the service of Charles I.

Ramsay's portraits are the work of a most competent and sensitive painter. Gainsborough's full-lengths of Henry Frederick, Duke of Cumberland (page 257) and his raffish Duchess (page 256), shown at the Royal Academy in 1771, are brilliantly witty variations, by a genius, on the same themes. Apart from Gainsborough's lively execution, the grandeur of the designs is charged with a new energy. The beautiful Duchess has an enigmatic smile; the vicious little Duke glides across the canvas, holding his coronet in his hand and nervously fingering his George.

The King and Queen, who were devoted to their children, and especially to the youngest, constantly employed painters to record them, from Ramsay in the early days of their nursery, to Hoppner and the young Thomas Lawrence in the 1780's. At Buckingham Palace is almost the whole of Benjamin West's series of portraits (e.g., page 258) of the King, Queen and their children, painted in 1776–9. The figures are stiffly articulated and the colour is pale and cold; but the series provides, in the backgrounds and accessories, an amusing record of the activities and interests of the royal family: the Queen and her eldest daughter work at a piece of embroidery under the gaze of Minerva and with music and Raphael drawings beside them; Prince Edward distracts his brother William's attention from a globe to a model of the ship on which Prince William was serving as a Midshipman; the younger children play with balls, toys and little carts.

The last years of the King's life were passed under the cloud of increasingly incurable illness. The royal family withdrew from London to Kew and Windsor. In 1804–5 a large number of the best pictures was sent down from Buckingham House to be hung at Windsor. For the historian of the royal collection the principal interest now shifts to Carlton House.

George III's eldest son, George, Prince of Wales, was Prince Regent from 1811 until he came to the throne on his father's death in 1820. He assembled at Carlton House a superb collection of pictures: less varied, it is true, than that of Charles I or Frederick, Prince of Wales, had been – there is no evidence that George IV had any feeling for Italian painting – but of the highest possible quality.[1] The pictures were, moreover, clearly hung with great taste and care; and it is significant that only a fairly small proportion of the Regent's pictures were hung on the walls of Carlton House – in 1816 some 245 pictures out of a total of about 530 were in store – and that the contents of the house were constantly being changed about by their restless owner. In May 1810 Lady Sarah Spencer went to Carlton House 'which is so magnificent just now . . . He [i.e., the Prince] changes the furniture so very often, that one can scarcely find time to catch a glimpse of each transient arrangement before it is all turned off for some other'.[2] The impression one gains from the plates in Pyne's *Royal Residences* is that each picture has been most carefully placed in order that it shall play the right part in Holland's beautiful rooms.

As a patron of living artists the Prince must have been easier to deal with than his father had been. He admired and patronised Gainsborough and did not share his parents' prejudice against Reynolds. Of his pictures by Reynolds there are at Buckingham Palace two of his interesting, but rather unhappy, mythological-historical subjects, *Cymon and Iphigenia* and the *Death of Dido* (page 259), and the sumptuous full-length in Garter robes of the Prince's brother, Frederick, Duke of York (page 259), which formed part of the series of family portraits which the Prince arranged in the old Throne Room at Carlton House. The Prince was clearly anxious to assemble a complete family portrait-gallery; and his passion for military matters (which has been shared by many of his family) led him to acquire a great many very inferior pictures of military subjects. After the death of Reynolds, the Prince employed Hoppner, Beechey and Lawrence (among others) to paint portraits of his family and friends; the most important Lawrence which is now at Buckingham Palace was, however, acquired at a later date: the spectacular full-length of the Prince's squalid and pitiable wife, Caroline of Brunswick, with their daughter Charlotte.

The Regent was always extremely generous in lending his pictures to exhibitions, or making them available to students; and at one time he was anxious to form a representative collection

[1]The most important sources for our knowledge of the pictures at Carlton House are the inventories of 1816 and 1819; these are in the Surveyor's office, with a very slightly later inventory and with the invaluable Day-Books kept by Benjamin Jutsham, Inspector of Household Deliveries. Pyne's account of Carlton House in Vol. III of the *Royal Residences* is important; in many of the illustrations of the interior the pictures can be easily identified.
[2]*Correspondence of Sarah Spencer, Lady Lyttelton,* ed. Mrs H. Wyndham (1912), pp.103–4.

of pictures by living British painters. In the summer of 1810 he was talking about this to the aged Benjamin West. As a start, he acquired Edward Bird's *Village Choristers* (page 260) and gave a commission to David Wilkie 'to paint a companion to it; leaving the subject & the price to Himself'; but by the end of the year the diarist Farington, who is the source for this episode, had been told by the painter Thomas Phillips that in this, as in so much else, the Prince was 'influenced by caprice, and has no steadiness'.[1] As a result, the Prince's collection of contemporary British painting is very unbalanced. It is particularly rich in the work of Lawrence and Wilkie. Lawrence's celebrated series of portraits of the sovereigns, statesmen and commanders who had contributed to the final overthrow of Napoleon has hung for many years at Windsor, but Buckingham Palace contains all the Regent's subject-pictures by Wilkie.[2] The picture which Wilkie painted for the Regent, as a companion to the *Village Choristers,* was *Blind-Man's Buff*; so pleased was the Regent with the picture that he commissioned a companion, the *Penny Wedding* (page 261), which was not finished until 1818. In both these pictures of Scottish *genre* subjects Wilkie's debt to Teniers is obvious; and the Prince's love for this form of highly-finished anecdotal painting led him to buy later two pictures from William Mulready (e.g., page 262). Some time later George IV bought from Wilkie two little pictures which he had painted in Rome and Geneva in 1827 (e.g., page 262) and in which his handling has become looser and his colour much more positive. More important are the four spirited, brilliantly painted subjects (e.g., page 263) which Wilkie executed in 1828 and 1830 under the influence of a visit to Spain and the legends of the Spanish resistance to the French occupation.

There can be no doubt that the King saw and admired in the work of Mulready and in the earlier pictures by Wilkie exactly the qualities of fine craftsmanship, beautiful paint and amusing narrative content that delighted him in Teniers, Steen or Adriaen van Ostade. As early as 1807 the collector and connoisseur Lord Mulgrave had said that 'He believed Wilkie wd. go beyond Teniers, Ostade & all who had preceded Him, as He not only gave exquisitely the ordinary expression of the human countenance but those of thought & abstraction'.[3] In the early years of the century the Prince had been spending fairly heavily on his pictures; by 1811, the year in which he became Regent, the collection had increased in quantity and in quality; and by May 1814, when he bought a famous consignment of nearly one hundred Netherlandish pictures from the collection of Sir Francis Baring, his collection had become so rich that the Prince sent to Christie's, for sale on 29 June 1814, pictures which he no longer considered worthy of a place at Carlton House. Thereafter, the rate of acquisition slightly slackened off, but very important purchases continued to be made up to the last years of his life. George IV's Flemish, Dutch and French pictures constitute one of the great riches of the Queen's collection, comparable in excellence and importance to George III's Venetian paintings, the Prince Consort's primitives, and what is left of Charles I's *cinquecento* pictures; and in the history of connoisseurship in this

[1] *The Farington Diary,* ed. J. Greig, Vol. VI (1926), pp.89, 219.
[2] The full-length of the Duke of Sussex in Highland Dress, now hanging on the staircase, was presented by the sitter to his niece, Queen Victoria, on 24 February 1838.
[3] *The Farington Diary, op. cit.,* Vol. IV (1924), p.101.

country, George IV's collection was among the best formed from the flood of pictures that passed into this country during the revolutionary and Napoleonic wars on the Continent.

It is impossible in this context to provide a complete survey of George IV's Dutch pictures,[1] but they fall into fairly well-defined groups, indicating incidentally the aspects of Dutch painting in the seventeenth century that George IV and his contemporaries most admired. Of the great painters of the Dutch interior, who had been popular in England since early in the eighteenth century, the King acquired two unsurpassed examples of De Hooch in his best period and two pictures by Ter Borch. The De Hoochs were among the King's last purchases: the *Courtyard in Delft* (page 264), a study in the fall of soft sunshine over red roofs into a partly white-washed courtyard: the *Card-Players* (page 265), a study in the effects of sunlight as it pours into the room in which they are sitting. The larger of the two Ter Borchs, on the other hand (page 266), is painted with the utmost attention to every detail within the group; but the modelling of the forms, especially of the faces, is sensitive and surprisingly free on this small scale, the light is soft and the colour extremely subtle. The two pictures by Gabriel Metsu (e.g., page 267) have, likewise, a richness of texture and tone in contrast with the detailed finish and lack of atmosphere —the atmosphere, that is, which suffuses De Hooch's *Card-Players* or Ter Borch's *Letter*—in such painters as Dou (page 267) or Frans van Mieris.

Among painters of more vigorous personality, George IV owned a particularly fine group of works by Jan Steen and Adriaen van Ostade. In the best of the Steens the fascinating intricacy and idiosyncrasies in subject-matter involve no lack of vigour in handling. Indeed, the touch is often as shrewd and lively as the character it defines (page 268) and the colour as subtle as Ter Borch's and more striking in its range. These technical qualities are seen at their finest in the enthralling *Morning Toilet* (page 269), where the warm grey-brown of the architectural framework, reminiscent of the opening into a trick perspective by Samuel van Hoogstraeten, serves to enclose the richer and particularly subtle colours of the interior; the light purplish-blue and silver curtains (thinly painted over pale brown underpaint), pale cerise and deep gold in the costume, dull red and gold in the cloth on the bedside table. One is reminded once again of Wilkie's debt to Dutch painting in the interiors by Adriaen van Ostade. The setting in the *Interior of a Peasant's Cottage* (page 270), the finest of the Regent's pictures by this painter, is very reminiscent of the large farm-house in which *Blind-Man's Buff* is played, but the colour is richer. The handling, though very fresh, is of extreme refinement; and the figures have Ostade's essentially mannered oddity. In the so-called *Dutch Courtship* (page 271), there seems to be a deliberate attempt to give the figures and their setting an archaic flavour—the woman could have sprung from a painting by Maerten van Heemskerck—and there is often a packed, if quietly exploited, narrative content in Ostade's pictures that reminds one of some forms of German book-illustration in the nineteenth century. His younger brother, Isack van Ostade, whose promise was cut short by an early death, painted in a rougher, less sophisticated style (page 271).

The fine quality and condition which distinguish the Regent's *genre* pictures is to be seen in

---

[1] A volume on the Dutch pictures, in the new *Catalogue Raisonné* of The Queen's Pictures, is in preparation.

his Dutch landscapes. His two little landscapes by Van der Heyden (e.g., page 274) are, indeed, miracles of delicate handling and meticulous finish, as if the painter was desperately anxious not to disturb by a single false stroke his peaceful scene. Jacob van Ruisdael is represented by the fine *Evening Landscape* (page 279) in which the artist displays a favourite device: allowing a shaft of light to fall from a lowering sky on to a field in the middle distance and keeping the watery foreground in shadow; and Hobbema by the *Water-Mill* and the more freely-painted *Lane through a Wood* (page 282). George IV acquired good pictures by Paul Potter and Wynants and a group of pastoral scenes by Adriaen van de Velde, as well as an unusual coast scene (page 272) and the *Hawking Party* (page 273), which is of exceptionally high quality. His pictures by Wouvermans are equally fine and quintessential examples of the sort of Dutch cabinet pictures which were so highly prized by contemporary collectors; but the Regent also secured an early *Cavalry Skirmish* (page 273) which is much more dramatic in design and less finished in texture. The finest of the Regent's sea-pieces is perhaps the *Calm* by Willem van de Velde the Younger (page 275); executed before the artist had settled with his father in London (probably late in 1672), it is painted much more tightly than the dashing pictures that the younger man painted for Charles II, James II and some of their leading naval commanders: the little canvas of the *Royal Escape*, for example, or the best canvases (e.g., page 275) in the series of naval battles which the two men painted for the Duke of York.

There is also at Buckingham Palace a very significant—and exceptionally beautiful—group of landscapes by those Dutch painters who at certain phases of their career were in Italy and whose paintings played a considerable part in the development of the classical landscape: Cornelis van Poelenburgh, Jan Both, Claes Berchem and Karel Du Jardin. Poelenburgh had actually been in London and painted a number of landscapes for Charles I. His little *Landscape with Shepherds and Ruins* (page 276) is perhaps the most important of the pictures of this type acquired by George IV. Painted *c.* 1620, not long after Poelenburgh's arrival in Rome, it is an example of the type of landscape by a Northern artist that would have influenced Claude and a reminder that it was these Northern painters who first appreciated and set out to paint the picturesque qualities in the Campagna. Among the earliest of the Berchems is the *Italian Landscape* (page 281), with its spacious view over a plain dotted with crumbling buildings, towards the distant mountains, and the crisply painted, loose-jointed figures which emphasise the importance of this type of Dutch landscape in the early development of Gainsborough's landscapes; in a *Landscape with Shepherds* (page 280), painted nearly twenty years later, Berchem's touch has become much freer and more liquid and there is a more purely decorative interest in the design. Distinct from Du Jardin's landscapes from the Regent's collection is one particularly fine example (page 277) of his work in a bambocciesque vein: a vein, that is, which had been evolved by the Haarlem artist, Pieter van Laer ('Il Bamboccio') after his arrival in 1625 in Rome, where he was fascinated by the picturesque qualities in the streets and poorer inhabitants. But the finest of the Regent's classical Dutch landscapes is probably the landscape by Jan Both (page 277) with the Baptism of the Eunuch taking place in a glow of evening light: the type of landscape that must have been profoundly influential in the North after Both's return to Utrecht in 1641.

The finest set of landscapes in the Regent's collection, however, were his magnificent pieces by Cuyp; indeed, it is remarkable that there should be in England so much richer a representation of this artist than in his native Holland. The three most splendid Cuyps at Buckingham Palace are perhaps the *Negro Page* (page 278) in which a misty classical landscape is bathed in evening light behind typically lumpish figures and horses; the *Passage Boat* (page 280) with its wonderfully bold design, superbly fresh handling in the reflections in the water, thundery clouds and squat figures; and the *Evening Landscape* (page 278), reminiscent of Jan Both in design, but entirely personal in the nervously fretted outline of the clouds and the soft cascade of lights among the plants and foliage in the foreground.

Finally come the Rembrandts, the crowning glory of the Regent's collection. The most important is the earliest and the first which the Regent acquired: *The Shipbuilder and his Wife* (page 283), painted in 1633, the year after the *Anatomy Lesson* and a comparable masterpiece in Rembrandt's early baroque style. In 1814, with the Baring collection, the Regent secured the *Self-Portrait* which is now at Windsor, the *Rabbi* which is now regarded tentatively as by Govert Flinck, and the puzzling *Adoration of the Kings,* which bears Rembrandt's signature and the date

A PHOTOGRAPH TAKEN OF THE PICTURE GALLERY BEFORE
ITS ALTERATION IN 1901

1657, but cannot now be accepted as by Rembrandt himself; nor can it be dated precisely to 1657, as it is painted in a curious *mélange* of Rembrandt's styles at different periods in his career. In 1819 were bought the two paintings which could be fairly judged to be the most moving pictures in the Regent's collection: the little *Noli Me Tangere* of 1638 (page 284) and the *Lady with a Fan* of 1641 (page 285). *Noli Me Tangere* is a magically poetical rendering of the moment when the Magdalen recognises the Risen Christ as a gardener, painted with a richer palette and conceived with a deeper tenderness than the series of scenes from the Passion which Rembrandt painted for the Prince of Orange. In the *Lady with a Fan,* one of Rembrandt's most sophisticated young female portraits, he creates in a baroque sense an illusion of the space from which the sitter gazes straight out at us, resting one hand on the side of the opening of a window and letting her fan fall forward over the ledge in front of her; in the companion portrait, which is now in Brussels, her husband leans on the ledge, looking out at us and from an identical frame.

With the Regent's love of narrative and fine quality in pictures, it is not surprising that he assembled a group of paintings by David Teniers the younger in which the artist is seen at the height of his powers. All are fresh, nervous and liquid in touch and clear and gay in colour. In the smaller pieces—the group of peasants outside a tavern or the *Card-Players* (page 286)—the touch has something of Brouwer's vigour, although Teniers's scenes and characters are always essentially less outspoken: painted, one always feel, for patrons who did not really wish to be told what went on in the taverns on the fringes of their estates or in the poorer quarters of the town. In others, such as the *Drummer* (pages 286-7) or the *Interior of a Gardener's House* (page 288), there is a brilliance in the painting of still-life which would have intrigued the Regent and David Wilkie. Of the outdoor scenes the finest is the *Dance in the Grounds of a Mansion* (page 289). The figures are clearly planted in their correct social relationships: the squire and his family are obvious portraits, the chaw-bacons are stock figures, mere puppets by contrast.

The landscape is painted in a style that derives from Rubens, though Teniers never went back to the highly-wrought, intricate, yet firmly-based landscapes of Rubens's earlier years, nor achieved the dream-like beauty of Rubens's last phase. A magnificent example of Rubens's first phase is the *Farm at Laeken* (pages 290-1), in which he is now starting to let the sunlight pour into the view; he also uses the design as a setting for magnificently drawn figures, cattle and still-life. From the later phase comes the *Landscape with St George* (pages 294-5) which the Prince secured in an exchange in 1814. It was a picture of peculiar fascination for an English buyer, evoking as it does the Thames landscape as a setting for the legend of St George and the Dragon enacted by the King and Queen of England.[1] Two years later the Prince bought the exquisite *Assumption of the Virgin* (page 292). This is a very carefully worked-out *modello,* in full colour, for an altarpiece which does not seem to have been carried out in exactly this form. It was conceived within a few years of Rubens's return to Antwerp from Italy in 1609.

It is unfortunate that, with his love of French furniture and works of art, the Regent did not show so much enthusiasm for French painting. He would surely have been fascinated by the

[1]There is in the Wellington Museum at Apsley House a *Landscape* by Teniers which in general disposition seems influenced by the *Landscape with St George.*

subject-matter in the works of Boucher, Lancret, Watteau and Pater or admired the rococo panache of Largillierre or Nattier. In fact, his purchases in this field are unimportant: the best are four scenes by Pater at Windsor and *Silence!* (page 293) by Greuze. His finest French pictures belong to the seventeenth, rather than to the eighteenth, century; and one sees once again his predilection for *genre* scenes and landscape in his early purchase of *The Young Gamblers* by Le Nain (page 297) and in one of his last acquisitions, the *Rape of Europa* (pages 296-7) by Claude: in every way one of the most magically beautiful of Claude's works and perhaps the loveliest, and certainly the most poetical, picture that George IV ever bought.

On 27 October 1821 Farington was told by Nash that the King 'had felt a dislike to Carlton House and wished to remove to Buckingham House'.[1] Soon after his accession, therefore, he must have planned to move his collection of pictures. Throughout the 1820's they were being dispersed. To the King's Lodge and Cumberland Lodge at Windsor were sent down many of the small portraits, military and *genre* subjects (including some of the Wilkies) and sporting pictures; indeed, the only fine example left, until recently, at Buckingham Palace from the King's superb collection of sporting pieces, is Stubbs's portrait of the dogs *Fino and Tiny* (page 300). In 1828 the King sent down for the new Corridor in Windsor Castle a large group of his father's fine Italian pictures which have ever since contributed to the special atmosphere of the Castle.[2]

His great continental pictures, however, the King seems always to have planned to display as a collection in his new Picture Gallery at Buckingham Palace. But he never saw them finally established there. In 1826 and 1827 a very large collection of them made up complete shows at the British Institution, to whose exhibitions in the past he had been a most generous lender. In 1830 the whole collection was at St James's Palace. In August 1835 the German connoisseur, Dr Waagen, on his first visit to England, saw the collection stored in five rooms in 105 Pall Mall. It was apparently intended that the pictures by Rubens and Van Dyck were to go to Windsor, the others 'to Buckingham House, the new Royal Palace in London'.[3] And so, although William IV had been considering in 1834 the construction of a picture gallery at St James's Palace, George IV's original intentions for his great collection were finally carried out. In 1841 a printed catalogue was issued of the pictures in the State Rooms of the Palace. In the Picture Gallery were hung 185 pictures, including a few acquired by Queen Victoria and the Prince Consort; in the catalogue of 1852, drawn up by Thomas Uwins, 182 pictures are recorded in the Gallery. In 1844 Mrs Jameson had published a description of the Gallery and adjacent rooms.[4] She found the Gallery 'too lofty, and the light not well contrived for such small and delicate pictures', many of which 'hang so high, almost out of sight'. This impression is confirmed by an old photograph (page 237). The cavernous gloom may not have been so frustrating as it appears, as it would have been impossible to see many of the finest pictures, however good the light.

[1] *The Farington Diary, op. cit.,* Vol. VIII (1928), p.289.
[2] The evidence for these moves is contained in Jutsham's Day-Books.
[3] G. F. Waagen, *Works of Art and Artists in England* (1838), Vol. II, pp.348-77.
[4] *Companion to the Most Celebrated Private Galleries of Art in London* (1844), pp.3-76.

The arrangement of the pictures throughout the Palace had been established by the Prince Consort. By 1898, thirty-seven years after his death, Sir J. C. Robinson, Surveyor of the Queen's Pictures, was keen to do something to improve their appearance. He reported that the Gallery was dark and inadequately lit, that the pictures themselves were darkening under the varnish applied by William Seguier in the time of George IV, and that many pictures, hanging high up, were literally invisible. These he wished to clean and hang elsewhere in the Palace. Robinson approached the Queen through her eldest daughter, the Empress Frederick. On the question of cleaning, the Queen, after speaking about it at Balmoral to A. J. Balfour, decided to take a second opinion. Sir Edward Poynter, Director of the National Gallery, and Claude Phillips, the writer and critic, were called in, to Robinson's chagrin. The Queen, perhaps because Phillips reported that it was in fact impossible to see the pictures in the Palace properly, agreed to Robinson experimenting with removing varnish and to the Office of Works attempting to improve the lighting. She was prepared for minor alterations within the Gallery, but no picture was to be taken out of it. 'The pictures at Windsor and Buckingham Palace were settled by the Prince Consort, and the Queen desires that there shall be no change'.[1]

Within a few weeks of Queen Victoria's death Robinson's place was taken, on 5 March 1901, by Lionel Cust. Edward VII, with his new Surveyor, went systematically through Windsor and Buckingham Palace. Many rearrangements were carried out and Cust employed F. H. Haines, the picture restorer, to remove the film of dirt which had settled on the pictures, especially on those that hung on the level of, or even above, the large gas-lit chandeliers in the Gallery.[2] The Gallery was further improved by the alterations carried out by King George V and Queen Mary in 1914: the walls were hung with olive-green damask, the roof was reconstructed and new lighting was installed. The pictures, however, continued to be hung–in modern eyes, at least–far too high and far too closely packed.[3] Queen Mary herself came to think the small pictures 'a little crowded, but they look all right'. The evacuation of the pictures on the outbreak of the Second World War provided an opportunity, after their return, to arrange the Gallery along more lucid and less oppressive lines. But it remains a monument to the taste of George IV and the disposition of the pictures in the adjoining state rooms and on the Principal Staircase (especially where full-length royal portraits have been let into the walls to form integral parts of the decoration) has changed very little since Queen Victoria and the Prince Consort authorised the printed catalogue in 1841.

Not long after the death of the Prince Consort, the Queen spoke about him to Sir Henry Cole, secretary to the School of Design. The Queen 'said she had no taste–used only to listen to him–not worthy to untie his latchet'.[4] As a girl, the Queen had shown a lively interest in the fine arts: she enjoyed visiting exhibitions and seeing country houses; she could etch and paint; and pictures and painters cropped up in her conversations with Lord Melbourne. On one

[1]Public Record Office, L.C.1/680, 117, 119, 127, 147–9, 153–4, 160; 697, 7, 9; 699, 4.
[2]For Cust's activities see Ch. II of his *King Edward VII and his Court* (1930).
[3]See the two views of the Picture Gallery in Clifford Smith, *op. cit.,* p. 186.
[4]Sir H. Cole, *Fifty Years of Public Work* (1884), Vol. I, p. 359.

occasion, on 13 July 1839, they talked 'of the beautiful pictures in the Gallery here, for some time; of their being all Dutch, which we agreed was a low style; our preferring the Italian Masters . . . Of my wishing in time to buy some Italian pictures'.[1]

She was thus ready to be educated by the Prince Consort, whose early travels and studies in Italy had, in his own words, 'intoxicated him with delight' and increased, above all, his 'power of forming a right judgment'. Apart from his arrangements of the pictures, Buckingham Palace does not now contain the most important fruits of the Prince's judgment and the Queen's enthusiasms. Their Garden Pavilion, decorated in fresco by eight leading Academicians – Stanfield, Uwins, Leslie, Ross, Eastlake, Maclise, Landseer and Etty – had become by 1928 so ruinous that it was beyond repair. The Prince's examination and arrangement of the Queen's prints and drawings were carried out during many happy evenings at Windsor. More important: the fine early Italian, Flemish and German pictures that the Queen and Prince acquired, mainly in the 1840's, were hung at Osborne, the Queen's house in the Isle of Wight; Edward VII brought them all up to London in April 1902, but after the Second World War King George VI gave permission for them to be put on show at Hampton Court.

There are, however, a number of interesting early Victorian pictures at Buckingham Palace. There are the portraits of the Queen herself as a girl by Richard Westall (page 299), painted in 1830 for her mother, the Duchess of Kent, and the full-length of the Duchess painted by George Hayter in 1835. The very early portrait by Watts of Lady Holland (page 300) was bequeathed by her to the Prince of Wales. In 1841 the Prince Consort bought John Martin's *Eve of the Deluge* (page 302). At the same period the Queen was patronising David Roberts and Clarkson Stanfield; at Christmas, 1846, she gave to the Prince Stanfield's picture (page 303) of the Royal Yacht passing St Michael's Mount. In 1838 she had bought two pictures by Maclise: *The Second Adventure of Gil Blas* and the *Scene from the Burletta of Midas* (page 303). She was later a patron of E. H. Corbould. But the finest contemporary picture that she acquired was Frith's *Ramsgate Sands* (page 304-5) with which she had been 'delighted' at the Royal Academy in 1854.

The two most lavishly patronised painters were, however, Sir Edwin Landseer and Frans Xaver Winterhalter. Landseer had been patronised by the Queen before her marriage. Among the paintings that she bought in 1839 is the picture (page 307) of the lion-tamer Van Amburgh lying in a cage with a lamb and a posse of lions, tigers and leopards. In 1836 her mother had given her a little portrait by Landseer of her spaniel 'Dash'. In 1838 she commissioned the group (page 307) of the parrot 'Lory' with 'Dash' and the more forbidding 'Hector' and 'Nero'. This is a fine example of Landseer's extreme skill at painting animals. One is almost reluctant to admit that, in the swagger arrangement of the design and the brilliant fluency of the handling, one is reminded of court portraits by Van Dyck or Lawrence. From this date until the end of his life Landseer lavished his formidable gifts on portraits of the Queen's pets, as well as of herself and her family, and on scenes of royal and wild life in the Highlands. Many of these pictures were sent up to Balmoral by Edward VII in 1901; there remain in the Palace, however, the

[1] *The Girlhood of Queen Victoria,* ed. Lord Esher (1912), Vol. II, p.223.

fascinating picture (page 306) of the Queen and her husband in gleaming mediaeval costume, a picture that makes a painful contrast with Landseer's grey and shadowed picture of the widowed Queen reading official papers at Osborne; and the *Baptismal Font,* the last picture that Landseer completed, bought by the Queen in 1872.

Winterhalter can probably be regarded as the last great court portrait painter, who could carry out with competence and conviction the duties of a fashionable court artist. He produced for the Queen and Prince Consort a vast number of pictures, ranging in size from monumental family groups to charming small sketches of the Queen's youngest children or such intimate family portraits as *The Cousins* (page 309) in 1852. Winterhalter was the last painter who could compose a thoroughly satisfying large family group, such as that of the royal family in 1846 (page 310), in the Van Dyck tradition, or tender and playful pictures of royal babies (e.g., page 308) that remind one, again, of Van Dyck or Lawrence. All through her reign the Queen also commissioned records of important events in the life of her family: her own Coronation (by Hayter), royal marriages, of which the best painting is John Phillip's of the marriage of the Princess Royal (pages 310-11), christenings by Hayter, Leslie, G. H. Thomas and others, Jubilee groups and processions, royal visits, trips on the Royal Yacht and naval or military reviews. And although the camera and the cinematograph can now record such events far more satisfactorily, they have been recorded in paint since 1901, accompanying the royal portraits from the time of Winterhalter to that of Sir Oswald Birley.

THE QUEEN'S GALLERY

Apart from the primitives, the most interesting earlier pictures at the Palace that the Queen and Prince Consort acquired were the Flemish and Spanish portraits which were bought at the sale of King Louis Philippe's Spanish pictures at Christie's in May 1853; the most important were the portraits by Sanchez Coello, including the signed portrait (page 246) of the Archduke Rudolf. After the Prince Consort's death, all the Queen's enthusiasm for pictures evaporated; and as she grew older she lost opportunities to acquire paintings which would have filled her with pleasure before 1861. Since 1901 a number of earlier portraits have been acquired. Perhaps the most important are John Russell's portrait of George IV when Prince of Wales (page 298), a puffy Florizel tightly buttoned into the uniform of the Kentish Bowmen, and Sanders's *Lord Byron* (page 301), which in 1914 was left to King George V by Lady Dorchester, daughter of Byron's friend John Cam Hobhouse.

In the Second World War, Queen Victoria's Private Chapel was gutted in an air raid. It has now been reconstructed as a small picture gallery–The Queen's Gallery–to which the public is admitted and in which are mounted exhibitions of works of art of all kinds and from all the royal palaces and houses. The Gallery was opened in the summer of 1962 with an exhibition of Treasures from the Royal Collection: pictures, furniture, jewels, drawings, china and miniatures of the highest quality and of many periods (page 242). Since that first show there have been exhibitions of certain schools or themes in which the royal collections are particularly rich. There seems no limit to the amount of fine, amusing or instructive exhibitions which could be drawn from the resources of the collections and shown in this small Gallery.

When news of George III's purchase of the Smith collection reached London, the *Public Advertiser* informed its readers on 20 December 1762 that 'as soon as the grand Collection of Drawings, etc. . . . arrive in Town, they will be deposited in the Queen's Palace, which with those already there, will make the finest Collection in Europe; and that Tickets will be given to the Nobility and Gentry to admit them to see it'.[1] Whether such tickets were ever issued, we do not know; but the public, in numbers larger than the *Public Advertiser* could ever have dreamed of, is now admitted to the Queen's Gallery to see a collection which has been substantially and continuously enriched since 1762.

NOTE. Two points must be made: first, that it is impossible in a brief survey such as this to do more than point out the more important pictures in Buckingham Palace; second, that the pictures in the royal collection are often moved between the royal palaces and that there is no guarantee that all the pictures mentioned here will always be found in the Palace.

Bibliographies for the history of the royal collection are to be found in O. Millar, *The Tudor, Stuart and Early Georgian Pictures* (1963), and M. Levey, *The Later Italian Pictures* (1964), *in the Collection of Her Majesty the Queen*. These are the first two volumes to appear in a new *catalogue raisonné* of the collection; volumes on the later Georgian, early Italian and Dutch pictures are in preparation.

[1] I am very grateful to Mrs Frances Vivian for bringing this reference to my notice.

JOHANNES VERMEER

THE MUSIC LESSON: A LADY AT THE VIRGINALS WITH A GENTLEMAN LISTENING

Purchased by George III with the collection of Consul Smith. It has recently been suggested that it is the picture 'con Donna alla Spineta' which was in the collection of Giovanni Antonio Pellegrini at the time of his death in 1741, may have been acquired when he was working in The Hague in 1718, and was subsequently bought by Smith.[1] At the time of its acquisition by George III, the painting was stated to be by Frans van Mieris, perhaps because the monogram *I. V. Meer* (on the frame of the picture within the painting) was read as being his. The picture is generally dated *c.* 1660. No really satisfactory explanation of the iconography of the painting has been put forward. The Latin inscription on the lid of the virginals reads: MVSICA LAETITIAE [COMES or CONSORS]/MEDECINA [DOLORIS or DOLORUM]: 'Music is a companion in pleasure, a remedy in sorrow'.[2]

Canvas: 29 by 25¼ in. *Signed.*

ANTONIO VISENTINI and FRANCESCO ZUCCARELLI

THE HOUSE OF GENERAL WADE

One of the eight surviving pictures by these two painters from the collection of Consul Smith. They represent famous English buildings in the Palladian style, painted by Visentini, in fancy settings and peopled by imaginary figures, both settings and figures being by Zuccarelli. In this example, Visentini, as on other occasions, used Colin Campbell's *Vitruvius Britannicus* for the architectural part of the design. General Wade's house was in Old Burlington Street and survived until 1935.[3]

Canvas: 31⅝ by 51⅜ in. *Signed by both artists and dated* 1746.

RVDOLFVS·VNGARIÆ·PRINCEPS·
ANNO·ÆTATIS·SVÆ· XVI

ALONSO SANCHEZ COELLO

THE ARCHDUKE RUDOLF

Bought by Queen Victoria at the sale of King Louis Philippe's pictures at Christie's, 14 May 1853 (302a). The Archduke was the eldest son of the Emperor Maximilian II, whom he succeeded in 1576; he reigned until 1612. He formed a vast and celebrated collection of pictures and works of art in his palace on the Hradshin in Prague. Among painters, he particularly admired Dürer and the elder Bruegel.

Canvas: 38¾ by 31½ in. *Signed and dated as painted in Madrid in 1567 and inscribed with the sitter's age, sixteen.*

FRANS HALS

PORTRAIT OF A MAN

Recorded in the time of George III, hanging in the Passage Room at Buckingham House. The earlier history of the portrait is not known, and it is conceivable that it had been acquired by Frederick, Prince of Wales.

The portrait is a good example of the simplicity of design and restrained tonality which Hals's portraits acquire in the 1630's.[4]

Canvas: $45\frac{3}{4}$ by $35\frac{1}{2}$ in. *Inscribed with the sitter's age, thirty-six, and dated* 1630.

247

IMP·CAES·FL·CONSTANTINO·MAXIMO
P·F·AVGVSTO·S·P·Q·R·
QVOD·INSTINCTV·DIVINITATIS·MENTIS
MAGNITVDINE·CVM·EXERCITV·SVO
TAM·DE·TIRANNO·QVAM·DE·OMNI·EIVS
FACTIONE·VNO·TEMPORE·IVSTIS
REMPVBLICAM·VLTVS·EST·ARMIS
ARCVM·TRIVMPHIS·INSIGNEM·DICAVIT

VOTIS·X·   VOTIS·XX·

ANT·CANAL·FECIT
ANNO·MDCCXLII·

GIOVANNI ANTONIO CANAL,
called CANALETTO

THE ARCH OF CONSTANTINE

Bought by George III with the collection of Consul Smith. It is one of a set of five large views of Rome by Canaletto, all signed and dated in the same year. There is apparently little evidence that Canaletto was himself in Rome around 1740; but it is possible that Bellotto had recently visited Rome and that Canaletto was stimulated by work which the younger man had brought back with him to Venice.[5]

Canvas: 72½ by 41½ in. *Signed and dated* 1742.

THE PIAZZA S. MARCO WITH S. GEMINIANO

One of a pair of views of the Piazza which, with the four upright pictures of Windsor, constitute a series of early works by Canaletto, *c.* 1727–9, magnificently free in handling and revelling in the play of light, shade and cloud. The view is towards the (now destroyed) church of S. Geminiano, with the base of the Campanile in the left foreground.[6]

Canvas: 53 by 67¾ in.

SIR ANTHONY VAN DYCK

CHARLES I ON HORSEBACK

Painted for Charles I to hang at the end of the Gallery at St James's. The King, in full armour and holding a baton, is seen riding towards the spectator, through an arch which must have served to open in the imagination the walls of the Gallery. The King is accompanied by the Seigneur de St Antoine, a riding-master and equerry, who had been sent over to England in 1603 by Henry IV of France with a present of horses for the Prince of Wales.

The painting, in its original position, clearly made a great impression on those who were confronted with it.

Canvas: 145 by 106¼ in.
Dated 1633.

THE FAMILY OF CHARLES I

Painted by Van Dyck soon after his arrival in London in 1632; on 8 August 1632 a warrant was issued for the payment to him of £100 for 'One greate peece of oᵣ royall selfe, Consort and children'. The King is shown with his wife, Henrietta Maria, who holds the infant Princess Mary, later Princess of Orange. At the King's knee stands the little Prince of Wales, the future Charles II.

The picture was first placed in the King's Long Gallery 'towards the Orchard' at Whitehall; beyond the royal group and the regalia is a view of the Thames and Westminster.[7]

Canvas: 146 by 108 in. (The original canvas was 117½ by 98 in; this area alone is reproduced; the remainder was probably added in the time of William III.)

JEAN-BAPTISTE VANLOO

FREDERICK, PRINCE OF WALES

The portrait shows the Prince in robes of state beside a table on which rests his coronet; it is a pendant to the portrait of the Princess.[8]

Canvas: 94½ by 61½ in. *Signed and dated* 1742.

AUGUSTA, PRINCESS OF WALES

The portrait of the Princess, the mother of George III, in a magnificently laced dress under robes of state, is a pendant to the portrait of the Prince of Wales in state robes.

The portraits are probably those recorded by Vertue in his note on Vanloo's departure from London on 16 October 1742: 'this last year having not begun any new works only imploy'd his time to finish those begun, particularly the Prince of Wales & princess done for Poultney, Earl of Bath – at whole, in their robes. finely drest'. The pair of portraits was bought by George IV in 1809. In these portraits Vanloo enlivens the tradition of the state portrait in a French manner that anticipates Ramsay's state portraits of George III and Queen Charlotte.[9]

Canvas: 94¼ by 61½ in. *Signed and dated* 1742.

ALLAN RAMSAY

GEORGE III

The King wears Coronation robes; the crown rests on a table at his side. The portrait is almost certainly the prime original of the state portrait painted of the new King. Ramsay himself states that soon after the King's accession on 25 October 1760 he was commissioned to compose a full-length 'dressed in Coronation robes'. At the end of 1761 Ramsay seems to have been working on two versions of the portrait, 'while I have the Royal robes set upon my figure'.

Soon after the Queen's arrival in England she sat to Ramsay and, in his own words, 'these two are the originals from which all the copies ordered by the Lord Chamberlain are painted'.[10] A very large number of repetitions of the portraits was produced in Ramsay's studio, at £84 a time, for presentation to diplomatic representatives overseas, fellow-sovereigns, friends and official institutions.[11]

Canvas: 98 by 64 in.

QUEEN CHARLOTTE

The pendant to the portrait of George III, painted soon after the Queen's arrival in England; it shows her in robes of state, resting her left hand on her crown (perhaps her Nuptial Crown) beside two sceptres.

It is finer in quality than the pendant and is the only known version of the portrait in which the Queen's head is dressed and placed in this way. Horace Walpole recorded in March 1762 that 'Ramsay has done another whole length of the king . . . This has more air, and is painted exactly from the very robes which the king wore at his coronation. The gold stuff and ermine are highly finished; rather too much, for the head does not come out so much as it ought. He has drawn the queen too, but it is much flattered, and the hair vastly too light'.[12]

Canvas: 98 by 63½ in.

THOMAS GAINSBOROUGH

RICHARD HURD

Queen Charlotte owned two portraits of Bishop Hurd by Gainsborough; the other is at Windsor. This may have been the portrait exhibited at the Royal Academy in 1781 (39); both portraits were hung at Buckingham House, one in the Queen's Bedroom, the other in the Wardrobe. Richard Hurd (1720–1808), scholar and critic, was a favourite with the royal family. In 1781 he became Bishop of Worcester and Clerk of the Closet; in 1776 he had succeeded William Markham as Preceptor to the Prince of Wales; and in 1788 he received the royal family at Hartlebury Castle when they attended the Three Choirs Festival.[13]

Canvas: 29⅞ by 24¾ in.

NATHANIEL DANCE

EDWARD, DUKE OF YORK

The Duke, younger brother of George IV, is seen in Garter robes. The portrait was probably painted for the set of family portraits which George III planned to install in the Dining Room at Buckingham House. The portrait may have been begun in Rome in 1764. Horace Walpole quotes a press report of 1 April 1764 that Dance had 'painted lately' the Duke of York in Rome.[14]

Canvas: 94¾ by 58½ in.

FRANCIS COTES

PRINCESS LOUISA ANN AND PRINCESS CAROLINE MATILDA

The Princesses were daughters of Frederick, Prince of Wales. Princess Louisa Ann is seated at a music-stand, holding a gittern or English guitar: her sister stands beside her, in front of an organ.
Probably painted for Augusta, Princess of Wales, mother of the two girls; her disbursements in the six months ending 1 April 1768 apparently included payment for a frame for the picture. By 1841 it had been hung in the Green Drawing Room at Buckingham Palace.[15]

Canvas: 104⅝ by 73½ in. *Signed and dated* 1767.

THOMAS GAINSBOROUGH

HENRY FREDERICK, DUKE OF CUMBERLAND

The Duke was a younger brother of George III, who deeply disapproved of his marriage in 1771 to the beautiful Anne Luttrell, widow of Christopher Horton. The Duke wears robes of state and carries his coronet.

The Cumberlands sat to Gainsborough on a number of occasions. The two full-lengths were shown at the Royal Academy in 1777 (131, 132). They were left by the Duchess to William IV and are first recorded in the State Dining Room at Buckingham Palace in the printed catalogue of 1841 (208, 209).[16]

Canvas: $94\frac{1}{4}$ by $56\frac{1}{4}$ in.

ANNE, DUCHESS OF CUMBERLAND

The companion portrait, showing the Duchess in her robes with her coronet on a ledge beside her. When the two portraits were cleaned in 1959, it became clear that in the course of painting the portraits Gainsborough had made considerable alterations, principally to the fall of the Duchess's draperies and to the background behind the Duke, of which part, at least, was at first going to be a landscape.

Canvas: 95 by 52 in.

BENJAMIN WEST

PRINCE ADOLPHUS,
LATER DUKE OF CAMBRIDGE,
WITH PRINCESS MARY
AND PRINCESS SOPHIA

One of the set of full-length portraits, painted by West for George III and Queen Charlotte in 1776–9, of the King, Queen and all their children. They seem to have been placed at first in the King's Closet at St James's. The background in this group is Kew Gardens with the Pagoda built by Sir William Chambers for the children's grandmother, Augusta, Princess of Wales. *Canvas: 95½ by 59½ in. Signed and dated 1778.*

SIR JOSHUA REYNOLDS

FREDERICK, DUKE OF YORK

The Duke is wearing Garter robes and stands against a Veronese-like backcloth. He sat to Reynolds in 1787 and 1788 and the portrait was exhibited at the Royal Academy in 1788 (88). It is not certain that it was painted for the Duke's elder brother, the Prince of Wales, but by 1813 it was in his possession and in 1816 we know that it was hanging with other family portraits in the Old Throne Room at Carlton House.

Canvas: $94\frac{1}{2}$ by $57\frac{3}{4}$ in.

THE DEATH OF DIDO

Exhibited at the Royal Academy in 1781 (160). Reynolds bequeathed the picture to his niece, the Marchioness of Thomond. At her sale, on 19 May 1821 (72), it was bought by George IV. The figure of Dido is based closely on a passage by Giulio Romano in his ceiling decorations in the Palazzo del Tè at Mantua.[17]

Canvas: $58\frac{1}{2}$ by $94\frac{1}{4}$ in.

EDWARD BIRD

THE VILLAGE CHORISTERS

A group of choristers and musicians rehearsing for the services on the following day. The picture was exhibited at the Royal Academy in 1810 (100). Later in the year it was bought by West for George IV 'who seemed much disposed to make a Collection of the works of British Artists'. Wilkie's *Blind-Man's-Buff* was later painted as companion to the *Village Choristers*, but the Regent – characteristically – did not pursue this project very assiduously.[18]

Canvas: 25 by 36½ in. Signed and dated 1810.

SIR DAVID WILKIE

THE PENNY WEDDING

When it was exhibited in the Royal Academy in 1819 (153), the scene was described as a marriage festival of a kind once common in Scotland. Each guest paid a contribution towards the cost of the feast and what money was left over was given to the newly-married couple to help in setting up house.

Wilkie had earlier painted *Blind-Man's-Buff* for George IV who was so pleased with it that he commissioned a companion piece. On 14 November 1818 Wilkie reported that the picture was ready for delivery to Carlton House; on 10 February 1820 Wilkie was paid £525 for it. There are preparatory drawings in the Royal Library, British Museum and the National Gallery of Scotland.[19]

Panel: 25⅜ by 37⅝ in. Signed and dated 1818.

WILLIAM MULREADY

THE WOLF AND THE LAMB

Exhibited at the Royal Academy in 1820 (106); later in the year it was bought by George IV for £210. £1000 was raised by Mulready for the Artists' Fund from Robinson's engraving of the picture.

Panel: 23⅝ by 20⅛ in. The panel is apparently signed, very obscurely, on a label attached to the gatepost on the right.

SIR DAVID WILKIE

'I PIFFERARI'

On 27 April 1827 Wilkie wrote to his brother from Rome that, after a long illness, he had taken up painting again and completed two small pictures. One of them was *I Pifferari*; and after Wilkie's return to England in 1828 it was sold to the King with a companion picture which Wilkie had painted in Geneva. Wilkie was paid £420 for the two pictures.

Both pictures were inspired by the gatherings of pilgrims in the streets of Rome for Holy Week in the Holy Year, 1825. *I Pifferari* illustrates a passage in one of Wilkie's letters to his brother: 'Each party of pilgrims is accompanied by one whose duty it is to give music to the rest . . . a piper or pifferaro . . . another man plays on a smaller reed . . . In parading the streets they stop before the image of the Virgin, whom they serenade . . . in imitation of the shepherds of old, who announced the birth of the Messiah.'[20]

Canvas: 18⅛ by 14¼ in. *Signed and dated* 1827.

THE DEFENCE OF SARAGOSSA

One of the three paintings, inspired by the heroism of the Spanish resistance movement, painted by Wilkie in Madrid between October 1827 and May 1828. After Wilkie's return to London, the King bespoke them for his collection; they were submitted to the King in February 1829 and on 18 March 1829 Wilkie signed a receipt for 2000 guineas for the three pictures.

The *Defence of Saragossa* commemorates a famous moment in the siege of the town by the French in the summer of 1808. On 2 July a French attack had nearly overrun the Portillo Gate, when Agostina Zaragoza, the 'Maid of Saragossa', seized a lighted match from her dying husband and fired a gun at point-blank range into the advancing French column. Her heroism was celebrated by Byron in the first canto of *Childe Harold's Pilgrimage*, stanzas 54–59. *Canvas*: 37 by 55½ in. *Signed and dated* 1828.

PIETER DE HOOCH

A COURTYARD IN DELFT

Bought for George IV at T. Emmerson's sale at Christie's, 2 May 1829 (152). Probably painted *c.* 1656. In the background are the towers of the Town Hall and the Nieuwe Kerk at Delft.[21]

Canvas: $27\frac{1}{4}$ by $21\frac{1}{4}$ in. *Signed.*

PIETER DE HOOCH

THE CARD-PLAYERS

Bought by George IV from John Smith in April 1825 for £700. One of the latest, and finest, of George IV's purchases and a superb example of De Hooch's style at its finest period.[22]

Canvas: 30 by 26 in. *Signed and dated* 1658.

GERARD TER BORCH

THE LETTER

Bought by George IV with the Baring collection in 1814; placed in the Dining Room at Carlton House. It is generally dated just after 1660.[23]

Canvas: $32\frac{1}{4}$ by $26\frac{3}{4}$ in. Perhaps faintly signed on the letter.

GABRIEL METSU

PORTRAIT OF THE ARTIST

Bought by George IV with the Baring collection in 1814. Probably painted *c.* 1660. The artist is seen apparently sketching at a window; under a box on the window-ledge is a print after the *Flagellation* by Gerard Seghers.

Panel: 15 by 12½ in. *Signed.*

GERARD DOU

A GIRL CHOPPING ONIONS

Bought by George IV with the Baring collection in 1814. It was hung in the room next to the Dining Room at Carlton House.[24]

Panel: 8¼ by 6½ in. *Signed and dated* 1646.

267

JAN STEEN

THE VIOLIN-PLAYER

Bought by George IV in 1818 for £170 from Joseph Waring; in 1819 it is recorded in the Dining Room at Carlton House.

Canvas: 32½ by 27½ in. *Signed.*

THE MORNING TOILET

Bought by George IV from Delahante in 1821; first recorded in a sale in Amsterdam in 1764.

It has been plausibly suggested that the lute, the book of music and the skull over which a vine is creeping, symbolise, as they lie on the sunlit threshold, the joy and sadness that the new day may bring; and that these earthly elements are to be compared with the cherub in the carving above. It is probable that a picture in the Rijksmuseum (2250–A6) is a study by Steen for the *Morning Toilet;* it shows the girl dressing in very much the same attitude, without the elaborate still life on the table; but there is no architectural framework in the foreground.[25]

Panel: 25½ by 20¾ in. *Signed and dated* 1663.

Steen

1663

ADRIAEN VAN OSTADE

THE INTERIOR OF A PEASANT'S COTTAGE

Bought by Lord Yarmouth for George IV at Lafontaine's sale at Christie's, 12 June 1811 (59); it was placed in the Bow Room on the principal floor at Carlton House.

Panel: 19⅜ by 16¼ in. Signed and dated 1668.

ISACK
VAN OSTADE

THE FIDDLER

Bought by George IV, recorded
at Carlton House in 1816 and
probably one of his earliest purchases.

Panel: 15½ by 13 in. *Signed and
dated* 1646.

ADRIAEN
VAN OSTADE

A DUTCH COURTSHIP

Bought by George IV with the
Baring collection in 1814.

Panel: 9¼ by 7¾ in. *Signed.*

ADRIAEN VAN DE VELDE

THE COAST OF SCHEVENINGEN

Bought by George IV with the Baring collection in 1814. It was placed in the room next to the Dining Room at Carlton House.

Canvas: 15¼ by 19½ in. Signed and dated 1660.

THE HAWKING PARTY

Bought by Lord Yarmouth for George IV at Lord Rendlesham's sale at Christie's, 28 May 1810 (32); recorded in 1816 in the Bow Room on the principal floor at Carlton House.

Panel: 19½ by 16¼ in. Signed and dated 1666.

PHILIPS WOUVERMAN

SKIRMISH BETWEEN CAVALRY AND PEASANTS

Bought by George IV.

Canvas: 32¼ by 46¼ in. Signed.

JAN VAN DER HEYDEN

THE APPROACH TO THE TOWN OF VEERE

Almost certainly bought by George IV from William Harris on 7 February 1811. With another equally beautiful picture by the same painter, it hung in the Little Blue Room at Carlton House.

Panel: 18 by 22 in. *Signed.*

WILLEM VAN DE VELDE THE YOUNGER

A CALM

Bought by George IV from the Baring collection in 1814. Placed in the Dining Room at Carlton House.

Canvas: $24\frac{1}{4}$ by 28 in. *Signed and dated* 1659.

A NAVAL ENGAGEMENT

Perhaps the finest of the pictures of 'Eleven sea fights' which were painted by the two Van de Veldes, father and son, for James II, when he was Duke of York. In his reign they hung at Whitehall.

Canvas: 49 by 70 in. *Signed and dated* 1677.

CORNELIS VAN POELENBURGH

LANDSCAPE WITH SHEPHERDS AND THEIR FLOCKS AMONG RUINS

Bought by George IV with the Baring collection in 1814. The picture belongs to a group of landscapes which were painted *c.* 1620, soon after the artist's arrival in Rome; other pictures of this type are in the Louvre, the Pitti and the Toledo Museum of Art.[26]

Copper: 12½ by 15¾ in. *Signed.*

KAREL DU JARDIN

A LOCANDA IN AN ITALIAN TOWN

Bought by Lord Yarmouth for George IV at Philip Hill's sale at Christie's, 26 January 1811 for 89 guineas; at the time of its purchase, and thereafter at Carlton House, the picture was attributed to Lingelbach or Jan Miel. Probably painted *c.* 1655; it has been suggested that the Spanish dress of the lady and gentleman behind indicate the district of Naples.[27]

Canvas: 25 by 28½ in. *Signed.*

JAN BOTH

LANDSCAPE WITH ST PHILIP BAPTISING THE EUNUCH

Bought by George IV at Lafontaine's sale at Christie's, 12 June 1811 (57), and placed in the Audience Room at Carlton House.[28]

Canvas: 50½ by 63 in. *Signed.*

AELBERT CUYP

AN EVENING LANDSCAPE

Bought by George IV with the Baring collection in 1814; placed in the Bow Room on the principal floor at Carlton House.

Canvas: 40 by 60½ in. *Signed.*

THE NEGRO PAGE

Bought for George IV at Lord Rendlesham's sale at Christie's, 20 June 1806 (56); placed in the Bow Room on the state floor at Carlton House. Probably painted *c.* 1650. The grey horse reappears, in almost the same position, in a smaller landscape with riders by Cuyp in the royal collection.

Canvas: 56¼ by 89¼ in.

JACOB VAN RUISDAEL

AN EVENING LANDSCAPE

Bought for George IV by Lord Yarmouth at the Walsh Porter sale at Christie's, 14 April 1810 (8); it was placed in the Little Blue Room at Carlton House. It was probably painted *c.* 1660.[29]

Canvas: 29¾ by 39¾ in. *Signed.*

AELBERT CUYP

THE PASSAGE BOAT

Probably bought by George IV with the Baring collection in 1814. It was placed by the King in the room next to the Dining Room at Carlton House.

Canvas: 49 by $56\frac{3}{4}$ in. *Signed.*

CLAES BERCHEM

LANDSCAPE WITH SHEPHERDS AND THEIR FLOCKS CROSSING A FORD

Bought by George IV with the Baring collection in 1814 and hung in the Colonnade Room at Carlton House.

Canvas: $27\frac{1}{4}$ by 36 in. *Signed and dated 1675.*

ITALIAN LANDSCAPE WITH A WOMAN ON HORSEBACK

Bought by George IV with the Baring collection in 1814 and placed in the room next to the Dining Room at Carlton House.[30]

Panel: 13 by $17\frac{1}{4}$ in. *Signed and dated 1655 ; the last digit is not entirely clear.*

MEINDERT HOBBEMA

A LANE THROUGH A WOOD

Bought by George IV with the Baring collection in 1814.

Panel: 24 by 43¾ in. *Signed and dated* 1668.

REMBRANDT

THE SHIP-BUILDER AND HIS WIFE

Bought by George IV at the Lafontaine sale at Christie's, 12 June 1811 (63); placed in the Audience Room at Carlton House. An etching after the picture by J. de Frey (1800) indicates that a strip of canvas, some 9 in. deep, has been cut off the top of the canvas; a mezzotint made in 1802 by C. Hodges, however, shows the picture approximately in its present shape.[31]

Canvas: 45 by 66½ in. *Signed and dated* 1633.

REMBRANDT

NOLI ME TANGERE:
CHRIST AND MARY
MAGDALENE AT THE TOMB

Acquired in 1819 from the dealer Lafontaine by George IV, who, in exchange, gave Lafontaine two *Calms* by Van de Velde, an *Alchymist* by Teniers, and a picture of Herodias with the Baptist's head which in 1816 had been attributed to Matsys.
On the back of the panel is a paper with a poem on the picture by Rembrandt's friend Jeremias de Decker.[32]

Panel: 24 by 19½ in. *Signed and dated* 1638.

REMBRANDT

THE LADY WITH A FAN

Bought for George IV at Lord Charles Townshend's sale at Christie's, 4 June 1819 (32). The sitter has been recently identified with Agatha Bas (1611–58); the companion portrait of her husband is in Brussels.

Canvas: 41½ by 33 in. *Signed and dated* 1641.

THE CARD–PLAYERS

Bought by George IV with the Baring collection in 1814; the King placed it in the Bow Room on the principal floor at Carlton House.

Panel: 9½ by 13½ in. *Signed.*

THE DRUMMER

Bought by George IV at the Walsh Porter sale at Christie's, 23 March 1803 (45), for £294; it was one of the first fine Dutch or Flemish pictures to be bought by the King when he was Prince of Wales.

Copper: 19⅝ by 25⅝ in. *Signed and dated* 1647.

DAVID TENIERS THE YOUNGER

THE INTERIOR OF A GARDENER'S HOUSE

Bought by George IV with the Baring collection in 1814.

Panel: 20 by 28 in. *Signed.*

THE DANCE IN THE GROUNDS OF A MANSION

Bought by George IV with the Baring collection in 1814. A group of peasants is dancing in the grounds of a country house; the owner and his family stand, rather detached from the festivities, on the left. There is a tradition that the panel once formed the lid of a harpsichord.

Panel: 32⅝ by 49¾ in. *Signed and dated* 1645.

SIR PETER PAUL RUBENS

THE FARM AT LAEKEN

Bought by George IV from the dealer Delahante in 1821. It appears to have belonged originally to the Lunden family in Antwerp, a family which was related to Rubens.

It is generally regarded as painted *c.* 1618 and as the earliest of the three landscapes of this type by Rubens. The comparable landscapes in Munich and Berlin are generally dated, respectively, *c.* 1620 and later; in all three pictures Rubens introduced the girl milking a cow, for which there is a preparatory drawing in the Musée des Beaux-Arts at Besançon,[33] and a preparatory drawing for the bullock in the middle of *The Farm at Laeken* is in Vienna;[34] the two figures in the foreground are reminiscent of two peasant women in the *Adoration of the Shepherds* in Marseilles, painted by Rubens *c.* 1617–18.[35]

Panel: 33¼ by 49½ in.

SIR PETER PAUL RUBENS

THE ASSUMPTION OF THE VIRGIN

Bought by Lord Yarmouth for George IV at the sale of Henry Hope's pictures at Christie's, 29 June 1816 (85); placed in the Bow Room on the ground floor at Carlton House. A finished *modello*, probably painted *c.* 1611, not long after Rubens's return to Antwerp from Italy. There is a *pentimento*, on the slab of the tomb, of the right hand of the kneeling Apostle in the foreground. No altarpiece of the Assumption by Rubens survives in which the subject is treated in precisely this way. The upper part of the *modello* was used by Rubens for an altarpiece, now in Vienna, for the Jesuit Church in Antwerp; the lower part is close to this area in the altarpiece in Brussels, painted *c.* 1615–16 for the high altar of the Carmelite church in Brussels. A drawing in Vienna has affinities with the *modello*.[36] The cloud of *putti* in the *modello* are very closely based on Pordenone's fresco (now destroyed) of God the Father in the Duomo at Treviso.[37]

Panel: 40¼ by 26 in.

JEAN-BAPTISTE GREUZE

SILENCE!

Purchased for George IV by Lord Yarmouth in Paris in 1817. It arrived at Carlton House on 9 January 1818, with other purchases from France.

Canvas: 24¾ by 20 in.

SIR PETER PAUL RUBENS

LANDSCAPE WITH ST GEORGE AND THE DRAGON

Painted during Rubens's visit to London, 1629–30, on a diplomatic mission to Charles I. The painter 'in honour of England & of our nation from whom he hath received so many courtesies, hath drawn with his pensill the History of St. George; wherin, if it be possible, he hath exceeded himself: but the picture he has sent home into Flanders, To remain as a monument of his abode & employment here'. It is possible that Charles I managed ultimately to secure the picture for his collection. In his catalogue is an entry, among pictures temporarily in store at Whitehall, for 'The great St George', containing an unspecified number of figures, 'Done by S[t]. Peet[r]. Paule Rubins'. It had been bought by the King from Endymion Porter and had been hanging in the King's Breakfast Chamber.[38]

The picture was thereafter in the collections of the Duc de Richelieu and the Duc d'Orléans. It was among the pictures sold from the Orléans collection and was ultimately bought by George IV in 1814 from the dealer Harris, who received four Dutch pictures in lieu of part of the purchase money. The picture was hung in the Crimson Drawing Room at Carlton House, was briefly at Windsor, but was hanging in the Picture Gallery at Buckingham Palace by 1841.

The parts of St George and the captive princess are traditionally said to be played by Charles I and Henrietta Maria; the design should be seen to some extent as a tribute to the King's interest in the Order of the Garter and its patron Saint, St George. The landscape is a *ricordo* by Rubens of the Thames Valley and of such buildings as Lambeth Palace and the church of St Mary Overy which he would have been able to see from his lodgings in York House.[39] X-ray, and comparison with a preparatory drawing in the Nationalmuseum, Stockholm,[40] reveal that Rubens, as on many other occasions, conceived the composition on a smaller scale and enlarged it in painting as his ideas flowered in his mind. Another drawing for the composition is in Berlin. It is possible that the decision to insert the King in the role of St George came fairly late in the development of the design.

Canvas: $59\frac{1}{2}$ by $78\frac{1}{2}$ in.

CLAUDE GELLEE,
called LE LORRAIN

THE RAPE OF EUROPA

One of the last pictures bought by George IV, for £2100 at Lord Gwydir's sale at Christie's, 9 May 1829 (81). Claude had been interested in the theme of Europa since at least 1634. Other versions of the painting, all closely alike, are known: one was painted in 1655 for Pope Alexander VII, and another in 1658 for Courtois; a drawing by Claude, dated 1670 (British Museum), is closely related to the Queen's picture.[41]

Canvas: 40 by 53 in. *Signed and dated* 1667.

MATHIEU LE NAIN

THE YOUNG GAMBLERS

Bought by George IV at the Walsh Porter sale at Christie's, 23 March 1803 (48). It was at that time attributed to 'Caravaggio or Le Nain', but by 1816, when it was in Carlton House, it went under Le Nain's name. It is now thought to be an early work of Mathieu, probably *c*. 1640, painted while he was still under the influence of his brothers Antoine and Louis. A version, with additional figures, is in the Louvre.

Canvas: 21½ by 25 in.

JOHN RUSSELL

GEORGE IV WHEN PRINCE OF WALES

Purchased by King Edward VII from Lord Colebrook in 1908. The Prince is seen in the green uniform of the Royal Kentish Bowmen; his buttons are decorated with the Prince of Wales's feathers and the initials R.K.B. In the background are archers shooting. The portrait is inscribed as painted in 1791; the head, however, is very close in type to a drawing and a pastel of the Prince, both inscribed with the date 1794. Bartolozzi's engraving of the design was published in 1795 with a dedication to the Bowmen.

Canvas: 102½ by 71 in.

RICHARD WESTALL

QUEEN VICTORIA AS A GIRL

The Princess is seen at the age of eleven; she is sketching out of doors, accompanied by her little terrier Fanny. The portrait was painted for her mother, the Duchess of Kent, and bequeathed to her in 1861. A preliminary study, dated 1829, is at Windsor. The portrait was shown at the Royal Academy in 1830 (64).[42]

Canvas: 57 by 44¾ in. *Signed and dated* 1830.

GEORGE SANDERS

GEORGE GORDON, 6TH LORD BYRON

The portrait was painted *c.* 1809 and probably commemorates a visit to the Highlands in 1807. Byron appears to have given the portrait to his mother: he wrote to her on 1 July 1810, 'I am glad you have received my portrait from Sandars. It does not *flatter* me, I think, but the subject is a bad one'.

The portrait eventually passed to Byron's devoted friend, John Cam Hobhouse, whose daughter, Lady Dorchester, bequeathed it to King George V in 1914.[44]

Canvas: 42½ by 35 in.

GEORGE FREDERICK WATTS

MARY, LADY HOLLAND

Lady Mary Coventry married the 4th Lord Holland in 1833. Her husband was British Minister in Florence during Watts's first visit to Italy and the portrait was painted at the Casa Feroni, where Watts was guest of the Hollands, soon after his arrival in 1843. It was exhibited at the Royal Academy in 1848 (307) and bequeathed by Lady Holland (d. 1889) to the Prince of Wales.[43]

Canvas: 31¾ by 25 in.

GEORGE STUBBS

FINO AND TINY

Painted for George IV. The two dogs are a small spaniel and a Pomeranian. They presumably belonged to George IV, as the larger dog appears in at least one other picture painted for him by Stubbs.

Canvas: 39½ by 49½ in. *Signed and dated* 1791.

WILLIAM CLARKSON STANFIELD

ST MICHAEL'S MOUNT

The Royal Yacht *Victoria and Albert* is seen steaming past St Michael's Mount, surrounded by a crowd of small vessels, during the voyage in early September 1846. The picture was given by the Queen to the Prince Consort at Christmas in the same year.

Panel: 12 by 18 in.

JOHN MARTIN

THE EVE OF THE DELUGE

Purchased by the Prince Consort from the artist, for £350, on 10 August 1841. It was at one period hanging in the Prince's Dressing-room at Buckingham Palace.

Canvas: 56½ by 85½ in. *Signed and dated* 1840.

DANIEL MACLISE

A SCENE FROM THE BURLETTA OF MIDAS

Exhibited at the Royal Academy in 1839 (6); it had been bought by Queen Victoria in 1838 and was placed in the Dining Room at Osborne.

The *Burletta,* by Kane O'Hara, had been first produced in 1762. In Maclise's picture Sileno is introducing Apollo disguised as a shepherd–'a strolling thrummer; What art thou good for?–speak, though ragged mummer'–to his wife and daughters.

Canvas: 40½ by 50½ in. Signed and dated 1838.

WILLIAM POWELL FRITH

RAMSGATE SANDS

The composition was based on studies made during Frith's summer holiday at Ramsgate in 1851. 'Weary of costume-painting I had determined to try my hand on modern life, with all its drawbacks of unpicturesque dress. The variety of character on Ramsgate Sands attracted me'. In September 1851 he made many sketches on the beach. In October and November he was at work on a careful oil sketch of the design. On 9 April 1852 he began work on the large picture. In the summer of 1853 Frith was back at Ramsgate, painting the background of the picture. It was finished early in 1854 and bought by Lloyd, a picture-dealer. It was shown at the Royal Academy in 1854 (157: 'Life at the sea-side') and acquired from Lloyd by Queen Victoria, who was 'delighted' with the picture when she saw it at the Academy.[45]

Canvas: 30 by $60\frac{1}{4}$ in.

SIR EDWIN LANDSEER

QUEEN VICTORIA AND PRINCE ALBERT

The Queen and her husband are shown in the costumes they wore, as Queen Philippa and Edward III, at their *'bal costumé'* at Buckingham Palace on 12 May 1842. Her courtiers were also to be dressed in correct medieval costume. Landseer was at work on the picture in the same month; on 18 May, for instance, he made sketches of the Queen and Prince in their costumes. The painting was placed in the Queen's Drawing Room at Osborne.[46]

Canvas: 55¼ by 42¾ in.

VAN AMBURGH AND HIS ANIMALS

Bought from the artist by Queen Victoria in 1839; she hung it in the Horn Room at Osborne. It had been shown at the Royal Academy in 1839 (351). Van Amburgh, a celebrated tamer of wild beasts, performed regularly at Drury Lane and Astley's in the 1830's and 1840's.

Canvas: 44¾ by 68¾ in.

FOUR PETS OF QUEEN VICTORIA

The three dogs, Hector, Nero and the little spaniel Dash, are seen with the parrot Lorey. The picture was painted for Queen Victoria in 1838 and shown at the Royal Academy in that year (213). It was placed in the Queen's Drawing Room at Osborne.

Canvas: 47½ by 59⅛ in.

FRANS XAVER WINTERHALTER

PRINCE ARTHUR, DUKE OF CONNAUGHT

Painted for Queen Victoria and given by her to the Prince Consort as a birthday present on 26 August 1851.

Canvas: 29 by 34½ in. Signed and dated 1851.

THE COUSINS: QUEEN VICTORIA AND
PRINCESS VICTOIRE, DUCHESSE DE NEMOURS

Princess Victoire was the daughter of Prince Ferdinand of Saxe-Coburg; she was Queen Victoria's 'much-beloved Vecto'. The group of the two cousins was given by the Queen to the Prince Consort on his birthday, 26 August 1852.[47]

Canvas: 28¼ by 20 in. Signed and dated 1852.

FRANS XAVER WINTERHALTER

THE ROYAL FAMILY IN 1846

Perhaps Winterhalter's most important picture for the Queen and the Prince Consort; he was paid £1000 for it. It was painted to hang in the Dining Room at Osborne; in 1901 it was brought up to Buckingham Palace by Edward VII.

The Queen has her arm around the Prince of Wales; Prince Alfred advances towards his sisters, Victoria, Princess Royal, Princess Alice, and the infant Princess Helena, who had been born on 25 June 1846. The group is almost the last completely successful royal group on a grand scale: perhaps, indeed, the last convincing work in the tradition established by court painters at the Tudor court and by Van Dyck in his 'Great Piece' of 1632. *Canvas: 98¼ by 124½ in. Signed and dated 1846.*

JOHN PHILLIP

THE MARRIAGE OF THE PRINCESS ROYAL

The marriage of Victoria, Princess Royal, Queen Victoria's eldest child, to Crown Prince Frederick William of Prussia, took place in the Chapel Royal, St James's Palace, on 25 January 1858. On the morning of the ceremony a daguerreotype was taken of the bride in her wedding dress, and with her parents; the Queen also commissioned Phillip to paint a picture of the wedding. By the beginning of 1859 she was very pleased with the progress of the picture, which was finally shown at the Royal Academy in 1860 (58), when the Queen thought it of all the pictures on show, 'out & out the best & quite resplendent'. The Queen also owned Phillip's study for the head of the Prince Consort, who stands behind his family with his uncle, Leopold I of Belgium, beside him.

Canvas: $40\frac{1}{8}$ by $71\frac{3}{4}$ in. *Signed and dated* 1860.

THE PAINTINGS
CAPTION NOTES

1 F. Vivian, 'Joseph Smith and Giovanni Antonio Pellegrini', *Burlington Magazine*, Vol. CIV (1962), pp.330–33.

2 R.A., *The King's Pictures*, 1946–47 (305); Mauritshuis, *Masterpieces of the Dutch School*, 1948 (10); in recent literature, see especially L. Gowing's *Vermeer* (1952), pp.119–27, and Chapter VI of A. Berendsen's *Verborgenheden uit het oude Delft* (1962).

3 Levey, *The Later Italian Pictures in the Collection of Her Majesty the Queen* (1964), No. 670.

4 Frans Halsmuseum, Haarlem, *Frans Hals*, 1962 (26).

5 Levey, *op. cit.*, No. 370.

6 Levey, *op. cit.*, No. 379.

7 Millar, *The Tudor, Stuart and Early Georgian Pictures* (1963), No. 150.

8 Millar, *op. cit.*, No. 536.

9 Millar, *op. cit.*, No. 537.

10 R. W. Goulding, *Catalogue of the Pictures . . . at Welbeck Abbey . . .* (1936), pp.470–72; letter in the Bute MSS.

11 David Martin and Philip Reinagle were the two assistants who worked on these copies for Ramsay.

12 *Anecdotes*, Vol. V, p.56.

13 Millar, *op. cit.*, No. 801.

14 *Anecdotes*, Vol. V, p.29; Millar, *op. cit.*, No. 701.

15 Millar, *op. cit.*, No. 719.

16 See W. T. Whitley, *Thomas Gainsborough* (1915), pp.142–43; E. K. Waterhouse, 'Preliminary Check List of Portraits by Thomas Gainsborough', *Walpole Society*, Vol. XXXIII (1953), pp.25–26.

17 E. Wind, '"Borrowed Attitudes" in Reynolds and Hogarth', *Journal of the Warburg Institute*, Vol. II (1938–39), pp.182–83.

18 *The Farington Diary*, ed. J. Greig, Vol. VI (1926), p.89.

19 Millar, *op. cit.*, No. 1176.

20 *See* Cunningham, *Wilkie*, Vol. II, pp.414, 454; Vol. III, pp.3, 4, 15–16, 527.

21 R.A., *The King's Pictures*, 1946–47 (347); Mauritshuis, *Masterpieces of the Dutch School*, 1948 (2).

22 R.A., *The King's Pictures*, 1946–47 (307); Mauritshuis, *Masterpieces of the Dutch School*, 1948 (3).

23 S. J. Gudlaugsson, *Gerard Ter Borch* (The Hague, 1959), pp.126–28, pl. 169; *Katalog . . .* (The Hague, 1960), pp.174–75.

24 R.A., *The King's Pictures*, 1946–47 (343).

25 The most recent account of the picture is in the exhibition catalogue, Mauritshuis, *Jan Steen*, 1958–59 (25).

26 Centraal Museum, Utrecht, *Nederlandse 17ᵉ Eeuwse Italianiserende Landschapschilders*, 1965 (12).

27 R.A., *The King's Pictures*, 1946–47 (299).

28 National Museum of Wales, Cardiff, *Ideal and Classical Landscape*, 1960 (11).

29 J. Rosenberg, *Jacob van Ruisdael* (Berlin, 1928), p.79.

30 Centraal Museum, Utrecht, *Nederlandse 17ᵉ Eeuwse Italianiserende Landschapschilders*, 1965 (77).

31 L. Münz, 'The Original Shape of Rembrandt's *Shipbuilder and his Wife*,' *Burlington Magazine*, Vol. LXXXIX (1947), pp.243–44; Mauritshuis, *Masterpieces of the Dutch School*, 1948 (5); J. Rosenberg, *Rembrandt* (Cambridge, Mass., 1948), Vol. I, p.65; Nationalmuseum, Stockholm, *Rembrandt*, 1956 (13).

32 Rijksmuseum and Museum Boymans, *Rembrandt*, 1956 (34).

33 J. S. Held, *Rubens Selected Drawings* (1959), Vol. I, pp.132–33; Vol. II, pl. 104.

34 Held, *op. cit.*, Vol. I, p.133; Vol. II, pl. 106.

35 R.A., *The King's Pictures*, 1946–47 (289), notes by L. Burchard.

36 Held, *op. cit.*, Vol. I, p.109; Vol. II, pl. 38.

37 A drawing by Rubens after this fresco is in the possession of Count Seilern (L. Burchard and R. A. d'Hulst, *Rubens Drawings* (Brussels, 1963), Vol. I, pp.43–45; Vol. II, p.24. The *modello* was engraved by Schelte a Bolswert, *c.* 1650.

38 'Abraham van der Doort's Catalogue', ed. O. Millar, *Walpole Society*, Vol. XXXVII (1960), p.171.

39 E. Croft-Murray, 'The Landscape Background in Rubens's *St George and the Dragon*', *Burlington Magazine*, Vol. LXXXIX (1947), pp.89–93.

40 P. Bjurström, 'Rubens's *St George and the Dragon*', *Art Quarterly* (Spring, 1955), pp.27–42. The best account of the picture is still that by L. Burchard in the R.A. catalogue, *The King's Pictures*, 1946–47 (288).

41 M. Röthlisberger, *Claude Lorrain: the paintings* (New Haven, 1961), Vol. I, pp.327–29.

42 The Queen's Gallery, *Royal Children*, 1963 (91).

43 R.A., *The First Hundred Years*, 1951–52 (332).

44 R.A., *British Portraits*, 1956–57 (382); L. A. Marchand, *Byron* (1957), Vol. I, p.178.

45 W. P. Frith, *My Autobiography and Reminiscences* (1888), Vol. I, pp.243–62.

46 R.A., *Sir Edwin Landseer*, 1961 (94).

47 The picture was first hung in the Queen's Bedroom at Osborne, but was brought up to Buckingham Palace in 1902.

Index

INDEX

NOTE: Italic figures throughout the index indicate an illustration of the subject mentioned

Blore's
Portico

Principal
Corridor

Chinese
Luncheon
Room

Grand
Entrance
Portico

Throne
Room

Green
Drawing
Room

Garden
Entrance

Queen's
Garden
Entrance

North-West
Conservatory

Orleans
Room

Cremorne
Room

18th-Century
Room

White
Drawing
Room

Buckingham Palace